Probation and Parole in Practice

Second Edition

Steven D. Dillingham
Reid H. Montgomery, Jr.
Richard W. Tabor

PROBATION AND PAROLE IN PRACTICE Second Edition

ISBN 0-87084-570-5
Library of Congress Catalog Number 89-81938

Kelly Humble *Managing Editor*

To the many dedicated criminal justice system practitioners for their untiring efforts in combatting crime and the illegal use of drugs in America.

PREFACE

The second edition of *Probation and Parole in Practice*, like the first edition, is designed to provide the reader with an overview and description of probation and parole systems, and to assist the reader in developing the skills for applying professional knowledge and current concepts to actual practice. The text is organized to provide coverage of the topics considered important in understanding the proper functions and dynamics of probation and parole systems and practices. Historical and descriptive information is detailed to acquaint the reader with past and present concerns of the profession. The text is unique in that it describes many of the actual responsibilities of probation and parole officers, and allows the reader to test his or her skills through the use of hypothetical cases and exercises. A careful reading and serious approach to the completion of the assigned tasks should provide the reader with broad insight into modern probation and parole operations and an accurate appraisal of probation and parole as a profession.

In the second edition, updated information has been included that reflects changes and events that have occurred since the early 1980s and which impact probation and parole practices. Predictably, the number of offenders on probation and parole has risen dramatically, placing new strains on a system already experiencing shortages in funds and resources. The continuing high levels of crime experienced across the nation are linked to the continuing national problem of drug abuse, a problem that defies simplistic solution. As a consequence of these and other developments, probation and parole practices are experiencing changes. Recent changes include the establishment of the United States Sentencing Commission and sentencing guidelines, the passage of Federal and state drug initiatives, and the creation of new punishment options. This text includes useful examples and exercises which provide the reader with an opportunity to develop his or her knowledge and skills, and to apply this talent in the dynamic and challenging role of a probation or parole officer.

CONTENTS

Chapter 1

INTRODUCTION:
MODERN PROBATION AND PAROLE
IN PERSPECTIVE

LEARNING OBJECTIVES

* Recognize the role of probation and parole within the American criminal justice system.

* Explain probation and parole in theory and practice.

* Identify professional and ethical standards governing probation and parole systems.

DISCUSSION TOPICS AND QUESTIONS

1. Is there a need for continued utilization of probation and parole options? Why?

2. What is probation? Explain key principles and dynamics.

3. What is parole? Explain key principles and dynamics.

4. What standards govern probation and parole practices?

IMPORTANT TERMS

Deterrence	Probation
Incapacitation	Rehabilitation
Intermediate Punishment	Restitution
Parole	Retribution

A CONTINUUM OF OPTIONS: SUPERVISION TO INCARCERATION

"Lock 'em up and throw away the key" is the immediate response that many Americans have of defendants involved in the criminal justice system. This single approach to punishment is an incomplete one, however, as it does not resolve the issue of confining crime in our society nor does it relieve the criminal justice system of its many problems. In fact, nearly all incarcerated offenders will eventually be released. As most students and practitioners of the criminal justice system (including law enforcement, corrections, the judiciary, and particularly probation and parole authorities) soon realize, reliance upon a single approach is impractical. As a result, numerous options are required to supplement prisons sentences and to cope with the staggering number of criminal offenders, while protecting society. For this reason, punishment should be viewed as continuum of options.

Today, some of the more critical problems impacting the criminal justice system involve increased prison and jail populations as well as inadequate resources for American prisons and jails. Nationally, the prison system is virtually exploding with an inmate population in excess of 600,000 (Department of Justice, September 11, 1988). Research has demonstrated deleterious conditions to be a major source of inmate dissatisfaction (Wenk & Moos, 1972; Montgomery, 1974; Moos, 1975) and even prison riots (Fox, 1972; Dillingham & Montgomery, 1982). In addition to the human costs of incarcerating ever-increasing numbers of offenders in prisons designed for far fewer occupants, the monetary costs are enormous. Recent research has estimated the operational cost of housing an inmate in the United States to be approximately $16,000 per year, in addition to the capital expenditures for each bed space that range between $50,000 and $100,000 (Abell, 1989). Still, these demands and costs must be weighed against society's need to control crime, protect citizens and assist victims. In many cases, incarceration is both cost-effective (Zedlewski, 1987) and deserved.

When attention is directed to those being processed through the criminal justice system, it becomes apparent that not all defendants or offenders pose equal dangers to the community. Indeed, a percentage are found to be nonviolent and possible candidates for alternative programs. Since the 1840s, when John Augustus instituted the first recognized probation program, the concept of probation has gained acceptance as an important component of the American criminal justice system when adequately funded and properly administered. On January 1, 1988, more than 32,000 persons were engaged in probation and parole careers nationally (Criminal Justice Institute, 1988). By the end of 1986, there were approximately 2.1 million state and Federal probationers in the United States. The states of Texas and California led the nation in numbers of probationers with 269,909 and 210,449 respectively (U.S. Department of Justice, Bureau of Justice Statistics (BJS), 1988).

Another option to imprisonment is parole, a process which permits inmates to avoid continued incarceration by obtaining early conditional releases. In 1986 the number of state and Federal parolees in the United States reached approximately 327,000 persons

(U.S. Department of Justice, BJS, 1988). The states of Texas and Pennsylvania led the nation in numbers of parolees with 47,471 and 34,785 respectively.

Having capsulized some of the demands placed on the correctional system and having outlined the advent and expansion of probation and parole practices, the question is posed whether or not a strong rationale exists for continuing to rely upon traditional probation and parole practices to supplement incarceration as punishment options. The answer to this question requires an understanding of the elements which should be incorporated into response strategies by government, and the roles of probation and parole within this continuum of options.

In recent years, policy makers have advocated that the following elements be included in strategies for responding to the prison and jail capacity crisis that is being felt across the nation:

1. Define appropriate *governmental roles and take action*
2. Involve the *private sector* and *volunteers* whenever appropriate
3. Improve *drug treatment and demand reduction* programs
4. Strengthen *pre-trial procedures and release procedures*
5. Expand *prison and jail capacities*
6. Refine *sentencing practices* and develop *new sanctions*

First, recognizing the enormous costs required for constructing and operating penal facilities and the federal government's limited ability to assume these costs for state and local governments, the involvement and leadership of federal, state and local officials can make a significant difference in the response to the prison and jail space crisis. At the Federal level, a leadership role can be assumed by the President and Administration officials. These officials can identify the problem, define the issues, adopt necessary policies and pursue a course of action. Congress may either support the policies and programs of the President, or it may propose and fund a separate course of action. It is preferable that both the executive and legislative branches reach agreement in their approaches to combatting crime and improving the criminal justice system, at least for purposes of providing innovative solutions and financial assistance to state and local governments. Similarly, at the state level, Governors and legislators should exercise leadership in defining appropriate state responses to identified criminal justice system needs and in funding those programs. Finally, local government units must provide leadership and resources for meeting their responsibilities, particularly local law enforcement activities and jail facilities.

Second, facility construction alone will not eliminate the serious problem of crime in America. Recent experience has shown that new prison space is filled quickly and design capacity standards are not easily maintained. This problem is coupled with the fact that facility construction projects extend over a period of years and that operational and service costs are escalating. These pressures force governments to find new options for meeting institutional and service needs. One option to be considered for reducing prison and jail construction costs is inmate labor (Carter and Humphries, 1987). Another option for reducing service costs is increased reliance on volunteer and public service organizations. A third option is the ability to contract with a private sector business or non-profit organization for the operation of prisons and jails. The *Report of the President's Commission on Privatization* (1988) strongly endorses such options. There are early indications that prison and jail facilities and services can be provided by the private sector in a manner similar to the provision of housing, educational and health facilities, and services.

Third, support must be given to improving those programs that have the greatest potential for reaching the underlying causes of the institutional capacity problem. This support would include the need to identify and promote effective drug treatment techniques and programs for offenders. The linkage between drug use and various criminal behaviors has been documented. Hence, both effective treatment and demand reduction programs are needed to break this link. A national Department of Justice study revealed that more than 60 percent of state prisoners released in 1983 were rearrested within three years following their release (Beck, 1989). Hence, programs that can be shown to change criminal behavior patterns are critical to meeting probation and parole requirements, and criminal justice system needs.

Fourth, the capacity overloads experienced by prisons and jails demonstrate the need to strengthen and improve pre-trial and pre-release procedures and practices. Jails house diverse populations, including defendants who have not had their cases adjudicated and those who are serving short terms, or awaiting custodial transfer to another location or to prison. Drug testing procedures are extremely valuable in determining whether release prior to trial is desirable, and also in monitoring offenders on release or parole. Furthermore, screening and classification procedures are important for identifying offenders who qualify for treatment, diversion and release programs without posing unnecessary risks to the community or to others.

Fifth, in nearly all states and communities, correctional and treatment facilities are in need of expansion and improvement. In each case, the need for differing levels of security and long-term care capabilities must be recognized. For instance, separation requirements for juveniles must be met. Similarly, intensive and direct supervision capabilities are favored in most settings, as are enhanced space standards and security safeguards. Accordingly, during the 1990s, prison capacities must be expanded.

Sixth, prison and jail capacity issues must be examined in context of the entire criminal justice system. The demands placed upon each component of the system are related. For this and other reasons, punishment and control of offenders should be considered as a continuum of options, many of which have yet to be developed. Sentencing options and practices must be refined to ensure that serious offenses merit serious punishments and that dangerous offenders are not allowed to pose continued dangers. In some instances, alternatives and less expensive intermediate sanctions may be appropriate for certain types of offenders. For instance, probation or parole may utilize innovative methods of intensive supervision, electronic monitoring, expanded drug testing, community service and victim restitution. Such programs should be designed to assist in the offender's reintegration into the community, assuming appropriate safeguards are present. Other options may include innovative shock incarceration "boot camp" programs and expanded prison industry alternatives.

As a consequence of the preceding factors, reliance upon existing resources and traditional practices of incarceration as exclusive remedies would seem most improbable in light of society's indecisiveness regarding the goals and justifications for punishment. Traditionally, punishment has been justified on the basis of at least four fundamental rationales: (1) retribution, (2) deterrence, (3) incapacitation, and (4) rehabilitation. *Retribution*, one of the oldest morality-based theories of punishment, generally serves a purpose of revenge or "just deserts." The theory of *deterrence* aims to prevent future criminal conduct, both individually (specific deterrence) and at large (general deterrence). *Incapacitation* requires restraint of persons through isolation from society, in an effort to render them incapable of performing criminal acts, at least while confined. *Rehabilitation* involves the reformation or treatment of individuals engaged in criminal activities with the aim to effect improvements in their behavior. For this reason, rehabilitation is sometimes not considered to be a form of punishment at all, but rather a treatment or therapeutic process. In recent years, the concept of *restitution* has gained wide acceptance as a response to criminal behaviors. Restitution generally refers to a sanction that requires the offender to provide compensation or services for victims in an effort to make them "whole" again (i.e., to pay for the harms that the offender caused).

It is the rationale of rehabilitation or treatment with which probation and parole operations have been traditionally associated, but in recent years other rationales have gained increased acceptance. As the organization and substance of this text indicate, probation and parole systems continue the pursuit of the rehabilitative goal when appropriate, but not to the exclusion of the others. More recently, probation and parole practices have been viewed as options included within a broad range of "intermediate punishments" (i.e., punishments or options that fall on a continuum between the extremes of either immediate probation or a sentence of prolonged incarceration.) An example of this is *shock incarceration* which generally combines a short term of disciplined incarceration with a probationary period of intensive supervision. In fact, probation and parole systems now emphasize control over the behavior of criminal offenders and the protection of society as primary concerns. During this era of tightening resources, changing intergovernmental relations, continuing crime and public apprehension, probation and parole officers should be familiar with the various goals and options of punishment and treatment.

WHAT IS PROBATION?

Probation, as practiced today, is far more encompassing than it was during its early history. The term *probation* is used in a number of contexts, including: a *disposition*, *status*, *system* and *process* (National Council on Crime and Delinquency, 1972). When a court suspends an offender's sentence and places the individual under conditions of supervision and conditional freedom, the term probation is viewed as a *disposition*. For example, the defendant may be given a five-year term of probation during which he or she enjoys freedoms that are greater than those of a confined inmate, but less than those of a free citizen. In this instance, the probationer may consider probation as a *status*, due to the limited rights and special duties to which he or she is subjected. Probation may also refer to a *system* which administers probation services. In this sense, probation (whether state, local, or Federal) is a system dedicated to the delivery of specific services, and is commonly considered a subsystem of the broader system of corrections or the even broader criminal justice system. Finally, probation may refer to a *process* encompassing a variety of operational activities, including investigatory and supervisory practices.

Elements of Probation

One author (Carney, 1977) identified the following elements in probation practices:

1. A *suspension of sentence*, resulting in
2. *Conditional liberty*, under
3. *Professional supervision*, subject to
4. *Improved conditions*, with a provision for
5. *Revocation* for serious breach of the conditions.

Based on these elements, the following description of probation emerges:

Probation is a judicially-imposed disposition which suspends the imposition of an original sentence by permitting the defendant to be conditionally released under the supervision of a governmental agency vested with the authority to revoke the privilege upon serious violation of the probation conditions.

Applying Probation

Generally, the defendant who is to be placed on probation is an offender who is not before the court for a serious or violent offense. A judge usually considers background information related to the defendant and his criminal behavior from a Presentence Investigation (PSI) report, for purposes of determining whether a sentence of incarceration is needed. If probation is granted, a probation plan may be devised for the offender, delineating his or her duties and responsibilities. Arrangements are made for ensuring a proper level of supervision for the individual. Counseling or treatment programs are frequently instituted. While on probation, the offender is advised that should he fail to comply with the conditions of probation, a revocation hearing may be instituted which can lead to the reinstitution of a term of incarceration. As a result, probation generally incorporates a "carrot and stick" approach to reintegration into the community: the incentive is provided and the leverage is maintained.

WHAT IS PAROLE?

When comparing parole to probation, important similarities and differences are to be noted. Both probation and parole require supervision of their clients within the community. The techniques of treatment utilized by parole and probation officers are generally indistinguishable. Due to these basic similarities, the two functions are typically combined under one agency, and officers often are assigned both responsibilities. Among the differences between probation and parole are those related to the prior criminal records of the offenders, and the problems encountered in reintegrating the individuals into society. Parolees usually have more extensive and/or serious criminal records. In addition, parolees experience a more difficult social readjustment process because of their institutionalization and status as an "ex-con."

Parole Defined

The word parole is of French origin and was first used in the context of its present meaning by Dr. S. G. Howe of Boston in 1846 in his correspondence to the Prison Association of New York (Carney, 1977). The literal translation of the French expression refers to words of honor, and were originally used in instances where captured soldiers pledged not to take up arms against their captors. In 1939, the Attorney General's Survey of Release Procedures provided a definition of parole that remains applicable today. The report defined parole as the "release of an offender from a penal or correctional institution, after he [or she] has served a portion of his [or her] sentence, under the continued custody of the state and under conditions that permit his [or her] reincarceration in the event of misbehavior." (U.S. Department of Justice, 1939: 4-5).

Elements of Parole

In examining parole in operation, numerous key elements deserve emphasis. Carney (1977: 257) identifies the elements as follows:

1. *Conditional release*;
2. Under *supervision*;
3. With *social reintegration* the agency objective; and
4. *Revocation* as the ultimate penalty.

A working definition of parole can be stated as follows:

Parole refers to the privilege of completing a criminal sentence outside an institutional setting, in accordance with conditions imposed by the governing authority, typically a parole board.

The American Correctional Association (1966: 114) has found that parole serves the following two basic functions:

1. Provision of supervision and control to reduce the likelihood of criminal acts while the offender is serving his or her sentence in the community (the "surveillance" function); and

2. Provision of assistance and services to the parolees, so that noncriminal behavior becomes possible (the "helping" function).

Parole in Practice

Generally the inmate who is placed on parole is someone the paroling authority considers capable of succeeding in the community and not posing a threat to the citizenry. The Model Penal Code (1962) proposed that an inmate can be released on parole when he is eligible, unless one of the following conditions exists:

1. There is a substantial indication that he will not conform to conditions of parole;
2. His release at that time would depreciate the seriousness of the crime or promote disrespect for the law;
3. His release would have substantially adverse effects on institutional discipline; or
4. His continued correctional treatment, medical care or vocational or other training in the institution will substantially enhance his capacity to lead a law-abiding life when released at a later date.

PROBATION AND PAROLE GUIDELINES

Probation and parole operations, like many other professional endeavors, have guidelines and professional standards to which personnel and clients are held accountable. These guidelines and standards are in addition to the constraints imposed by law. Guidelines may be found within: codes of ethics of professional associations; policy standards of agencies; and professional practices adhered to by persons in the field. Examples of guidelines are presented below.

Correctional Standards

Since probation and parole are typically considered subsystems of the broader correctional system, reference to the code of ethics of the American Correctional Association provides some guidance for correctional personnel. The American Correctional Association adopted a Code of Ethics in August, 1975 at the 105th Congress of the American Correctional Association. This Code established a very high ethical standard of conduct for its members by incorporating numerous professional goals (see Table 1-1).

TABLE 1-1

CODE OF ETHICS
AMERICAN CORRECTIONAL ASSOCIATION

The American Correctional Association expects of its members unfailing honesty, respect for the dignity and individuality of human beings, and a commitment to professional and compassionate service. To this end, we subscribe to the following principles.

Relationships with clients/colleagues/other professions/the public:

* Members will respect and protect the civil and legal rights of all clients.
* Members will serve each case with appropriate concern for the client's welfare and with no purpose of personal gain.
* Relationships with colleagues will be of such character as to promote mutual respect within the profession and improvement of its quality of service.
* Statements critical of colleagues or their agencies will be made only as these are verifiable and constructive in purpose.
* Members will respect the importance of all elements of the criminal justice system and cultivate a professional cooperation with each segment.
* Subject to the client's rights of privacy, members will respect the public's right to know, and will share information with the public with openness and candor.
* Members will respect and protect the right of the public to be safeguarded from criminal activity.

Professional conduct/practices:

* No member will use his official position to secure privileges or advantages for himself.
* No member will act in his official capacity in any matter in which he has personal interest that could in the least degree impair objectivity.
* No member will use his official position to promote any partisan political purpose.
* No member will accept any gift or favor of a nature to imply an obligation that is inconsistent with the free and objective exercise of his professional responsibilities.
* In any public statement, members will clearly distinguish between those that are personal views and those that are statements and positions on behalf of an agency.

* Each member will be diligent in his responsibility to record and make available for review any and all case information which could contribute to sound decisions affecting a client or the public safety.
* Each member will report without reservation any corrupt or unethical behavior which could affect either a client or the integrity of the organization.
* Members will not discriminate against any client, employee or prospective employee on the basis of race, sex, creed or national origin.
* Each member will maintain the integrity of private information; he will neither seek personal data beyond that needed to perform his responsibilities; nor reveal case information to anyone not having proper professional use for such.
* Any member who is responsible for agency personnel actions will make all appointments, promotions or dismissals only on the basis of merit and not in furtherance of partisan political interests.

Probation and Parole Officer Ethics

In addition to the comprehensive guidelines dealing with corrections, more specific ethical codes are designed for probation and parole functions. One such code is that of the Federal Probation Officers' Association. The following code was adopted by that organization in 1960 (see Table 1-2).

Client Responsibilities

Probation and parole agencies have established their own standards and guidelines for their clients. These standards and guidelines provide direction for agency personnel in performing their duties. For example, in the state of South Carolina, the conditions of probation (see Table 1-3) are part of the responsibility of a state agency entitled the Parole and Community Corrections Board.

Officer and Agency Requirements

The American Correctional Association (ACA), in *Standards for Adult Probation and Parole Field Services*, establishes guidelines for probation and parole agencies. Below are shown the ACA (1981: 37) parole guidelines (See Table 1-4).

TABLE 1-2

CODE OF ETHICS
FEDERAL PROBATION OFFICERS' ASSOCIATION

As a Federal Probation Officer, I am dedicated to rendering professional service to the courts, the parole authorities, and the community at large in effecting the social adjustment of the offender.

I will conduct my personal life with decorum, will neither accept nor grant favors in connections with my office, and will put loyalty to moral principles above personal considerations.

I will uphold the law with dignity and with complete awareness of the prestige and stature of the judicial system of which I am a part.

I will be ever cognizant of my responsibility to the community which I serve.

I will strive to be objective in the performance of my duties; respect the inalienable rights of all persons; appreciate the inherent worth of the individual; and hold inviolate those confidences which can be reposed in me.

I will cooperate with my fellow workers and related agencies and will continually attempt to improve my professional standards through the seeking of knowledge and understanding.

I recognize my office as a symbol of public faith and I accept it as a public trust to be held as long as I am true to the ethics of the Federal Probation Service. I will constantly strive to achieve these objectives and ideals, dedicating myself to my chosen profession.

TABLE 1-3

CONDITIONS OF PROBATION

The Parole and Community Corrections Board is charged with the responsibility of supervising those offenders who have received a sentence of probation. These offenders, it is believed, can derive the greatest benefit from this noninstitutional program.

The following are conditions for probation:

1. Refrain from the violation of any State, Federal or Municipal Law.

2. Refrain from associating with any person who has a criminal record.

3. Refrain from the unlawful use of intoxicants and you will not frequent places where intoxicants are sold unlawfully.

4. Refrain from the unlawful use of narcotic drugs and you will not frequent places where drugs are sold, dispensed or used unlawfully.

5. Refrain from having in your possession firearms or other weapons.

6. Work diligently at a lawful occupation.

7. Remain within the state unless permitted to leave by your supervising probation agent.

8. Agree to waive extradition from any state of the United States.

9. Follow the advice and instructions of the probation agent. 10.Permit the probation agent to visit your home, place of employment or elsewhere at any time.

11. Report to the probation agent as directed.

12. Pay all fines as ordered by the court.

13. In accordance with [the law of this state], I shall pay [a specified] yearly supervision fee.

TABLE 1-4

SUPERVISION GUIDELINES FOR PAROLE AGENCIES

Unless precluded by statute or court order, parole agency policy specifies that no inmate is released on parole until the parole program is verified by a designated parole officer. (Essential)

DISCUSSION: To ensure that the inmate is being released to a legitimate parole program, policy should provide for authorizing release on parole only when the release program has been investigated and verified by a parole officer. The verification process should include field visits by the parole officer to the parolee's prospective employer, and family or friends with whom the parolee plans to reside. This investigative procedure should include the option to reject or modify the release program if circumstances warrant.

Unless precluded by statute or court order, written policy and procedure provide that the parole agency receives pertinent information about a prospective parolee in advance of the parole date to allow for parole program development and/or verification. (Essential)

DISCUSSION: Adequate time is needed to develop a sound program for the individual about to be paroled. In cases where the parole officer must develop a parole program, particularly where a number of community resources and relatives may be involved, early receipt of referral material is essential. Even in cases where only verification of a job and residence is needed, early receipt and completion of this task by the parole staff eases the anxiety of the inmate. The options of placing the parolee in transitional release programs, such as work release and halfway houses, and the possible need to advance or modify the release date to accommodate a particular release program, require that the parole officer receive the referral material three months in advance of the parole date.

The parole agency supports release policies that require employable inmates to have visible means of support or a reasonable assurance of employment, rather than a promise of a specific job, before release on parole. (Essential)

DISCUSSION: Often inmates cannot be released on parole until there is a specific and verified job waiting for them. This results in many inmates being "overdue", or retained past their parole date in the institution. This is an expensive policy, both in terms of institutional costs and inmate anxiety and motivation. Family help, public assistance, halfway house placement, and direct financial assistance can maintain parolees adequately until they are self-supporting. A number of studies have shown that releasing parolees with "reasonable assurance" of employment does not adversely affect recidivism rates, and that offenders do as well or better if they can find their own jobs.

Confidentiality

Problems arise for the probation or parole officer who does not follow appropriate ethical and agency standards. The responsible probation officer, for example, does not usually encourage irrelevant "off the record" admissions by a defendant upon whom he is conducting a presentence investigation. For instance, if the probation officer directly solicits "off the record" statements which indicate the commission of possible wrongs, the officer is faced with a dilemma of reporting or withholding the information. This places law enforcement responsibilities upon the officer which may conflict with his duties, and potentially may jeopardize the processing of the case. These activities generally are best left to specially trained law enforcement and investigative officers.

Another problem relates to the discussion of a presentence investigation outside the office. Professional probation officers do not discuss investigations in public or to non-privileged parties. This could constitute a serious ethical violation and possibly result in actions and directives by the court.

The probation officer will face a different ethical question if he is assigned to conduct a presentence investigation on a friend or relative. The officer should ask that the presentence investigation be assigned to a different probation officer, because his objectivity might be questioned. A probation or parole officer, much like a judge, should avoid even the appearance of impropriety.

TEXT OVERVIEW

Probation and Parole in Practice, Second Edition is designed to provide the reader with an overview and description of probation and parole systems, and to assist in the development of skills for applying basic knowledge and concepts in practice. The organization of this text reflects this purpose. First, a brief examination is made of the early introduction of probation and parole to America. Second, an overview of both the organization and operation of the Federal and state systems is presented. The organizational structures serve to illustrate the roles and resources of probation and parole systems as important components of a broader criminal justice system. Similarly, an examination of the operations of probation and parole systems is intended to promote an understanding of their essential dynamics. Third, the numerous duties and responsibilities of probation and parole officers are discussed, indicating the variety of activities in which they are engaged. Fourth, attention is directed to the effective application of counseling and treatment techniques in the probation and parole setting. These techniques are of increasing importance to professionals in the performance of their jobs which require effective counseling skills. Fifth, an examination of future trends and issues in probation and parole is made to promote an awareness of recent developments and to provide insight as to how they will impact the delivery of services. Finally, an exercise section is included to evaluate the reader's ability to perform some of the major responsibilities of probation and parole officers. With an improved understanding and familiarity of the probation and parole systems, it is anticipated that readers will be better able to understand, appraise, and contribute to the probation and parole functions within America's criminal justice system.

REFERENCES

Abell, R.B. (1989, Winter). Beyond Willie Horton. *Policy Review*, 47, 32-35.

American Correctional Association. (1966). *Manual of Correctional Standards*. Washington, DC: Author.

American Correctional Association. (1981). *Standards for Adult Probation and Parole Field Services*. (2nd ed.) Rockville, MD: Author.

American Justice: ABCs of How it Really Works. (1982, November 1). *U.S. News & World Report*.

American Law Institute. (1962). *Model Penal Code*. Philadelphia: Author.

Beck, A.J. (1989, March). Recidivism of Prisoners Released in 1983. U.S. Department of Justice, National Institute of Justice. *Special Report*. Washington, DC: U.S. Department of Justice.

Bureau of Justice Statistics (BJS). (1987, December). Probation and Parole 1986. U.S. Department of Justice, BJS *Bulletin*. Washington, DC: U.S. Government Printing Office.

Burne, J.M. (1988). Probation. U.S. Department of Justice, National Institute of Justice. *Study Guide*. Washington, DC: U.S. Government Printing Office.

Carney, L.P. (1977). *Corrections and the Community*. Englewood Cliffs, NJ: Prentice-Hall.

Carter, S.A. & Humphries. (1987, December). Inmates Build Prisons in South Carolina. U.S. Department of Justice, National Institute of Justice. *Bulletin*. Washington, DC: U.S. Department of Justice.

Cullen, F.T. (1986, March). The Privatization of Treatment: Prison Reform in the 1980s." *Federal Probation*, Vol. L (1).

Dillingham, S.D. & Montgomery, R.H., Jr. (1982, October). Can Riots be Prevented? *Corrections Today*, 44 (5), 50-52, 54-56.

Dressler, D. (1969). *Practice and Theory of Probation and Parole* (2nd ed.). NewYork: Columbia University Press.

Fox, V. (1972, August). Prison Riots in a Democratic Society. *Police*, 16, 35.

Friel, C.M., Vaugh, J.B. & Carmen, R. (1987, June). Electronic Monitoring and Correctional Policy: The Technology and Its Application. U.S. Department of Justice, National Institute of Justice. *Research Report*. Washington, DC: U.S. Government Printing Office.

McCarthy, B.R. (ed.). (1987). *Intermediate Punishments: Intensive Supervision, Home Confinement and Electronic Surveillance*. Monsey, NY: Willow Tree Press.

Montgomery, R.H., Jr. (1974). *A Measurement of Inmate Satisfaction/Dissatisfaction in Selected South Carolina Correctional Institutions*. Doctoral dissertation, University of South Carolina, Columbia, SC.

Moos, Rudolph H. (1975). *Evaluating Correctional and Community Settings*. New York: John Wiley & Sons.

National Advisory Commission on Criminal Justice Standards and Goals. (1973). *Report on Corrections*. Washington, DC: U.S. Government Printing Office.

National Council on Crime and Delinquency. (1972). *Policies and Background Information*. Hackensack, NJ: Author.

President's Commission on Privatization. (1988, March). *Privatization: Toward More Efficient Government*. Washington, DC.

South Carolina Department of Parole and Community Corrections. (1981). *South Carolina Parole and Community Corrections Annual Report*. Columbia, SC: Author.

U.S. Department of Justice. (1939). *Attorney General's Survey of Release Procedures*. Washington, DC: U.S. Government Printing Office.

U.S. Department of Justice. (1988). *Probation and Parole 1986.* Bureau of Justice Statistics. Washington, DC: U.S. Government Printing Office.

Wenk, E.A. & Moos, R. H. (1972, July). Social Climates in Prison: An Attempt to Conceptualize and Measure Environmental Factors in Total Institutions. *Journal of Research in Crime and Delinquency*, 9, 141.

Zedlewski, E.W. (1987, July). Making Confinement Decisions. U.S. Department of Justice, National Institute of Justice. *Research Brief*. Washington, DC: U.S. Department of Justice.

Chapter 2

THE EVOLUTION
OF PROBATION AND PAROLE

LEARNING OBJECTIVES

* Trace the historic development of probation practices.

* Trace the historic development of parole practices.

* Explain American influences on probation and parole practices.

* Outline major developments and continuing issues in modern probation and parole practices.

DISCUSSION TOPICS AND QUESTIONS

1. What role did early English history play in the development of probation and parole?

2. How did probation and parole practices differ in their development?

3. To what extent have modern probation and parole practices been accepted in the United States?

4. What recent improvements have been experienced in probation and parole systems?

IMPORTANT TERMS

Benefit of clergy
Recognizance
Surety
Common law
Equity law
Filing of cases

"Earned work" credit
"Good time" credit
Ticket-of-leave
Parole Boards
Resource brokerage
Prediction Model

NAMES TO REMEMBER

Athelstane
Matthew Hill
John Augustus
Peter Thacker

Colonel Montesinos
Alexander Maconochie
George Obermaier
William Crofton

THE ORIGIN AND HISTORY OF PROBATION

In tracing the evolution, acceptance and implementation of probation theories and practices, attention is focused upon at least four major developments which served to transform traditional orientations toward punishment from purely retributive goals to more rehabilitative goals. This progression was slow and began with the expanded use of numerous common law antecedents to probation, such as benefit of clergy, judicial reprieve, release on personal recognizance and others. A second important stage in the development of modern concepts of probation was the introduction of probation practices to America by John Augustus in 1841. This introduction initiated a movement in America which led to a recognition of probation officers as professionals. Finally, the employment and utilization of probation officers grew nationally, resulting in the state and federal probation systems as Americans know them today.

Early English Developments

England, like other early European countries, experienced a harsh and violent history during the Middle Ages. Nowhere was the harshness more evident than in the treatment of criminals, who were typically subjected to trial by combat or ordeal. Nevertheless, over several centuries, a variety of practices gradually evolved which served to ameliorate the severity of punishment practices.

One of the earliest recorded forms of relief granted to English subjects was a declaration of Athelstane, the Anglo Saxon King (895-940), that forbade the execution of anyone under the age of 15 years. King Athelstane also instituted an early type of "bail" system in which an offender could be released to a responsible person providing surety and monitoring of the offender's behavior (Smith & Berlin, 1979).

A second common law antecedent of probation which evolved in England was a privilege known as benefit of clergy. This device emerged in the 1200s during the reign of Henry II. The practice originally permitted arrested clergy (later including all persons capable of reading, and some who could "fake" the skill) to have their cases transferred to ecclesiastical courts for disposition. By claiming benefit of clergy, which included the recitation of a biblical passage, a lenient sentence would typically be received, as opposed to the traditional death sentence of a secular court. Many illiterates qualified for this privilege by memorizing a passage from the psalm *Miserere me* ("Have mercy on me"). This practice was introduced to America where it was accepted prior to the American Revolutionary War (Henningsen, 1981). The benefit of clergy was officially abolished for commoners in England in 1827, and was dealt its final blow in 1841, when it was terminated for aristocrats as well.

The practice of recognizance, or "binding over for good behavior," was a practice which gained acceptance in the 14th century English courts. Similar to Athelstane's original concept, this process allowed an offender to escape conviction through release to another person who stood as surety or provided bail. Such release was contingent upon continued good behavior, and required supervision and monitoring by the person acting as surety. The first recorded use of recognizance in the United States occurred in 1830 in the case of *Commonwealth v. Chase*, heard in the Municipal Court of Boston (Callison, 1983). In this case Judge Peter Oxenbridge Thacker heard a guilty plea by the defendant, Jerusha Chase. The judge released the defendant at the request of her friends, but the offender was subject to return to the court at its insistence. The rationale for this sentence was to guarantee future compliance with the law (Hussey & Duffee, 1980). In 1836, Massachusetts passed a statute which permitted the release of petty offenders on their own recognizance. Increased reliance upon bail also became an accepted practice during this period. In instances where release on one's own recognizance appeared inappropriate, bail provided additional guarantees for court appearance by mandating sureties. These sureties became responsible for the defendant's supervision. As a result, release on one's own recognizance and bail evolved into valuable techniques for early probation efforts.

Judicial reprieve, another forerunner of probation, experienced a gradual and circuitous acceptance as an official judicial procedure in England. As the English courts developed a sophisticated *common law* (based upon judge-made law through the use of precedents), a parallel system of *equity law* emerged. Equity was administered by a royal chancellor who was authorized to issue decrees based upon then-developing principles of equity, such as injunctive relief. By the 16th century, a common law system of both law and equity, with overlapping principles, was firmly in place. Judicial reprieve, involving the suspension of a sentence, was one device that developed from this body of law. A judge who had reservations about the verdict of a trial could grant a reprieve enabling the offender to seek a conditional or absolute pardon at a later date. Some courts would grant a reprieve and impose conditions of transportation to a colony. This device came to be viewed as a precedent for the modern practice of suspending sentence.

Judicial practices known as *filing of cases* gained acceptance in Massachusetts during the 19th century. This practice usually occurred in cases involving mitigating circumstances or cases where an appellate decision relating to the case was anticipated. It involved suspending the imposition of sentence after a verdict of guilty (Henningsen, 1981). Both the defendant and the prosecutor were required to consent to the filing. By delaying the imposition of a final judgment, a defendant's case might never reach a final verdict (Smith & Berlin, 1979). This device provided the leverage for making a defendant's freedom dependent upon continued good behavior.

Probation Introduced to America

When examining the introduction of probation in America, brief mention must be made of a simultaneous development in England. In 1841, an English barrister and magistrate of the City of Birmingham, England, Matthew Davenport Hill, instituted a practice of completely suspending sentences for youthful offenders by placing them under the supervision of approved adult guardians. This rehabilitative approach depended upon the assistance of local police in monitoring the behavior of the probationed juveniles, although it lacked a formal mechanism for revoking the privilege or reinstituting the original sentence. Still, it has come to be recognized as a precursor to the modern concept of probation.

The year 1841, however, is better known for a development in America which formally introduced probation in the criminal justice systems of the world. It was in that year that John Augustus, considered to be the true "father of probation," championed probation practices which serve as the foundation of contemporary probation systems.

John Augustus, born in Massachusetts (1784), became a successful businessman at an early age. In addition, he had a strong sense of public service and civic responsibility which he later directed toward the rehabilitation of criminal offenders. In 1841, at the age of 57, Augustus began his "probation" career. As he was leaving a courthouse after delivering a pair of boots to a judge, a "ragged and wretched looking" man was brought in for sentencing. The man had been found guilty of being a "common drunkard." Augustus spoke with the man before his sentencing and believed the man sincere in his desire to be reformed. To be saved from the House of Correction, the man agreed to refrain from future drinking. To the shock of the court, John Augustus offered bail for the man and suggested a period of probation. The judge accepted the proposal and ordered the man to return in three weeks. After three weeks, Augustus accompanied the man back to court. The former "drunkard" was clean-shaven, well-dressed, and had refrained from alcohol consumption. The judge, impressed by Augustus' results, fined the man only one cent plus court fees for his crime (Augustus, 1852).

Because of Augustus' efforts and hard work, it soon became a rule of the court in Boston that a person charged with being a common drunkard could be granted probation. Augustus eventually enlarged the scope of his work to include juveniles and female offenders.

TABLE 2-1

THE EVOLUTION OF PROBATION: KEY DEVELOPMENTS

895-940	Anglo-Saxon King (Athelstane) pioneered bail by surety
1200s	*Benefit of clergy* evolved during reign of Henry II
1300s	English courts practiced recognizance (*binding over for good behavior*)
1827	*Benefit of clergy* officially abolished in England
1830	Practice of *binding over* introduced in the United States
1836	Massachusetts passed statute allowing for use of recognizance
1841	English barrister, Matthew Hill, instituted suspended sentences
1841	John Augustus ("The Father of Probation" in United States) began probation work
1878	Professional probation officers hired in Boston, Massachusetts
1880	Statewide authorization of probation officers in Massachusetts
1887-9	Missouri, Vermont, Rhode Island, Illinois and Minnesota pass original probation legislation
1907	National Association of Probation Officers (NAPO) formed in Minneapolis, Minnesota
1911	NAPO expanded into National Probation Association (NPA)
1916	U.S. Supreme Court overruled Federal court authority to suspend sentences
1925	President Coolidge established Federal Probation System
1940	Federal probation transferred from Federal Bureau of Prisons to Administrative Office of the United States Courts
1984	Sentencing Reform Act of 1984 passed as part of the Comprehensive Crime Control Act of 1984
1987	Federal sentencing guidelines (Federal) become effective
1989	U.S. Supreme Court decides constitutionality of U.S. Sentencing Commission and Federal guidelines (*Mistretta v. U.S.*)

John Augustus' duties increased as he undertook the following: finding temporary homes for the destitute; feeding and clothing the needy; and helping to find work for those who could be employed. He provided additional assistance to thousands of neglected and homeless women. His work was done on a voluntary basis, eventually leading to the failure of his own business. He spent much of his money on bails and fines for his "charges". Recognizing the worth of his endeavors, his friends assisted him financially, thus enabling him to continue his philanthropic work. The records of John Augustus' service reveal the effectiveness of his work. Of his first 1,100 recorded cases, only one failure was recorded. Of the more than 2,000 people he bailed, only 10 proved ungrateful or absconded. Much of his success was attributed to his personal involvement and fundamentally sound probationary techniques.

There were five fundamental steps in Augustus' approach to probation, which laid the foundation of many modern probation systems. First, there was a careful screening of candidates for service. Second, the sentence was suspended. Third, the defendant was granted conditional liberty. Fourth, some sort of supervision with conditions was devised. Fifth, revocation of probation was implemented for breach of any conditions. In this process, Augustus soon discovered the importance of various factors to ensuring success. Screening was extremely important. In the selection of a probationer, Augustus would consider the previous character of the person, his or her age, how promising the person's future looked, and whether or not it was a first offense. Once a person was placed on probation, Augustus assumed additional responsibilities. He reviewed the general conduct of the probationer, focusing on whether the person attended school or engaged in honest employment. He often arranged living accommodations for the offender, and maintained a careful register of all the cases he handled. Augustus had a reputation for making impartial, honest reports to the court concerning the probationer when requested. The practices of John Augustus, which included investigating cases, interviewing clients, supervising releases, and providing services for the probationer, were later accepted as basic techniques in almost all probation systems.

The innovation and farsightedness of Augustus were not always recognized, however, and reform did not always come without a price. As well as suffering the hardships of monetary failings, Augustus faced a great deal of personal opposition. Law enforcement officers resented losing the normal monetary "lock-up fee." The fact that Augustus was providing bail "in all proper cases" also annoyed many of the clerks, officers, and prosecutors, who attempted to sway public opinion against him and his reforms. Some people even believed that his methods were incentives to crime and called him a mock philanthropist. Still, Augustus remained steadfast through it all, gathering support from judges and the press, and eventually many of the citizenry.

Probation Develops as a Profession

Early probation practices, modeled after those pioneered by John Augustus, gained a gradual but steady acceptance after Augustus' death. In 1878, the city of Boston hired its first probation officer who worked with both male and female offenders under the supervision of the municipal police. Following a two-year trial period, the Massachusetts legislature, in 1880, approved the nation's first statewide hiring of probation officers. The law removed probation officers from the employment of police departments (Henningsen, 1981).

Following the example of Massachusetts, Missouri became the second state to enact a probation law, in 1897. In Missouri's legislation, the prerequisites for receiving a sentence of probation were numerous and the term "parole" was synonymous with probation. This legislation may be viewed as the forerunner of many modern probation statutes, frequently fraught with confusion and complexity. In 1898, Vermont enacted probation laws which were county-based. Rhode Island, on the other hand, adopted a state-administered system in 1899. Illinois and Minnesota also passed probation statutes in 1899, although they were limited to juveniles (Smith & Berlin, 1979). By 1900, numerous states had recognized probation as a profession and had implemented various probation practices and offices to fulfill the newly recognized occupation.

The national use of probation was enhanced by developments in the juvenile courts. Beginning in 1899, the states of Illinois, Minnesota and Colorado enacted new laws for use in juvenile cases. By 1925, every state had some type of probation alternative for juveniles, although it was not until 1967 that all the states in the United States had laws authorizing probation for adults (Smith & Abadinsky, 1982).

In 1907, a small group of probation officers met in Minneapolis to form a National Association of Probation Officers. In 1911, the group reorganized under the name of the National Probation Association (NPA). The NPA has since evolved into the current National Council on *Crime and Delinquency* (NCCD), which publishes the Crime and Delinquency journal.

While most states authorized probation alternatives during the early 1900s, the United States was without such laws for the Federal courts. Predictably, the authority of the Federal courts to grant probationary sentences came into question. In 1916, the U.S. Supreme Court addressed the issue in the landmark *Killits* decision (*Ex parte United States*, 24 U.S. 27, 37 S.Ct. 72, 61 L.Ed. 129). In this decision, the U.S. Supreme Court decided that the Federal courts had *not* been granted the power to indefinitely suspend a defendant's sentence. To indefinitely suspend sentences, the court reasoned, would be a refusal to enforce applicable laws. Such a refusal would constitute usurping legislative powers. By refusing to recognize such an inherent judicial power, the court explicitly recognized the authority of the legislative branch to enact such laws. By 1925, probation advocates were able to convince Congress of the need for such legislation.

The Federal Probation Act was passed by Congress in 1925 and signed by President Coolidge. It officially established the Federal Probation System. In 1930, two changes were made to this legislation which had substantial impact on the system's development. One change removed the system from the U.S. Civil Service and placed it under the power of the Federal district courts with the power of appointment of probation officers, while the second change extended supervisory responsibilities for parolees to probation officers (Federal Judicial Center, 1976).

In 1940, the Federal Probation System underwent another important change by transferring its authority from the Bureau of Prisons in the U.S. Department of Justice to the Administrative Office of the United States Courts. This shift from the executive branch to the judicial branch was hotly debated for numerous years, but further attempts to transfer the office failed. While an argument existed for combining all agencies dealing with corrections under one department, a countervailing interest of insulating probation from the influences of the prosecution side was recognized.

THE ORIGIN AND HISTORY OF PAROLE

The origin and history of parole, like that of probation, had its roots in early English practices and experienced a gradual development until the 19th century. During the 1800s, significant contributions were made by several countries. In 1870, the concept of parole began to receive acceptance in the United States. The term "parole" is derived from a French expression which means "conditional liberation" and was developed as a procedure which permitted the early release of an inmate from prison on a conditional basis. If the inmate failed to fulfill the parole requirements, his or her sentence could be re-imposed. Evolving over a 75-year period, this device eventually gained acceptance in the United States as a supplement to, and alternative for, incarceration.

Early English Practices

As early as 1597, England had passed laws which punished dangerous criminals by banishing them from their homeland. Such an approach to the problem of crime was common for the age and by the 17th century the practice of transporting criminals from England had become commonplace. Not only were dangerous criminals transported, but due to harsh economic conditions and high unemployment, many others suffered the ordeal. The English parliament expressly authorized the
shipment of many criminals to the American colonies in hopes of supplying desperately needed manpower (Smith & Berlin, 1979). To create an incentive for the transported convicts to provide such labor, the prisoners were granted pardons and clemency for their crimes. A problem soon arose, however, when some of the pardoned criminals managed to surreptitiously return to England. As a result, in 1655, a law was passed nullifying all pardons for prisoners returning to England and subjecting them to execution. The transported criminals in America did not always passively accept their fate and, in 1670, they encouraged a rebellion among slaves in Virginia. In response to this uprising, a Virginia court issued a directive prohibiting any further importation of criminals. The effort was futile, of course, and the practice continued until the American Revolutionary War.

TABLE 2-2

THE EVOLUTION OF PAROLE: KEY DEVELOPMENTS

1597	English law provided for banishment of dangerous criminals
1655	English law nullified pardons for returning prisoners
1670	Virginia court banned importation of criminals to colony
1787	Australia established as a colony for transported criminals
1790	England authorized colonies to reduce criminal sentences
1811	England authorized work credit to reduce sentence length
1817	New York passed first "good time" law, shortening terms of imprisonment
1821	England adopted guidelines for awarding "work credit"
1835	Colonel Montesinos instituted sentence reduction for good behavior in Valencia, Spain
1840	Englishman Alexander Maconochie ("Father of Parole") instituted parole concepts in Australia
1842	German prison head, Obermaier, initiated prison reforms reducing recidivism in Munich
1853	English Penal Servitude Act of 1853 formalized conditional releases
1867	Transportation of prisoners to Australia terminated
1870	American Prison Association introduced Crofton reforms to United States
1876	Elmira Reformatory (NY) adopted concept of parole
1884	Ohio extended parole throughout state prison system
1913	Wisconsin passed Huber law, permitting inmates to support dependents
1944	Last state adopted parole system – Mississippi
1984	Sentencing Reform Act of 1984 phases out federal parole

Although the Revolutionary War ended the importation of English criminals to the United States, it marked the beginning of transporting offenders to Australia. In 1787, Prime Minister Pitt established Australia as a colony for criminals only 17 years after the continent's discovery by Captain Cook. Unlike the preceding banishment practices with America, the English government did not relinquish control of the prisoners sent to Australia. The government paid all transportation expenses and assigned the prisoners to the local governor with *property in service* rights, a form of involuntary servitude. These rights were normally reassigned by contract to free settlers. In 1790, however, a special provision was passed which empowered the Australian governors to remit or shorten the sentences of the imported convicts. While some convicts received absolute pardons, a process of granting *tickets-of-leave*, or conditional pardons, soon became the standard practice. The ticket-of-leave was very similar to a grant of freedom for an indentured servant. It enabled the individual to legally accept employment and entitled the person to various privileges, such as the freedom to marry.

The ticket-of-leave practice was modified in 1811 in a manner which permitted transported criminals to work off a prescribed sentence (a forerunner of modern "earned work" and "good-time" credits). This concept took root in America, as evidenced by the passage of a "good time" law in New York in 1817, which authorized a shortened term of imprisonment to reward good conduct. In 1821, specific minimum sentences were assigned in England which enabled convicts to serve a finite number of years, knowing that freedom would follow although only a portion of the original sentence was served. Some of these minimum sentences reduced the original sentence by as much as one-half.

Acceptance and Expansion of Parole

The role of early English practices in shaping parole comprises an important correctional influence, but not an exclusive one. Not to be overlooked were the contributions of other European countries, notably Spain, Germany and Ireland.

On 1835, the governor (warden) of the prison at Valencia, Spain, Colonel Montesinos, instituted a plan emphasizing discipline, vocational training and education which provided for a one-third reduction in sentence length for good behavior and personal progress. Following implementation of these reforms, recidivism at the Valencia prison decreased from 35 percent to almost none, indicating a highly successful and well-managed program of treatment (Killinger & Cromwell, 1977).

During the period when Colonel Montesinos was experiencing success in Spain, an Englishman, Alexander Maconochie, was applying his own ideas to the penal system, earning him the title of "Father of Parole." In 1837, Maconochie made a proposal to the English parliament to modify penal policy by requiring the length of a convict's criminal sentence to hinge upon the individual's demonstrated "good behavior and industry." Records were to be kept to measure each convict's progress. The system had numerous additional innovations including: (1) public inmate trials with procedural safeguards; (2) improved living environments and social amenities; (3) a "mark system" whereby inmates earned money as work incentives; and (4) a five-stage program of "graduated release," culminating in full freedom for successful inmates. In 1840, Maconochie assumed the role of Governor of an Australian penal colony where his experimental reforms were tested over a four-year period of tenure. Gradually, criticism of his methods increased until he was forced to resign his position, preventing any final determination regarding the long-term success of his reforms.

George Obermaier, a German contemporary of Montesinos and Maconochie, served as governor of a Munich prison in 1842. Upon assuming supervision of a crowded and rebellious prison population, he instituted numerous successful rehabilitative reforms that relied upon earning the confidence and respect of the inmates. Much of the credit for his success was largely attributed to the indefinite sentences his inmates faced and the close supervision practices imposed on the discharged inmates.

The Penal Servitude Act of 1853 was passed in England, giving legal status to the ticket-of-leave system, for the purpose of creating an alternative plan to the compulsory transportation of inmates to Australia. In many cases, the plan called for a minimum period of incarceration prior to receiving a ticket-of-leave. The objectives of enticing inmates to engage in good behavior and making their release conditioned upon rehabilitation were not usually met by this poorly administered plan.

In 1854, Sir William Crofton became Director of the Irish Prison System and began a new method of administering the ticket-of-leave device. Under his direction, tickets-of-leave were awarded only to inmates demonstrating desirable attitudes and proven accomplishments. Among the features of Crofton's system were the following: (1) Maconochie's supervised stages of imprisonment; (2) indeterminate sentences; (3) improved prison conditions; (4) supervised release; and (5) public confidence. Perhaps due to the emphasis on public support, Crofton's accomplishments received widespread recognition and acceptance.

The English practice of transporting prisoners to Australia underwent modification as the new settlers increased their protests, similar to events in the American colonies. The English government responded by initiating a "selection system" of training prisoners before being transported. An assigned "board" (precursor to modern "parole boards") was used to evaluate inmate readiness. Ultimately, the program failed and, in 1867, England ended transportation of convicts to Australia.

Development of Parole in the United States

The American parole system naturally drew most of its impetus and ideas from the European experiences. Still, many of the key developments had distinctive American qualities and even came to later serve as models for European reforms. An event important in the development of parole in America occurred in 1870 when the National Congress of the recently organized American Prison Association advocated a philosophy of rehabilitation based upon the principles Crofton had implemented in the Irish prisons. The participants issued a "Declaration of Principles" on prison reform which incorporated many widely held ideas in contemporary society. These included: (1) rehabilitation as a goal of incarceration; (2) a progressive classification of prisons; (3) a system rewarding good behavior in prison; (4) an evaluation of prisoner reformation; and (5) comprehensive programs of supervision and assistance upon release from prison.

One response to the 1870 conference was the establishment of Elmira Reformatory in 1876 which included a system of parole supervision. Prisoners were carefully selected for parole; indeterminate sentences enhanced rehabilitation; privileges were dependent upon behavior and progress; organization and discipline were enforced; and requirements for parole had to be met. Once paroled, the parolees had to report monthly to their assigned guardian who supervised their activities. Prison reformer Zebulon Brockway served as the Elmira superintendent and is credited with having ensured much of the program's success.

Following the example at Elmira, parole systems were soon adopted by the other states, although sentencing reforms lagged behind. In 1884, Ohio became the first state to extend parole throughout its state prison system (Parker, 1975). By 1922, the number of states with parole statutes increased to 45. Meanwhile, the state of Wisconsin passed the Huber Law in 1913, a statute which allowed jailed inmates to support their dependents. Finally, in 1944, Mississippi became the last state to adopt parole. Sentencing schemes, however, still varied among the states.

MODERN PROBATION AND PAROLE PRACTICES

As the history of probation and parole reveals, today's practices evolved over a number of centuries and have precedents in numerous countries. Yet, modern probation and parole practices in the United States have a number of distinctly American features. The following discussion will present a brief analysis of some of the recent developments experienced in probation and parole systems, some of the pressing issues confronting the systems, and several innovative features of the systems which deserve closer attention.

Recent Developments in Probation and Parole

How have the changes since the impact of John Augustus shaped probation and parole today? The best method for assessing the current dimensions of probation and parole today is to view the growth that has occurred and to identify major developments and trends.

In 1966, the Task Force on Corrections noted that: "probation in the United States is administered by hundreds of independent agencies operating under a different law in each state and under widely varying philosophies, often within the same state" (Task Force on Corrections, 1966: 28). In 1978, the U.S. Bureau of Census found that more than 1900 agencies offered adult probation services and more than 2100 agencies provided juvenile probation services. In both cases, more than 55 percent of the services were offered at the county or municipal level (Abadinsky, 1982).

The use of probation has also experienced increasing acceptance as an alternative to incarceration. In 1980, of all adults processed through the criminal justice system, approximately 60 percent were given probation as opposed to the remaining 40 percent who were incarcerated (Bartollas, 1981). During the mid-1980s, the probation and parole systems experienced continued growth, as did the prison systems. In 1985, more than one million adults were placed on probation, and approximately 180,000 adults began parole terms (U.S. Department of Justice, BJS, 1987). By the 1980s, only 11 states operated on a county basis; the remaining 39 were statewide. Thirteen of the statewide systems retained a combined state/county service delivery system.

The administration of parole is comparatively simple in organization, since it generally consists of one agency per state. Still, there are two basic models for administering parole services. Under one model, parole authority is granted to an independent parole board, while a second approach gives parole authority to the respective corrections agency. Both approaches have advantages and disadvantages and the optimum approach may well depend upon the current operations and leadership within the corrections or parole authority (Task Force on Corrections, 1966).

Issues in Probation and Parole

What are some of the problems and issues in the field of probation and parole work? One publication sets forth key issues in probation and parole as including: (1) consideration of the termination of parole as a release alternative; (2) the possible release of all offenders under some form of supervision similar to parole; (3) probation agencies having to provide a growing range of services to an increasing number of clients, frequently without an increase in resources; (4) demands for probation to provide both pretrial services and for misdemeanant probation; and (5) demands that probation agencies assume a surveillance rather than a treatment posture (University Research Corp., 1980: 13). As will be discussed, recent Federal sentencing guidelines have been designed to eliminate parole for Federal offenders.

A nationwide survey of probation administrators identified the following issues as being of paramount concern to the profession: (1) increasingly scarce resources; (2) higher numbers of offenders; (3) more severe offenders on probation; (4) longer sentences; (5) judicial pressure for accountability; (6) poor image of probation services; (7) lack of knowledge about program effectiveness; (8) lack of agreement of outcome measures; and (9) inadequate use of management skills (University Research Corp., 1980).

As a result, the modern probation and parole officer must act as a "resource broker." The officer must assess the needs of the client, find the community resources to deal with the particular problem(s) of the client and make contracts with the community agencies to provide services to the client.

Prediction Models

The modern probation and parole officer should be knowledgeable about prediction models. Such models provide methods for systematically evaluating offender experiences. These models assist a probation officer in writing a presentence recommendation, in deciding what level of supervision a probationer or parolee should be under and on predicting when an inmate will be eligible for parole consideration.

Using such a model, for example, the probation officer is able to predict with a higher degree of precision how a defendant is likely to behave if placed on probation. If the prediction model strongly indicates that the defendant will succeed on probation, the probation officer may recommend that the judge sentence the defendant to a period of probation.

Research conducted nationwide by the Comptroller General of the United States revealed that models were generally more successful in predicting behavior than the subjective feelings of probation officers. Models may vary in form. The following table demonstrates a typical prediction model, accompanied by a success rate scale.

TABLE 2-3

ILLUSTRATIVE PREDICTIVE MODEL

Significant Characteristics	Model Value	Individual's Score
No history of opiate use	9	--
Family has no criminal history	6	--
Not an alcoholic	6	--
Married	4	--
No prior arrests	4	--
Total possible score for probationer	29	--

SUMMARY RISK TABLE

Score	Success Rate	Individual's Assessment
23-29	(90%)	--
10-22	(70%)	--
00-09	(10%)	--

Source: *State and County Probation: Systems in Crisis, 1976.*

Salient factor scores have been used in prediction models of the U.S. Parole Commission to measure the amount of time a federal prisoner will serve in prison before being considered for parole. The higher the salient factor score the less time a prisoner must serve, as compared to a prisoner with the same charge but a lower salient factor score. A prisoner's salient factor score is based on his or her prior criminal record, employment history, drug history and family situation.

Change: A Continuing Process

The modern probation and parole officer is aware that model guidelines can be changed depending upon the prevailing philosophies. A news article in 1983 illustrates how guidelines changed. In an interview with the U.S. Parole Commission concerning recent changes, the following comments were made: "The Reagan Administration, having failed to get Congress to eliminate parole for federal prisoners, issued tough, new parole guidelines...designed to keep violent criminals and offenders in prison longer." (*The* (S.C.) *State*, Jan. 25). Subsequently, Congress passed the Crime Control Act of 1984 which provided for a phasing out of parole under its new sentencing guidelines. In 1988, Congress passed the Anti-Drug Abuse Act of 1988 which provides, in part, new and severe penalties for various drug offenders, and stresses the need for "user accountability." Also on January 18, 1989, the constitutionality of the United States Sentencing Commission was decided by the United States Supreme Court (*Mistretta v. U.S.*, 57 LW 4102).

If agents of change are underestimated and public sentiments ignored, dysfunctional consequences may occur within an organization (More, 1977). Since probation and parole systems are currently experiencing enormous pressures critical to their future, recognition of changing programmatic needs and new coping strategies are of increasing importance.

Volunteers: A New Resource

Although probation work originated from the volunteer work of John Augustus in the 1840s, the modern probation and parole officer is still aware of the value of the volunteer. Until the 1960s, little attention was directed toward the use of volunteers or paraprofessionals in probation and parole operations (Smith & Berlin, 1976).

Scheier (1970) points out the many services a volunteer can perform including: (a) acting as behavior models for probationers; (b) assisting probationers in finding employment; (c) helping to recruit and train other volunteers; (d) acting as tutors for probationers with limited reading ability; and (e) offering many other talents and forms of assistance. A major task of the modern probation officer is the recruiting, selecting and training of volunteers. The college student, for example, who takes advantage of the opportunity to work as a volunteer, greatly increases his or her understanding of the criminal justice system and develops special professional skills applicable to numerous employment opportunities.

SUMMARY

Probation and parole are related concepts and have experienced roughly parallel development and professional acceptance in America. Both evolved from a number of early English common law practices. Similarly, both concepts were embraced in America during the 1800s, reflecting recognition of their successful, though limited usage abroad. As the nation and American criminal justice expanded, a need to professionalize treatment and manage a growing offender population was recognized. Thus, individuals, groups, and Federal, state and local units of government realized the need to develop formalized and professional systems for implementing probation and parole practices.

Today, probation and parole comprise important components of our overall criminal justice system. Both concepts require comprehensive guidelines and regulations, and are administered by professional staffs. Although applicable laws and administrative authorities differ among the states, both components are experiencing shared pressures and changes in areas of expanding programs and the management of resources. Recently, the issue of abolishing parole has come to the forefront of debate as federal sentencing guidelines are implemented, and the constitutionality of the U.S. Sentencing Commission has been decided. In meeting these challenges, modern probation and parole practices have incorporated additional features and techniques, ranging from prediction models to increased reliance upon volunteerism. In all likelihood, further innovations will occur as new problems and pressures surface.

REFERENCES

Abadinsky, H. (1982). *Probation and Parole: Theory and Practice* (2nd ed.). Englewood Cliffs, NJ: Prentice-Hall.

Augustus, J. (1852 reprint). *A Report on the Labors of John Augustus*. Haddam, CT: Connecticut Criminal Justice Training Academy.

Bartollas, C. (1981). *Introduction to Corrections*. New York: Harper and Row Publishers.

Callison, H.G. (1983). *Introduction to Community-Based Corrections*. New York: McGraw-Hill, Inc.

Federal Judicial Center. (1976). *An Introduction to the Federal Probation System*. Washington, DC: Author.

Henningsen, R.J. (1981). *Probation and Parole*. New York: Harcourt Brace Jovanovich.

Hussey, F.A. & Cromwell, P.F., Jr. (1978). *Corrections in the Community: Alternatives to Imprisonment* (2nd ed.). St. Paul,MN: West Publishing.

More, H.W., Jr. (1977). *Criminal Justice Management*. St. Paul, MN: West Publishing.

O'Leary, V. & Hanrahan, K.J. (1977). *Parole Systems in the United States* (3rd ed.). Hackensack, NJ: National Council on Crime and Delinquency.

Parker, W. (1975). *Parole*. College Park, MD: American Correctional Association.

Scheier, I.H. (1970, June). The Volunteer in Probation. *Federal Probation*.

Smith, A.B. & Berlin, L. (1976). *Introduction to Probation and Parole*. (1st and 2nd ed.). St. Paul, MN: West Publishing.

Smykla, M.J. (1983, January 25). *Community-Based Corrections: Principles and Practices*. New York: Macmillan Publishing.

Sniffen, M.J. (1983, January 25). New Rules Tighten Federal Paroles. *The* (Columbia, S.C.) *State*: Associated Press.

Task Force on Corrections. (1966). *Task Force Report: Corrections*. Washington, DC: U.S. Government Printing Office.

University Research Corporation. (1979). *Improved Probation Strategies: Trainer's Handbook*. Washington, DC: U.S. Government Printing Office.

SELECTED READINGS

Carter, R.M. & Wilkins, L.T. (Eds.). (1976). *Probation, Parole and Community Corrections*. New York: John Wiley and Sons.

Fox, V. (1977). *Community-based Corrections*. Englewood Cliffs, NJ: Prentice-   Hall.

Miller, E.E. & Montilla, R.M. (Eds.) (1977). *Corrections in the Community*. Reston, VA: Reston Publishing.

Glaser, D. (1964). *The Effectiveness of a Prison and Parole System*. Indianapolis: Bobbs-Merrill.

Dressler, D. (1951). *Practice and Theory of Probation and Parole*. New York: Columbia University Press.

Shouer, N. & Einstadter, W.J. (1988). *Analyzing American Corrections*. Belmont,   CA: Wadsworth Publishing.

Chapter 3

ORGANIZATION AND OPERATION
OF PROBATION AND PAROLE SYSTEMS

LEARNING OBJECTIVES

* Understand both the organization and operation of the federal probation and parole system.

* Be familiar with the general organizations and operations of state probation and parole systems.

* Learn the important probation and parole functions of supervision, investigation, revocation and pretrial services.

* Provide an overall comparison of federal and state probation and parole systems.

DISCUSSION TOPICS AND QUESTIONS

1. How does the federal probation and parole system operate?

2. What components of the criminal justice system should a probation and parole officer be familiar with? Explain.

3. Compare how the budgets (including salaries) of probation and parole operations compare with other criminal justice functions and budgets.

4. Explain the supervisory and investigatory functions of probation and parole. Give examples.

5. What is parole revocation and how is it applied?

6. What are pretrial services and how do they operate?

FEDERAL SYSTEM

Federal probation and parole services are basically standardized and uniform, resulting in a professional and qualitative level of service considered by many to be superior to that of most state systems. Other variables important to this professionalization of services include: improved resources, reduced caseloads and different a clientele. Many state probation and parole systems consider the Federal system as a model deserving emulation.

Overview of Organization and Operation

The Federal Probation System, prior to 1940, was administered by the Bureau of Prisons in the Department of Justice. On July 1, 1940, the administration of probation was transferred to the Administrative Office of the United States Courts. The Division of Probation, established within the Administrative Office, developed uniform standards of professional performance (e.g., standards for writing a pre-sentence investigation). Unlike many government agencies, considerable autonomy is given to each of the 95 Federal District Courts. The District Courts, under the Probation Act, 18 U.S.C. §3654, have the sole power to appoint and dismiss federal probation officers. The chief probation officer in each district directs the work of all probation officers. The number of federal probation officers has increased from the first three appointments in 1927 to approximately 2,400 officers in 1988.

The following typically comprises the chain of command in a federal probation office: the probation officer directly reports to a supervisor; the supervisor reports to the deputy chief; and the deputy chief reports to the chief probation officer.

The Federal Probation Service works closely with many individuals and agencies in the federal criminal justice system. To have an effective system, there must be close working relationships between the Federal Bureau of Prisons, the U.S. Parole Commission, and the Federal Probation System. For example, federal probation officers perform parole duties in agreement with the U.S. Parole Commission. The accompanying diagram depicts the variety of persons and entities with which a federal probation officer works at various times (see Figure 3-A).

As the figure demonstrates, the federal probation officer works with law enforcement officials. The probation officer, for example, may consult with an FBI agent who participates in the arrest of an offender who faces sentencing. The probation officer may ask the FBI agent what role the offender played in the crime.

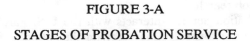

FIGURE 3-A

STAGES OF PROBATION SERVICE

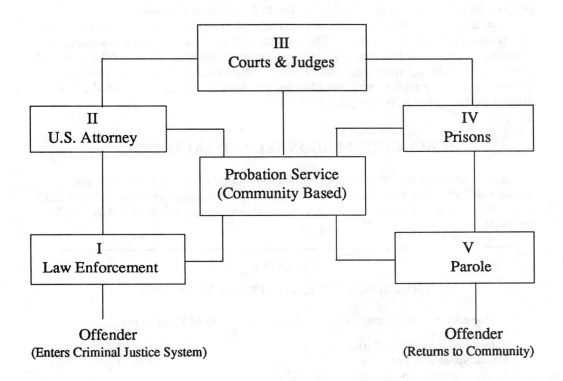

The U.S. Attorney or Assistant U.S. Attorney is frequently contacted by a probation officer. The probation officer, for example, may request the U.S. Attorney's help in seeking to revoke the probation of someone who has left the district without permission, or otherwise violated his or her conditions of parole.

The court personnel and the Federal judges have extensive contact with the probation officers. For example, the probation officer checks with court clerks to find out the exact date the defendant pleaded guilty. Federal judges, on the other hand, depend on Federal probation officers to investigate the background of a defendant and to recommend what sentence should be imposed by the court.

The Federal Bureau of Prisons contacts Federal probation officers when a Federal prisoner is going to be released on furlough. The Federal probation officer may need to assist this person in a job search.

The Federal Probation Service interacts with the U.S. Parole Commission. The federal probation officer at this stage may take on the role of a federal parole officer. The supervision of federal parolees is a major task. For example, annual supervision reports on all parolees must be submitted to the Federal Parole Commission.

The federal probation officer must also submit monthly statistical reports to indicate changes in his or her caseload. The probation officer who receives a new parolee to supervise, indicates on the monthly statistical report an increase in the total number of parolees he or she is supervising. All of the statistical records on Federal parolees and probationers are compiled and recorded by the Administrative Office of the United States Courts located in Washington, D.C.

BUDGETS, PERSONNEL AND SALARIES

The financial resources to support probation and parole services are one portion of the over-all expenditures of the judiciary. As Table 3-1 indicates, in Fiscal Year 1985, 10 cents of every budget dollar for the federal court system was spent for salaries of POs and staff.

TABLE 3-1

THE JUDICIAL DOLLAR (FISCAL YEAR 1985)

Major Expenditure Items	% of Total Expenditures
Salaries of Supporting Personnel	24
Office Space and Facilities	14
Salaries and Expenses, Bankruptcy Courts	12
Court Operations and Maintenance	11
Salaries of Probation Officers and Staff	10
Salaries of Judges	8
Defender Services	6
Fees of Jurors and Commissioners	4
Administrative Office and Federal Judicial Center	4
Court Security	3
Salaries of Magistrates and Staff	3
National Courts	1
	100

Actual Total Amount: $1,021,680,000

Source: Administrative Office of the United States Courts, Annual Report, 1985.

Federal probation officers are only a portion of the total personnel comprising the judiciary of the United States. In fact, in 1987, federal probation officers and staff represented approximately 17 percent of the total federal judicial work force (see Table 3-2).

TABLE 3-2

PERSONNEL IN THE U.S. JUDICIARY (JUNE 1987)

Judges:	1,011	(5.2 percent)
Judge's Staff:	3,330	(17.2 percent)
Other Court Staff:	200	(1.0 percent)
Clerk's Offices:	4,255	(22.0 percent)
Bankruptcy Judges and Staff:	3,965	(20.5 percent)
Probation Officers and Staff:	3,311	(17.1 percent)
U.S. Magistrates and Staff:	1,010	(5.2 percent)
Public Defenders and Staff:	460	(2.4 percent)
Administrative Office and Federal Judicial Center:	686	(3.5 percent)
Other Court Personnel:	1,124	(5.8 percent)
	19,352	

Federal probation officers are hired by the United States District Court in which they will work. The salary scale, however, is uniform for the entire system. Based on the recent job classification system, a new federal probation officer starts at a grade 9 and is promoted, as a general rule, to grade 11 after one year; and then to grade 12 after two years.

Normally, a federal probation officer will remain at grade 12 the remainder of his or her working career. The person will still be eligible for step increases in pay at the grade 12 level. If a federal probation officer is promoted to a supervisory position, the person may have a grade of 13 and, if promoted to a deputy chief, a grade of 14. A chief of a federal probation district is generally a grade 15 or 16, depending on variables such as office size and approval of the chief judge of that district. The following are the grade salary ranges in Federal probation as of January 1, 1989: grade 9 - $23,800; grade 11 - $28,900; grade 12 - $34,600; grade 13 - $41,100; grade 14 - $48,600; grade 15 - $57,200; grade 16 - $67,000.

Supervision

Supervision is one of the primary responsibilities of the federal probation officer. The following table illustrates the types of supervision over which a probation officer is responsible, and the relative demand represented by each.

TABLE 3-3

PERSONS RECEIVED FOR SUPERVISION
FOR TWELVE MONTH PERIODS ENDING JUNE 30, 1984 AND 1985

Type of Supervision	1984		1985	
	Number	Percent	Number	Percent
Judge Probation	4,634	42.3	15,044	42.7
Magistrate Probation	7,582	21.9	7,662	21.8
Pretrial Diversion	2,175	6.3	2,269	6.4
Parole	6,250	18.1	5,830	16.6
Mandatory Release	2,192	6.3	2,488	7.1
Military Parole	231	0.7	279	0.8
Special Parole	1,518	4.4	1,627	4.6
All Cases	34,582	100.0	35,199	100.0

Source: Administration Office of the United States Courts, Annual Report, 1985, 23.

Approximately 80 percent of the Federal probation officers are actively engaged in supervising probationers and parolees. The following table indicates the number of officers and their caseloads during the years 1978 through 1985.

TABLE 3-4

PERSONS RECEIVED, REMOVED, AND UNDER SUPERVISION IN THE FEDERAL PROBATION SYSTEM FROM 1978 THROUGH 1985

	Received	Removed	Remaining Under Supervision
1978	43,060	42,399	66,681
1979	41,863	44,049	66,087
1980	39,040	41,964	64,450
1981	36,723	43,550	59,016
1982	38,773	39,439	58,373
1983	41,019	39,151	60,180
1984	42,456	38,134	63,092
1985	42,812	39,249	65,999

Source: Administrative Office of the United States Courts, Annual Report, 1985: 22.

Investigation

The federal probation officer is responsible for numerous types of investigations. The annual reports of the Administrative Office of the United States Courts reveal that the types of investigations may vary over the years, reflecting changes in crime, caseloads, sentencing practices, prison populations and other variables. The following table indicates the types and numbers of investigations undertaken over a two-year period.

TABLE 3-5

INVESTIGATIVE REPORTS BY PROBATION OFFICERS
FOR TWELVE-MONTH PERIODS ENDING JUNE 30, 1984 & JUNE 30, 1985

Type of Investigation	1984	1985	Change
Presentence Investigation	30,745	32,669	6.3
Collateral Investigation for another district	23,057	25,055	8.7
Preliminary Investigation to assist U.S. Attorney	2,375	2,178	-8.3
Postsentence Investigation for Institution	1,375	1,323	-1.8
Pretransfer Investigation (Probation and Parole)	7,292	8,550	8.5
Alleged Violation Investigation (Probation and Parole)	12,585	13,289	5.6
Prerelease Investigation for a Federal or Military Investigation	7,292	6,955	-4.6
Special Investigation regarding a prisoner in confinement	6,605	6,853	3.8
Bail Interviews	25,569	27,365	6.6
Furlough and Work-Release Reports for Bureau of Prisons Institutions	5,350	5,490	2.6
Parole Supervision Reports	22,412	24,471	9.2
Parole Revocation Hearing Reports	1,806	1,747	-3.3
Total	147,124	55,945	6.0

Revocation

A federal probation or parole violation is any act or omission on the part of a probationer or parolee which is contrary to the express or implied conditions under which the individual is being supervised. Violations of a probationer are reported to the court and violations of a parolee are reported to the U.S. Parole Commission. Otherwise, the two processes are very similar. The figure below illustrates such a process.

FIGURE 3-B

STAGES OF REVOCATION PROCESS

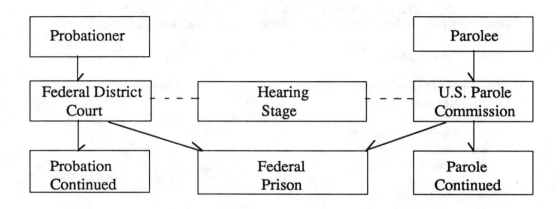

Two major court decisions have had enormous impact on the revocation process. *Morrissey v. Brewer*, 408 U.S. 471 (1972) established due process rights for a parolee and required that two separate hearings be undertaken prior to revocation of parole. The Supreme Court expanded this due process requirement in 1973 in *Gagnon v. Scarpelli*, 411 U.S. 778 (1973). The court ruled in this case that probationers were entitled to the same rights and procedures as parolees in revocation proceedings. In addition, the court ruled that probationers and parolees had a right to a court-appointed attorney, where a need was demonstrated. A summarization of parolee rights at preliminary hearings established by the *Morrissey* decision include: (1) prior notice of the inquiry; (2) prior notice of the alleged offense; (3) right to appear in person; (4) right to present documents and witnesses; (5) right to a hearing before a neutral hearing officer; and (6) right to be given reasons for the determination made.

Those rights guaranteed at a final revocation hearing include: (1) written notice of the asserted parole violations and evidence in support thereof; (2) opportunity to be heard in person; (3) opportunity to present witnesses and documentary evidence; (4) right to confront and cross-examine adverse witnesses; (5) right to a neutral hearing body (e.g., Federal Parole Examiner); and (6) a written statement of the evidence relied on and the reasons for revoking parole.

Pretrial Services

The role of pretrial services within the overall criminal justice process is extremely important for many of the same reasons described in support of alternatives to incarceration. Although all federal probation officers are called upon to render pretrial services of various forms from time to time, Congress enacted special legislation formalizing this pretrial service on an experimental basis in a limited number of districts in 1974. This legislation was an important part of the Speedy Trial Act of 1974 (Pub. L. No. 93-619, 88 Stat. 2076, 18 USC 3152 *et seq*.). This act contained two titles: Title I provided a schedule for decreasing the amount of time for indictment, arraignment, and disposition of a criminal case to 100 days by July 1, 1979; Title II provided that 10 demonstration pretrial service agencies be established to interview defendants, verify information for judicial officers, and supervise and coordinate (or provide services) for certain persons on bail.

Title II of the Speedy Trial Act of 1974 authorized the Director of the Administrative Office of the United States Courts to establish, on a demonstration basis, 10 pretrial service agencies in representative judicial districts. Five of the agencies were to be governed by a seven member Board of Trustees appointed in each of the five separate districts. The agencies in the remaining selected districts were to be administered under the Probation Division of the Administrative Office of the United States Courts with the chief probation officer serving as the chief pretrial service officer.

The Act authorized the Chief Justice of the United States, with the concurrence of the Attorney General, to designate the 10 district courts in which agencies were to be established. In accordance with the criteria set forth in the statute, the Chief Justice designated that pretrial service agencies be established on a demonstration basis.

The designations were made on the basis of a study conducted by the Administrative Office of the United States Courts in accordance with the criteria established by the Speedy Trial Act. All 10 agencies were located in large metropolitan centers where the volume of criminal litigation was substantial and the types of criminal cases varied. Funds in the amount of $10 million, as authorized by the Speedy Trial Act, became available on July 1, 1975, and the task of organizing the agencies began immediately. In October 1975, the pretrial services agency in the Northern District of Illinois commenced operations, and by April 1976, pretrial agencies had been fully established in all 10 districts. By 1988, there were 29 federal districts with pretrial service officers (Administrative Office of the U.S. Courts, 1988).

Pretrial service agencies generally make pre-bail investigations for judicial officers and maintain supervision as well as provide supportive services to defendants released pending trial. More specifically, pretrial service agency functions include: (1) the compilation and verification of background information on persons charged with the violation of federal criminal law for the use of the Federal District Judge or a United States Magistrate in setting conditions of release pursuant to the Bail Reform Act (18 U.S. Code, 3141 et seq.); and (2) the supervision of persons released from custody prior to trial or conviction, including the provision of counseling and other pretrial services. In performing these functions, the federal pretrial service officer presents a completed form to the federal judge/magistrate which: (1) identifies the defendant; (2) summarizes his/her history (e.g., family ties, financial resources, drug use, health, prior record, record of appearance); and (3) contains a recommendation. The possible recommendations include the following options: (a) personal recognizance, (b) unsecured bond, (c) 10 percent deposit, (d) surety bond, (e) collateral, (f) third-party custody, (g) pretrial service agency supervision, and (h) other conditions.

The stated objectives of the Speedy Trial Act are to reduce pretrial detention and recidivism. Included among the services to be rendered by pretrial services agencies to persons released from custody prior to trial or conviction are assistance in securing necessary employment, medical, legal, or social services. The agencies are sometimes authorized to operate, or contract for the operation of, appropriate facilities for the custody or care of persons released from custody. Apparent violations of the conditions of pretrial release are reported to the court with recommended modifications in the terms of release.

The Pretrial Services Act of 1982 established pretrial services for each of the federal court districts (other than the District of Columbia, which already had pretrial services in operation), with supervision responsibilities vested in chief probation and pretrial services officers. The functions of pretrial services under the Act include the following:

(1) Collect, verify and report to the judicial officer, prior to the pretrial release hearing, information pertaining to the pretrial release of each individual charged with an offense, including information relating to any danger that the release of such person may pose to any other person or the community and recommend appropriate release conditions for such individual.

(2) Review and modify the reports and recommendations for persons seeking release.

(3) Supervise persons released into its custody under this chapter.

(4) Operate or contract for the operation of appropriate facilities for the custody or care of persons released under this chapter including residential halfway houses, addict and alcoholic treatment centers, and counseling services.

(5) Inform the court and the United States Attorney of all apparent violations of pretrial release conditions, arrests of persons released to the custody of providers of pretrial services or under the supervision of providers of pre-

trial services, and any danger that any such person may come to pose to any other person or the community, and recommend appropriate modifications of release conditions.

(6) Serve as coordinator for other local agencies which serve or are eligible to serve as custodians under this chapter and advise the court as to the eligibility, availability and capacity of such agencies.

(7) Assist persons released under this chapter in securing any necessary employment, medical, legal or social services.

(8) Prepare, in cooperation with the United States Marshall and the United States Attorney, such pretrial detention reports as are required by the provisions of the Federal Rules of Criminal Procedure relating to the supervision of detention pending trial.

(9) Develop and implement a system to monitor and evaluate bail activities, provide information to judicial officers on the results of bail decisions, and prepare periodic reports to assist in the improvement of the bail process.

(10) To the extent provided for in an agreement between chief pretrial services officers in districts in which pretrial services are established, collect, verify and prepare reports for the United States Attorney's office of information pertaining to the pretrial diversion of any individual who is or may be charged with an offense, and perform such other duties as may be required under such agreement.

(11) Make contracts, to such extent and in such amounts as are provided in appropriation acts, for the carrying out of any pretrial service functions.

(12) Perform such other functions as specified [by law or regulation].

The future of pretrial services has been a matter of continuing concern, especially in view of increasing system demands. In recent years, evaluation results have indicated that such programs are indeed valuable for monitoring and supervision purposes. With the increasing incorporation of new requirements (such as drug testing) into pretrial services, the programs are likely to expand despite their considerable costs.

STATE SYSTEMS

State probation and parole systems differ in many ways from one another, and also from the federal systems. An accurate portrayal of individual state operations involves in-depth analysis within each state environment. While acknowledging the differences in the state systems, certain elements and problem areas are common to all. The following discussion will delineate some of the major differences between state systems, and also describe some of their similarities. Specific examples will be provided regarding one state's approach for purposes of illustration.

Overview of Organization and Operation

One of the significant differences in the organization of state probation systems concerns whether they are located under the state's executive or judicial branch. An argument in favor of placement within the executive branch is that offender services normally exist under executive branch authority and this will result in closer, more effective coordination. This position was favored by the President's Task Force on Corrections in 1973 (*Report on Corrections*). The Task Force noted the benefit of uniform standards and coordinated staff training.

Although parole boards, unlike probation agencies, are by nature executive bodies, the structure of the parole boards may differ. In most states, the parole board administers an integrated probation and parole agency. The American Correctional Association (1971) identified four basic parole board structures:

(1) those administering an integrated probation and parole agency;
(2) those administering the parole function only;
(3) those that are a subordinate component of a department which administers the correctional institutions; and
(4) those that are part of an agency which administers the institutional and probation services.

The major duty of a parole board is to decide whether parole is to be granted or denied. Once the parolee is in the community, the parole board must also decide if parole should be revoked or continued.

The selection process of parole board members varies. An American Correctional Association research project (1975) surveyed the process by which various jurisdictions appoint parole board members (*Parole*, 1975). The study found that in 40 of the 54 jurisdictions studied, the appointing authorities were Governors; in two jurisdictions, Board Members were Civil Service appointees; and in the remaining 12 jurisdictions, members were selected by a variety of methods, most including the participation of Governors, but not exclusively. In the federal system (U.S. Parole Commission) the President of the United States appointed the commissioners with the advice and consent of the Senate.

The number of parole board members also varies among the states. The American Correctional Association study found that board membership ranged from three to 12 members. Most jurisdictions are relatively small, with 24 having five members and 16 with three members. The U.S. Parole Commission has eight members.

A national survey of parole board members (*Selection for Parole*, 1966) revealed that the items considered by them to be most important in parole decisions were related to the risk of violation. The following table indicates the study results.

TABLE 3-6

ITEMS CONSIDERED BY PAROLE BOARD MEMBERS
TO BE MOST IMPORTANT IN PAROLE DECISIONS

Item	Percent Including Item as One of Five Most Important
1. My estimate of the chances that the prisoner would or would not commit a serious crime if paroled.	92.8
2. My judgment that the prisoner would benefit from further experience in the institution program or, at any rate, would become a better risk if confined longer.	87.1
3. My judgment that the prisoner would become a worse risk if confined longer.	71.9
4. My judgment that the prisoner had already been punished enough to "pay" for his crime.	43.2
5. The probability that the prisoner would be a misdemeanant and a burden to his parole supervisors, even if he did not commit any serious offenses on parole.	35.3
6. My feelings about how my decision in this case would affect the feelings or welfare of the prisoner's relatives or dependents.	33.8
7. What I thought the reaction of the judge might be if the prisoner were granted parole.	20.9

Source: National Parole Institutes, *Selection for Parole* (New York: NCCD, 1966).

Some state parole boards have responsibilities in addition to the granting of parole. The following table points out some of the additional responsibilities assumed by parole boards, as revealed by a national survey.

TABLE 3-7

ADULT PAROLING AGENCIES
RESPONSIBILITIES OTHER THAN PAROLE

Additional Responsibility	Number of Boards
Holds clemency hearings	28
Commutes sentences	24
Appoints parole supervision staff	24
Administers parole service	20
Paroles from local institutions	19
Grants or withholds "good time"	17
Supervises probation service	14
Grants pardons, restorations, and remissions	1
Fixes maximum sentence after six months	1
May discharge prior to sentence expiration	1
Sets standards for "good time"	1
Acts as advisory board on pardons	1
None	5

Source: NCCD, *Corrections in the United States* (New York: NCCD, 1967).

Budget

Unlike the budget of the federal probation system which is only a portion of the judicial budget, the overall budgets of the "hodge-podge" of state agencies cannot be so easily apportioned. Nevertheless, the United States Department of Justice has gathered valuable budgetary data by which comparisons might be made, including the expenditures for institutions and corrections administration. The figures reveal the proportionally small expenditures allotted to probation and parole functions (typically 10 to 20 percent) of the overall correctional budgets (see Table 3-8).

TABLE 3-8

DIRECT EXPENDITURES FOR STATE AND LOCAL
CORRECTIONS ACTIVITIES
(Dollar Amounts in Thousands)

Level of Government	Total Direct Expenditures	Correctional Institutions	Probation, Pardon and Parole
State-Local, total*	$12,327,568	10,291,080 (83.5%)	1,506,331 (12.2%)
States*	8,080,703	6,776,610 (83.9%)	773,936 (9.6%)
Local, total	4,246,865	3,514,470 (82.8%)	732,395 (17.2%)
Counties	3,197,603	2,550,263 (79.8%)	647,340 (20.2%)
Municipalities	1,049,262	964,207 (91.9%)	85,055 (8.1%)

*   An additional $530,157,000 was expedited for other state correctional activities resulting in inexact total percentages for these categories.

Source: U.S. Department of Justice, Bureau of Justice Statistics, *Sourcebook of Criminal Justice Statistics* -- 1987, 1988.

The salaries of the probation and parole officers in the state settings are generally less than those of federal probation officers. In recent years, recruitment difficulties have been reported at both the federal and state levels. As the table below illustrates, the variation between states is also substantial.

TABLE 3-9

STATE SALARIES OF LINE OFFICERS BY REGION

Region	Entry Level	After Five Years	Region	Entry Level	After Five Years
Western					
Alaska	$32,424	$38,712	Oregon	$21,987	$26,225
Arizona	20,571	23,836	Utah	18,730	26,416
California	33,228	40,044	Washington	19,500	23,820
Colorado	24,564	32,910	Wyoming	20,271	22,151

continued

TABLE 3-9 *continued*

Region	Entry Level	After Five Years	Region	Entry Level	After Five Years
Idaho	17,388	22,755	Hawaii	21,900	27,900
Montana	15,332	19,307	AVERAGE:	22,363	27,618
Nevada	22,461	27,342			
Northeast					
Connecticut	$21,245	$35,612	New York	$30,833	$38,138
Delaware	16,980	18,167	Pennsylvania	19,007	27,000
Maine	22,164	29,452	Rhode Island	21,423	24,796
Massachusetts	27,893	34,867	Vermont	21,279	NoRept
New Hampshire	20,292	25,908	AVERAGE:	22,246	29,313
New Jersey	21,343	29,877			
Southeast					
Alabama	$17,394	$23,951	So. Carolina	$18,006	NoRept
Florida	16,990	21,300	Tennessee	13,536	17,628
Georgia	17,000	22,000	AVERAGE:	16,061	21,627
Mississippi	13,441	23,258			
Mid-Atlantic					
Kentucky	$16,000	$20,000	Wash.,DC		
Maryland	15,958	18,465	(Superior Ct.)	$22,907	$35,432
North Carolina	18,349	22,212	West Virginia	16,872	18,528
Virginia	20,933	28,000	AVERAGE:	18,503	23,773
Central					
Arkansas	$15,000	$20,000	New Mexico	$17,388	$19,200
Iowa	21,000	26,000	North Dakota	16,920	19,860
Kansas	20,136	23,304	Oklahoma	18,504	24,792
Louisiana	16,212	20,400	South Dakota	16,848	17,500
Minnesota	20,200	27,000	Texas	21,744	27,036
Missouri	16,788	20,000	AVERAGE:	18,135	22,174
Nebraska	16,883	21,000			

Source: Federal Probation Officers Association, national survey, 1988.

In evaluating the comparative investments made by the states to probation and parole functions per client, the following table examines the recent indicators provided by selected southeastern states. Notice the comparatively low expenditures compared to the national average, and the wide range in expenditures.

TABLE 3-10

COMPARATIVE ANNUAL EXPENDITURES FOR PROBATION IN 10 SOUTHEASTERN STATES AND THE UNITED STATES (1985)

State	Annual Probation Budget ($1,000)	Cost of Number of Probationers	Supervision per 1,000 Clients
Alabama	$7,936	16,520	400
Florida	48,156	71,951	635
Georgia	28,079	86,487	325
Maryland	30,974	75,797	290
Mississippi	54,432	6,604	259
North Carolina	25,000	57,506	456
South Carolina	12,800	16,770	400
Tennessee	8,400	13,635	613
Texas	44,662	269,909	365
Virginia	13,958	13,958	697
Federal	125,000	51,011	1,500

Source: Criminal Justice Institute, *The Corrections Yearbook*, South Salem, New York, 1986.

Supervision

Many probation and parole officers have contended for years that supervision of their cases would improve if their caseloads were reduced in number. Some feel that an ideal caseload should not exceed 50 clients. The San Francisco Project (1969) studied the issue of caseload size. Four levels of workloads were established: (1) ideal (50 cases); (2) intensive (25, half the ideal); (3) normal (100, twice the ideal); and (4) minimum supervision (with a ceiling of 250 cases). As part of the study, persons in minimum supervision caseloads were required only to submit a monthly written report; no contacts occurred except when requested by the probationer. It was found that offenders in minimum caseloads performed as well as those under normal supervision. The minimum and ideal caseloads had almost identical violation rates. In the intensive caseloads, the violation rate did not decline, but technical violations increased.

The San Francisco Project suggested that the number of contacts between probationer and staff had little relationship to success or failure on probation. The study concluded that the concept of a caseload is meaningless without some type of classification and matching of offender types with services to be offered, and effective staffing to accomplish the goal.

Probation and parole officers across the United States must also work together in the supervision of probationers and parolees. Clegg (1970) reported that states entered into agreements (compacts) for supervision of parolees and probationers, beginning with the passage of the Inter-State Parole and Probation Compact in 1934. Compacts permit parolees and probationers to return to their home residence and still be under proper supervision by local probation and parole authorities.

Clegg (1970) also observed that the Inter-State Compact accomplished two objectives: (1) It protected the community by providing supervision for the offender and (2) It increased the chances of successful reformation for the offender by permitting his return to a locality where he had a family, acquaintances and job opportunities.

Investigation

The major duties of parole and probation officers include investigation as well as supervision. Some officers have a difficult time with the dual functions. How can an officer be a "helper" on the one hand and a "watch-dog" on the other? Ohlin, Piven and Pappenfort (1956) made a study of probation officers and their work roles. They determined that three work orientation types were prevalent: (1) the *punitive officer*, (2) the *protective agent* and (3) the *welfare worker*.

Generally, the *punitive officer* assumes that he is the protector of "middle class" values, with an overriding duty to protect society from his clients. The *protective agent* is ambivalent. He is protective of both community and client. The officer's reaction (e.g., praise or rejection) depends on the factual circumstances, not his basic value or philosophic preferences. The *welfare worker*, on the other hand, is oriented toward the client. This officer goes out of the way to meet the needs of the probationer or parolee. While these rules may be handy in categorizing officer roles, it should be obvious that modern probation and parole needs require a continued balancing of these overlapping and competing roles.

It should be noted, however, that some states do not regularly perform presentence investigations. The failure to undertake presentence investigations usually reflects a probation and parole authority that is lacking in necessary resources, or a judiciary that is resistant to change.

Revocation

The requirements of the revocation process may differ among the states. The due process and procedural safeguards mandated by judicial decisions, however, are applicable to both the federal and state systems. The previously mentioned *Morrissey* case is a prime example of a landmark judicial decision that required modifications in many state procedures.

The revocation of parole by a parole authority has been traditionally justified on three theoretical grounds: *the privilege theory*, the *contract theory* and the *continuing custody theory* (Palmer, 1973). The *privilege theory* considers parole to be within the total discretion of the state, thus a privilege. Such an approach appears to ignore the realities of parole's importance and prevalence within the criminal justice system. The *contract theory* views parole as an agreement between two contracting parties, the violation of which subjects the violator to the penalties provided. The logic of this rationale, however is somewhat strained, as the relationship of the contracting parties is hardly equal or voluntary in nature. Finally, the *continuing custody theory* considers parole only as an extension of the confinement process, thus subject to the same restrictions. This theory of treating parolees as inmates is also faulty in that the freedoms enjoyed by each are not truly comparable. As evidenced by recent judicial decisions, the courts have been unwilling to embrace any single theory of parole, and have severely limited the application of each through imposition of due process requirements. This had led to a recognition of a fourth theory by some observers, understandably referred to as the *due process theory*, which reflects recent judicial decisions and legal mandates. Parolees are either discharged from their parole conditions by completing their terms, or by obtaining early discharges.

Pretrial Services

State pretrial service programs, like those of the federal system, permit intervention into a case before it comes to court. Frequently, the defendant enters a program of counseling and guidance, since supervised pretrial programs generally offer rehabilitation or treatment for eligible defendants, especially those charged with non-violent crimes. Restitution to the victim is also sometimes required of participants. States exercise substantial latitude in their individual programs, but the following requirements may be considered typical of those imposed on defendants:

> Program requirements differ from charge to charge and from defendant to defendant. There are, however, several ground rules. All defendants are assigned a counselor and are responsible for making contact with him for a duration of a minimum of 90 days and a maximum of one year. The defendant is required to attend an organized tour of a correctional facility, perform a minimum of 15 hours volunteer work, and seek meaningful employment. Defen-

dants who have special needs or problems may be referred, on a contract basis, by their counselors to other agencies such as Alcohol and Drug Abuse, Mental Health, Vocational Rehabilitation, Technical Education, Department of Social Services, etc. In cases where it is appropriate to compensate victims for their losses, restitution is required from the defendant before he can complete the diversion program (South Carolina Pretrial Intervention Report, 1983).

The factors leading to the increased emphasis on state pretrial services are numerous. The programs may be made self-supporting by requiring funding by participants. Since many of the programs require restitution, direct benefits accrue to the victims. Other advantages may include: (a) immediate treatment and counseling; (b) criminal record avoidance; (c) vocational training; (d) reduced jail populations; and (e) relief to taxpayers. These benefits should not be sought at the expense of public safety, however. In summary, the benefits of pretrial services should be carefully considered and safeguards implemented (e.g., drug testing).

REFERENCES

Administrative Office of the United States Courts. (1988, October 21) (statistical data).

Administrative Office of the United States Courts. (1988, September 22) Workload memorandum by D.L. Chamblee.

Administrative Office of the United States Courts. (1985) *1985 Annual Report of the Director*. Washington, DC: U.S. Government Printing Office.

Administrative Office of the United States Courts. (1981) *Speedy Trial Act of 1974*. Washington, DC: U.S. Government Printing Office.

Administrative Office of the United States Courts (1981) *1981 Annual Report of the Director*. Washington, DC: U.S. Government Printing Office.

Administrative Office of the United States Courts. (1980) *1980 Annual Report of the Director*. Washington, DC: U.S. Government Printing Office.

Administrative Office of the United States Courts. (1980) *Federal Judicial Workload Statistics*. Washington, DC: U.S. Government Printing Office.

Administrative Office of the United States Courts. (1976) *Report on the Implementation of Title I and Title II of the Speedy Trial Act of 1974*. Washington, DC: U.S. Government Printing Office.

American Correctional Association. (1971). *Manual of Correctional Standards*.

Bureau of the Census, National Criminal Justice Information and Statistics Service. (1978). *State and Local Probation and Parole Systems*. Washington, DC: U.S. Government Printing Office.

Clegg, R.K. *Probation and Parole*. (1970). Charles C Thomas Publisher.

Criminal Justice Institute. (1986). *The Corrections Yearbook*. South Salem, NY. Camp, G. & C. (eds.).

Federal Judicial Center. (1976). *An Introduction to the Federal Probation System*. Washington, DC: Author.

Gagnon v. Scarpelli. 411 U.S. 471 (1973).

Morrissey v. Brewer. 408 U.S. 471 (1972).

National Advisory Commission on Criminal Justice Standards and Goals. (1973). *Report on Corrections*. Washington, DC: U.S. Government Printing Office.

National Parole Institutes. (1966). *Selection for Parole*. New York: National Council on Crime and Delinquency.

Ohlin, L.E., Piven, H. & Pappenfort, D.M. (1956). Major Dilemmas of the Social Worker in Probation and Parole. *NPPA Journal*, 2 (3), 215

Palmer, J.W. (1977). *Constitutional Rights of Prisoners*. Cincinnati: Anderson Publishing Co.

Parker, W.C. (1975). *Parole*. College Park, MD: American Correctional Association.

Prus, R.C. & Stratton, J.R. (1976). Parole Revocation Decisionmaking: Private Typings and Official Designations. *Federal Probation*, March.

Reports of the Proceedings of the Judicial Conference of the United States. (1980). Washington, DC.

Robinson, J. et al. (1969). *The San Francisco Project*. Berkeley, CA: University of California School of Criminology.

Ryan, D.B. (1977). The Federal Pretrial Services Agencies. *Federal Probation*, March, 15-22.

United States Courts. (1976). *Pretrial Services*. Washington, DC: U.S. Government Printing Office.

United States 93rd Congress. *Speedy Trial Act of 1974*. Public Law 93-619, Section 18 U.S. Code 3152-3.

United States Department of Justice. (1980) *Parole in the United States*. Washington, DC: U.S. Government Printing Office.

United States Department of Justice. (1980). *Sourcebook of Criminal Justice Statistics*. Washington, DC: U.S. Government Printing Office.

Chapter 4

PROBATION AND PAROLE OFFICERS:
DUTIES, RESPONSIBILITIES
AND NEW DEVELOPMENTS

LEARNING OBJECTIVES

* Understand the operations of effective case management.

* Knowledge of the importance and substance of presentence investigations.

* Learning the requirements of proper probation and parole supervision.

* Developing strategies for providing referrals and treatment.

DISCUSSION QUESTIONS

1. What is a Client Management Classification (CMC) System and how does it operate?

2. What are the important elements of presentence investigations?

3. How does a probation or parole officer determine the appropriate form of supervision? What type of conditions may be imposed on the offender?

4. Why are treatment and referral programs important? How may a probation or parole officer become aware of treatment and referral alternatives?

CASE MANAGEMENT

Modern case management is increasingly being utilized through the implementation of new Client Management Classification (CMC) Systems. CMC Systems are designed to meet two specific needs. First, these systems are designed to help in management by determining the level of surveillance that should be employed in each probation/parole case (National Advisory Commission, 1973). A second purpose is to determine offender needs as well as identifying resources to meet them. This second concern is not of recent origin, but was a concern for some of the earliest students of criminology, including Lombroso, Ferri and Garofalo (Schafer, 1969). Classification processes continue to receive much attention in the corrections setting, where classification schemes are critical to both inmate assignments and institutional priorities (Abadinsky, 1983).

In recent years, newly designed client management classification models have been developed to meet both the needs of caseload management and classification. One such model has been the Client Management Classification System (CMC), first developed and utilized in Wisconsin in 1975, and adopted by the National Institute of Corrections (NIC Draft Report, 1983).

The NIC embraced CMC as a pragmatic and easily administered classification and case handling approach for adult probation and parole (NIC, 1983). The procedures incorporated within CMC assist officers in three ways: (1) gaining a quick appreciation and understanding of the offender's problems and needs; (2) identifying impediments to solving the offender's problems; and (3) developing an appropriate and effective casework plan.

The CMC is employed at the earliest intake phase, enabling offenders to be assigned to casework groups based upon an empirically scored, structured review, a device that saves time and assists in developing coherent treatment strategies. Early evaluations of the CMC have documented its accuracy in classifying offenders, its effectiveness in saving time and resources, and its acceptance by probation and parole officers implementing it.

The Client Management Classification System is comprised of four specific treatment modalities: (1) Selective Intervention, (2) Environmental Structure, (3) Casework/Control and (4) Limit Setting. These labels identify the characteristic supervision strategy to be employed with each group, and serve as a framework for developing a working relationship. A brief description of each modality follows:

1.   *Selective Intervention*. This group is designed for offenders who enjoy relatively stable and prosocial lifestyles (e.g., employed, established in community, and minimal criminal records). Such offenders have typically experienced an isolated and stressful event, or neurotic problem. With effective intervention, there is a higher chance of avoiding future difficulty. The goals of treatment for these individuals include the development of appropriate responses to temporary crises and problems, and the reestablishment of pro-life patterns.

2. *Environmental Structure*. The dominant characteristics of offenders in this group consist of deficiencies in social, vocational, and intellectual skills. Most of their problems stem from their inability to succeed in their employment or to be comfortable in most social settings, an overall lack of social skills and intellectual cultivation/ability. The goals for these persons include: (a) developing basic employment and social skills; (b) selecting alternatives to association with criminally-oriented peers; and (c) improving social skills and impulse controls.

3. *Casework/Control*. These offenders manifest instabilities in their lives as evidenced by failures in employment and domestic problems. A lack of goal-directedness is present, typically associated with alcohol and drug problems. Offense patterns include numerous arrests, although marketable job skills are present. Unstable childhoods, family pressure and financial difficulties are typically present. The goals appropriate for this group include promoting stability in their professional and domestic endeavors, and achieving an improved utilization of the individual's potential along with an elimination of self-defeating behavior and emotional/psychological problems.

4. *Limit Setting*. Offenders in this group are commonly considered to be successful and career criminals because of their long-term involvement in criminal activities. They generally enjoy "beating the system," they frequently act for material gain, and they show little remorse or guilt. Because of their value system, they easily adapt to prison environments and return to crime upon release. Goals for the group are problematic, but include changing the offender's basic attitudes and closely supervising his behavior within the community.

CMC utilizes the above categories by placing the offender into the proper modality based upon a structured interview of less than one hour. Upon classification, an individualized treatment plan is developed based on the following guidelines (NIC Draft Report, 1983): (a) General description of participants: (b) Suggested treatment goals; (c) Anticipated officer-offender relationship (positive and negative); (d) Auxiliary referral sources likely to be used; and (e) Suggested techniques for approaching persons in each group.

Early results of this plan in Wisconsin found that offenders generally were classified in each mode in the following manner: (1) Selective Intervention treatment (40 percent), (2) Environmental Structure model (15 percent), (3) Casework Control mode (30 percent) and (4) Limit Setting group (15 percent).

In conclusion, the CMC seems to offer the following advantages to adult probation and parole agents: (a) effective and simplified intake interviewing procedures; (b) systematic methods for integrating information regarding offender needs; (c) the formulation of in-depth case plan; and (d) an objective basis for classifying and managing offender programs, free of individual and hidden bias. In addition, advantages accruing to probation and parole agencies are likely to include (a) the assignment of cases based upon agents' skills and preferences; (b) the creation of higher expectations among supervisors by promoting increased training, better strategies and a basis for evaluating performance; and (c) the production of better-trained and more knowledgeable agents, capable of dealing more productively with offenders.

PRESENTENCE INVESTIGATION

Presentence investigations (PSIs) comprise the primary investigative duties of most probation officers. As previously indicated, however, some states do not utilize presentence investigations to their full potential. One system which does place heavy reliance upon these reports is the federal probation system. Because of the high degree of professionalization, extended experience and its use in designing state systems, the traditional methods of the United States Probation Office will serve as examples for describing the potential for utilization of presentence investigations.

The basic duties and responsibilities of Federal probation officers are derived from four sources: (1) statutes, (2) Federal rules, (3) court directives and (4) administrative agreements. Many pertinent statutes relating to the duties of a probation officer are found in Title 18 of the United States Code. For example, Section 3655 requires the probation officer to furnish each probationer a copy of his or her probation conditions, and supervise and monitor the probationer's compliance. The Federal Rules of Criminal Procedure impose responsibilities on probation officers. For example, the probation officer is required to supply the court with a presentence report prior to imposing a sentence, unless otherwise directed. Court directives are also important to the probation officer. For example, by statute, a U.S. Magistrate may direct the provision of investigation reports in a case, upon the approval or direction of a Federal District Court Judge. Finally, some duties of the probation officer are derived from administrative agreement. These agreements promote cooperation and greater efficiency between agencies which may sometimes have overlapping responsibilities, such as the Bureau of Prisons and the military services. As a result, Federal probation officers must be knowledgeable of specific and unique responsibilities in addition to those related to the community.

Presentence Investigations required of a federal probation officer include:

(a) *Presentence Investigation Reports* (which are written reports to assist the court in disposing of criminal cases);

(b) *Selective Presentence Investigations* (which are generally used in misdemeanor cases);

(c) *Collateral Investigation Reports* (which are prepared in districts other than the district in which final dispositions of the case are made);

(d) *Preliminary Investigation Reports* (which assist United States Attorneys in determining whether the cases of alleged offenders should be diverted or deferred);

(e) *Postsentence Investigation Reports* (which are completed after the disposition of cases).

ILLUSTRATION 4-A

AUTHORIZATION TO RELEASE
GOVERNMENT (STATE OR FEDERAL) INFORMATION
TO PROBATION OFFICER

I,_____, the undersigned, hereby waive my rights under the Privacy Act, 5 U.S.C. 552a (Supp. IV, 1974), and authorize the disclosure to the United States Probation Office of the_____District of _____, or its authorized representative(s) or employee(s), any and all information pertaining to me, contained in the files or systems of records maintained by any government agency subject to the Privacy Act, which such agency sees fit to convey, either orally or in writing, to the aforementioned Probation Office.

I hereby waive any rights I may have under the Privacy Act to prior notice of such disclosure or of any rights I may have to an accounting of such disclosure to the aforementioned Probation Office.

I understand that this consent will be used by the aforementioned Probation Office to request disclosure of information pertaining to me from any or all Federal agencies.

This information is to be obtained for the purpose of conducting a presentence investigation and making a report for supervision.

authorizing signature	full name	date
	parent/guardian signature, if required	
	attorney signature, if available	
WITNESS	probation officer	date

An individual undergoing a presentence investigation is instructed by the probation officer to bring important information and selected papers to assist in the presentence investigation. These papers help in the verification of facts reported to the probation officer. The following items are frequently requested by probation officers:

Birth/baptismal certificate
School diplomas
Proof of residence (rent receipts, etc.)
Draft registration card
Military discharge papers
Military disability information
Marriage certificate
Divorce decree
Income tax reports for last three years

Employment verification (pay stubs)
Immigration papers or passport
Naturalization papers
Professional papers (license)
Car registration
Medical reports
Social Security number
Department of Welfare records

The accompanying illustrations of authorization demonstrate how a defendant must sign a release to the government and private persons and organizations regarding information pertinent to the presentence investigation.

ILLUSTRATION 4-B

AUTHORIZATION TO RELEASE INFORMATION
(PRIVATE PERSON OR ORGANIZATION) TO PROBATION OFFICER

TO WHOM IT MAY CONCERN:

    I,_____, the undersigned, hereby authorized the United States Probation Office for the_____District of_____or its authorized representative(s) or employee(s), bearing this release or copy thereof, to obtain any information in your files pertaining to my employment; credit or educational records including but not limited to academic, achievement, attendance, athletic, personal history and disciplinary records; medical records; and credit records. I hereby direct you to release such information upon request of the bearer. This release is executed with full knowledge and understanding that the information is for the official use of the aforementioned United States Probation Office.

    I hereby release you, as custodian of such records; any school, college, university or other educational institution; hospital or other repository of medical records; credit bureau; retail business establishment including its officers, employees, or related personnel, both individually and collectively, from any and all liability for damages of whatever kind which may at any time result to me, my heirs, family or associates because of compliance with this authorization and request for information or any other attempt to comply with it.

    The information hereby obtained by the aforementioned Probation Office is to be used for the purpose of presentence investigation and report or for supervision.

authorizing signature	full name	date

WITNESS

probation officer	date

The presentence report is the basic working document for the Federal Probation Service and the courts as well. It is usually the most detailed and comprehensive report, serving the following five purposes: (a) assisting the court in deciding upon appropriate sentences; (b) guiding the probation officer in matters of supervision; (c) assisting prison officials in classifying and treating offenders; (d) aiding in the consideration of parole;

and (e) providing valuable information for statistical and research purposes. From these reports, valuable information is developed which provides an insight into the character and personality of the defendant and also the defendant's special problems or needs. The report demonstrates the defendant's social circumstances, relationships with people and other information which helps to reveal the nature of his or her offense and general conduct.

The following discussion will outline the proper preparation of the PSI, describing the report's important details. In illustrating the report, refer to the hypothetical presentence investigation of client John Doe in the exercise section of the text.

An interview process must be undertaken by the probation officer prior to completion of a PSI report. During the interview process, the Federal probation officer must gather special information about the defendant (his or her background and other pertinent facts) which will assist in the completion of the PSI Report. This information is detailed in the accompanying exercises following the text.

The face sheet of the PSI requires numerous items of basic information. The Plea/Verdict section indicates the count(s) to which the defendant either pleaded or was found guilty. The Custody section notes the date that the defendant was released on bond, or how long he has remained in confinement. Regarding codefendants, information is provided as to what sentences they received and the sentencing judge. Regarding Detainers or Warrants pending, information details what the charges are, the jurisdiction and the next hearing date.

The presentence investigation report should include the following 12 items of information:

(I) OFFENSE

The *who, what, when, how* and *where* of newspaper parlance would seem to be applicable here. Be brief, but indicate the specifics of the charge, such as the location and time of the official version of the offense. Although not essential to the official version of the offense, it is important to note supplemental information (e.g., the current condition of any victim, the recovery of property, the nature of the drug offense).

(II) DEFENDANT'S VERSION OF OFFENSE

Here one should note the defendant's side of the story, then ascertain any discrepancies between the official version and the defendant's version. In addition, questions concerning why the defendant was at the scene of the crime, or what type of weapon was used, may be appropriate. Finally, and very important, does the defendant now admit the offense (even though the offender may have denied the charges at the trial)? If a plea of guilty was entered, does the defendant now contend that he did not commit the offense? As a final point, the probation officer should ask questions in a careful and appropriate manner in order to gain the most accurate and relevant information from the defendant.

(III) PRIOR ARREST RECORD.

Entries should be noted chronologically, beginning with the earliest arrest. If the charges are serious, or the defendant received a sentence of probation for them, one should attempt to get some official statements regarding the charges *and* obtain the defendant's comments regarding the arrests. If probation was granted, some attempt should be made to determine how the defendant behaved while under probation supervision. If the defendant has been arrested on new charges while out on bond in the current case, one should detail this in the presentence report, and try to get information regarding the offense. If possible, schedule a definite hearing date.

(IV) PERSONAL AND FAMILY DATA

Here the aim is simply to indicate to the Court, without a great deal of unnecessary information, what might be termed a *social history*. Specifically include: (a) date and place of birth; (b) who reared the defendant, whether his home was intact; (c) defendant's relationship with family and their comments about the defendant (through an interview); (d) when the defendant left home and what he has been engaged in since. NOTE: Obviously, the older the defendant, the less emphasis one would place on a discussion of his formative years. If any of the family members impress you as concerned about the defendant, and comment on what they believe are the reasons for his getting involved in the offense, then you should so indicate. Also, it is very important that one determine whether any of the family members could be considered a resource for the defendant should the Court decide to grant probation.

(V) MARITAL HISTORY:

Numerous important items of information should be covered here, including: (a) date and place of marriage (along with spouse's name), and verification, if possible; (b) whether marriage is *meretricious* (unlawful) or *common law*, along with such information as to how long the couple has been living together, number and ages of children, whether the children are with them; (c) the number and ages of any children born out of wedlock, the name of the biological parent of the children, where the children are, whether the defendant is providing for their support, and if defendant is under court order to do so; and (d) if the defendant claims to have a girlfriend/boyfriend, and whether he/she plans to marry soon or not. NOTE: An interview with the defendant's wife, husband, common law partner, or girlfriend/boyfriend may be important.

(VI) EDUCATION:

Here one should note how much education the defendant claims, any "special" training he or she may have received and what basic level of intellect the defendant appears to have (i.e., below average intelligence, borderline, average, superior, etc.). Also, if a relatively young defendant, it might be helpful to the court if his or her I.Q. is determined.

(VII) HEALTH

This section can be very important or routine, depending on the defendant and the offense. Generally, a simple statement that "the defendant states that his/her present mental and physical health is satisfactory" will suffice. If the defendant denies the excessive use of alcohol, or claims that he has never taken what might be considered narcotics in any form (including the smoking of marijuana), the statements themselves will be helpful. However, if one detects the possibility of a history of mental or emotional illness, or the defendant is before the Court on a drug charge and admits to the use of narcotics, or other unusual conditions are present, more information must be provided. NOTE: Many courts are now requiring urine samples on *all* drug cases and on all defendants (whether a drug case or not) who have a history of drug abuse or may be suspected of possible drug abuse. Efforts and programs are under way in some courts expanding drug testing even further.

(VIII) EMPLOYMENT

This section should begin with the defendant's present employment status. List the most current employment, month and year of claimed employment, the name and address of the firm, the position held and claimed salary (see Illustration 4-C).

ILLUSTRATION 4-C

DEFENDANT'S WORK HISTORY

(1) Current employment:

6/88 to date of arrest. Ace Wrecking Co. 1215 Va. Ave., NE (Laborer) ($500/wk). Information verified that the defendant was considered an excellent worker and that the company would rehire the defendant if probation is granted.

(2) Past employment:

5/87 to 5/88. During this period the defendant states that he held a number of short-term jobs as a day laborer, none for longer than a few days at a time. He was usually paid around $8.00 an hour.

4/85 to 4/87. The defendant candidly admitted that he held no salaried employment at all during this time, stating that he supported himself by "hustling," gambling, and from the proceeds of the sale of various merchandise which he shoplifted from area department stores.

7/81 to 3/87. In custody at the U.S. Penitentiary, Atlanta, Georgia during this period, serving a 3 to 9 year term for manslaughter (see PRIOR ARREST RECORD).

(IX) MILITARY

This section is not as applicable as it once was. However, if the defendant has had military service, it should be noted (e.g., branch, dates of service, or discharge, any AWOL and other disciplinary charges, or any time served in confinement). If he/she is within the required age range, it should be noted whether he or she registered for the draft.

(X) FINANCIAL CONDITION

The importance and necessity for data here will, as with some of the other sections of the report, depend on the defendant, his/her background and the nature of the offense. If the offender is an income tax violator, stock manipulator or involved in a complex fraud case, for instance, it may be necessary to have the defendant submit an itemized "statement of net worth." If the defendant is young, with no obvious resources, this section can be handled simply by indicating what he/she claims in the way of assets and liabilities.

(XI) EVALUATIVE SUMMARY

This section will probably be considered the most important part of your report, for it is here that one should be able to: (a) develop a profile of the defendant for the court; (b) bring together, in some meaningful manner, all of the historic and other data that has previously been reported; (c) give the court some possible reasons for the defendant's involvement, what his/her strengths and weaknesses are, and the personal impression the defendant gives; (d) indicate whether the defendant appears to be a good probation risk or might pose a threat to the community, with reasons to support the conclusions. NOTE: It is not necessary or desirable to simply repeat what has been previously stated in the report. On the contrary, two or three paragraphs of *evaluation*, *diagnosis* and *prognosis* would appear to be all that is necessary.

(XII) RECOMMENDATION

The recommendation for or against the use of probation should be obvious. If probation is recommended, one should indicate any special conditions of probation that will be called for, such as restitution, participation in drug aftercare program, involvement with Alcoholics Anonymous, along with a tentative plan of treatment which may or may not be a specific conditions of probation (see Illustration 4-D).

ILLUSTRATION 4-D

SUPERVISION PLAN

Should the Court concur with a recommendation for probation, the following tentative community plan has been developed for the defendant:

(a) Residence: Will return to the home of his parents at 1102 First Street, Washington, D.C.
(b) Employment: Arrangements will be made to assist the defendant with a job through the Employment Counseling Service Division of the City Government. We will also explore with this agency the possibility of securing a program of trade training for the defendant as a computer technician.
(c) Other: For at least the first six months of his probation supervision, the defendant has agreed to attend and participate in a weekly group counseling program where the defendant will receive job counseling.

It should be noted that the Federal Rules of Criminal Procedure permit a federal judge to exclude certain information from review by an offender and his attorney. For instance, a psychological report, if read by a defendant, might interfere with his future prospects for rehabilitation. Generally, however, a defendant and his attorney will be permitted to read a presentence investigation report except for the sentence recommendation page (which is for the judge only).

OFFENDER SUPERVISION

Supervision of an offender is a fundamental area in which a probation or parole officer (PO) should become proficient. Since interviews and on-site visits are essential activities, proper supervision generally requires a command of various counseling techniques. The PO must be able to assist the probationer/parolee in the development of social skills and in problem-solving. Frequently, the officer must gather information from the client's employer, associates, and relatives. He must also establish and maintain accurate case files, which include data on the person's treatment, attitudes and behavior. In addition, the accuracy and availability of these records become especially important when a probationer or parolee changes jurisdiction, or when research data are needed.

When an offender has been placed on probation or parole, one of the first steps an officer takes is to read and explain the conditions of supervision. Typical conditions are included in the federal conditions of probation (see Illustration 4-E).

ILLUSTRATION 4-E

CONDITIONS OF PROBATION FOR THE U.S. DISTRICT COURT

It is the order of the Court that you shall comply with the following conditions of probation:

(1)   You shall refrain from violation of any law (federal, state and local). You shall get in touch immediately with your probation officer if arrested or questioned by a law enforcement officer.

(2)   You shall associate only with law-abiding persons and maintain reasonable hours.

(3)   You shall work regularly at a lawful occupation and support your legal dependents, if any, to the best of your ability. When out of work, you shall notify your probation officer at once. You shall consult with him prior to job changes.

(4)   You shall not leave the judicial district without permission of the probation officer.

(5)   You shall notify your probation officer immediately of any change in your place of residence.

(6)   You shall follow the probation officer's instructions.

(7)   You shall report to the PO as directed.

It is required that each individual under supervision submit written reports as ordered by the court. Each individual completes the forms and submits them by a designated time period, usually each month. If a probationer or parolee desires to travel to a different jurisdiction, he must complete a permission to travel form. This form protects the probationer or parolee if he is questioned by law enforcement officials about his presence in their jurisdiction.

A federal PO generally uses a Risk Prediction Scale (RPS) on a new probationer to determine what type of supervision is needed. A new federal parolee has a similar scale, the Salient Factor Score (SFS), which determines if the supervision level should be low or high activity.

Using the risk score, the PO determines a level of supervision. In some cases, there are circumstances where the probation officer may need to increase the level of supervision. During the initial months of supervision, the supervision level is not to be less than what the predictive device indicates (Administrative Office of the U.S. Courts, 1981).

There are two basic levels of supervision, low activity and high activity. The purpose and value of differentially designating persons to one of these two levels is to free the PO to direct systematically his/her skills and energies to those in greatest need of services and monitoring. Persons in the low activity supervision level, as reflected in their histories, have usually experienced relative success in establishing personal stability. Although occasionally it is necessary for the probation officer to respond to crisis situations, sustained contact is seldom necessary. The PO attempts to manage these cases through the use of referred services and collateral contacts. The PO should not encourage more than one personal contact per quarter and three personal contacts per quarter should be the exception rather than the rule. Persons in the high activity supervision level have usually experienced difficulty in establishing and maintaining personal stability. The PO should direct the greatest effort toward persons in the high activity supervision level. There is no upper limit on the number of times a given person may be seen in a month's time. All persons in this supervision level, however, are to be seen at least once a month. The purpose, frequency and location of personal and collateral contacts are shaped by the supervision plan. Once a new probationer has been rated by the RPS scale, a classification and initial supervision plan is designed.

A case review is completed by a PO after the person has been under supervision for a brief period of time. The case review explains the progress or lack of progress made by a person during a certain period of time. The PO also keeps a chronological record of the activities of the client. This chronological record points out the dates the client reported to the office, and what problems he/she has faced during the period of supervision. The PO similarly keeps a travel record to plan out his/her day in the field. The record lists the individuals he/she visited and the cases which were investigated. The field sheet of the PO gives address and employment information on a client. The PO keeps an accurate record of contacts on a record of reports/visits forms.

TREATMENT AND REFERRALS

The PO must develop helpful strategies to deal with problem areas of a probationer or parolee's life. Problems can range from drug abuse to employment difficulties. If the problems facing a probationer or parolee need the assistance of a specialist, a referral is required. Major studies reveal a positive association between receiving some services and success on probation (See *State and County Probation: Systems in Crisis*, 1976). One report recommends that departments try to provide clients with as many services as possible.

Many probationers and parolees need intensive supervision which may be provided by house arrest or a halfway house. A judge or a parole board can require offenders to live in a halfway house as a condition of their release. A national study by Donald Thalheimer (1975) pointed out the following goals for halfway houses: (a) development of attributes conducive to good employment; (b) placing the inmate in employment which he or she may retain after release; (c) providing an atmosphere suitable for education; (d) reducing confinements to state institutions; and (e) offering an effective residential program at less cost per offender than institutions.

A PO often finds that a client with a drinking problem should be referred to Alcoholics Anonymous (AA). This organization was founded in Akron, Ohio in 1935 (The Society of Alcoholics Anonymous, 1949). AA members meet on a regular basis to hear testimonials from individuals who have successfully abstained from drinking. The AA group reinforces for the probationer or parolee that he/she is not alone in the struggle with alcohol dependency.

Drug usage other than alcohol is a related major problem for offenders. Carney (1977) reports that up to 25 percent of all crime is drug related. The probation officer must seek out innovative programs to deal with this problem and obtain client participation. Frequently, the PO must learn the classification, use and slang terms that are associated with drug usage (see illustrations below).

ILLUSTRATION 4-F

DRUG TYPES, CLASSIFICATIONS AND USE

DRUGS	SCHEDULE**	METHOD OF USE***	DURATION (HRS)
NARCOTICS			
Codeine	II,III,V	O,I	3-6
Heroin	I	I,SN,SM	3-6
Hydromorphone	II	O,I	3-6
Meperidine (Pethidine)	II	O,I	3-6
Methadone	II	O,I	12-24
Morphine	II,III	O,SM,I	3-6
Opium	II,III,V	O,SM	3-6
Other narcotics	I,II,III,IV,V	O,I	var
DEPRESSANTS			
Barbiturates	II,III,IV	O	1-16
Benzodiazepines	IV	O	4-18
Chloral hydrate	II,III,IV	O	5-8
Glutethimide	III	O	4-8
Methaqualone	III	O	4-8
Other depressants	III,IV	O	4-8
STIMULANTS			
Cocaine*	II	SN,SM,I	1-2
Amphetamines	II,III	O,I	2-4
Phenmetrazine	II	O,I	2-4
Methylphenidate	II	O,I	2-4
Other stimulants	III,IV	O,I	2-4

continued

ILLUSTRATION 4-F *continued*

<u>DRUGS</u>	<u>SCHEDULE**</u>	<u>METHOD OF USE***</u>	<u>DURATION (HRS)</u>
HALLUCINOGENS			
Amphetamine variants	I	O,I	var
Lysergic acid (LSD)	I	O	8-12
Mescaline & peyote	I	O,I	8-12
Phencyclidine	II	SM,O,I	days
Phencyclidine analogs	I	SM,O,I	days
Other hallucinogens	I	SM,SN,O,I	var
CANNABIS			
Marijuana	I	SM,O	2-4
Tetrahydrocannabinol	I	SM,O	2-4
Hashish	I	SM,O	2-4
Hashish oil	I	SM,O	2-4

---

*   A narcotic under the Controlled Substances Act (Comprehensive Drug Abuse Prevention and Control Act of 1970).

**   The Drug Enforcement Administration (DEA) schedule

*** Oral (O), Injected (I), Sniffed (SN), Smoked (SM)

I   (a) *high* potential for abuse;
     (b) *no accepted medical use* in the USA; and (c) lack of accepted safety for use of the drug even under medical supervision

II   (a) *high* potential for abuse;
     (b) *no accepted medical use* in USA (often with severe restrictions); and
     (c) abuse may lead to *severe* psychological or physical dependence

III (a) potential for abuse *less* than Schedule I & II;
     (b) currently accepted medical use in USA; and
     (c) abuse may lead to *moderate or low physical* dependence or *high psychological* dependence

IV (a) *low* potential for abuse relative to Schedule III;
     (b) currently accepted medical use in USA; and
     (c) abuse may lead to *limited physical or psychological* dependence relative to Schedule III

V   (a) low potential for abuse;
     (b) currently accepted medical use in USA; and
     (c) abuse may lead to limited physical or psychological dependence relative to Schedule IV

Source: Johnson, N.P. (ed.). *Dictionary of Street Alcohol and Drug Terms*, 2nd Ed., 1987.

ILLUSTRATION 4-G

IMPORTANT TERMS FOR EFFECTIVE DRUG ENFORCEMENT

Official Terms: **Slang Terms:**

A. Opiates/Opioids
   codeine   schoolboy/subs
   codeine used with other drugs
   alcohol and codeine (schoolboy)   schoolboy Scotch
   elixir of terpin hydrate w/ codeine   GI gin/syrup/turps
   dihydrocodienone   hykes
   heroin   A-bomb/black gum/black tar/
                                                       brown sugar/dope/flea powder/
                                                       foolish powder/hard stuff/horse/junk

   heroin and other drugs
      heroin and methamphetamine   poor man's speedball
      heroin and Ritalin   pineapple
      heroin, barbiturate, caffeine
         and strychnine   purple rock/red rock
      heroin, PCP and marijuana   space base/space blast
      marijuana dipped in heroin   dynamite
      methylene-dioxyamphetamine   MDA

   hydromorphone   D's/lords
   meperidine   doctors
   methadone   dollies/dolls/fizzies/methadose
   morphine   blue heavens/brown heroin/cube
                                                       juice/drugstore dope/Miss Emma
   opium   Allah/big O/black/stuff/dope/
                                                       gum/mud/tar
   oxycodone   percs/perks/pink spoons

B. CNS Stimulants
   amphetamines (generic)   AAA/accelerator/amps/black beauties/
                                                       black bombers/black Mollies/
                                                       bumble-bees/candy/jellybeans/
                                                       pep pills/speed/uppers/whites
      Benzedrine   bennies/beans/black beauties/black
                                                       bombers/black cadillac/boxcars/
                                                       hearts/peaches/roses/ups
      Biphetamine   black beauties/black bombers/black
                                                       cadillacs/black dex

Dexedrine	black dex/brown and/clears/cartwheels/Christmas trees/peaches/speed/ups
dimethylamphetamine	AMT/pep pill/speed/stimulants/upper
methamphetamine	crank/crystal meth/speed/water/white cross/yellow bams/ice
caffeine	black/brew/cup/decaf/go juice/mud/perk/pick me up/starter/stay awake/unleaded
cocaine	base/Bernice/big bloke/big C/big flake/big rush/coke/crack/crystal/eight ball/eight track/gold dust/happy dust/noise candy/rock/Roxanne/snowflake/toot

cocaine and other drugs

cocaine and heroin	girls and boys/Frisco speedball
cocaine and marijuana	C & M
cocaine and morphine	C & M
cocaine and PCP (smoked)	dusty roads/ghostbusting/space basing/space blasting
LSD and mescaline	pink wedges
LSD, STP, methedrine or cocaine, and strychnine	four way
LSD, STP, speed, strychnine, and cocaine	orange cupcake
*m*ethylene-*d*ioxy*a*mphetamine	MDA

C. **CNS Depressants**

alcohol

beer	brew/suds
distilled spirits	booze/corn
wine	short dog/cooler
nonbeverage alcohol	alley juice/squeeze

barbiturates

amobarbital	blue angel/blue dolls
pentobarbital	yellow jackets/yellows
phenobarbital	phennies
secobarbital	devils/reds
secobarbital/amobarbital	blue & reds/trees

benzodiazepine

| chlordiazepoxide (Librium) | downers/libs |
| diazepam (Valium) | vals/downers |

other CNS depressants

chloral hydrate	jellie bean/joy juice
glutethimide (Doriden)	goof balls/goofers
ketamine	purple/super acid
lidocaine	Florida snow
methaqualone (Sopor)	disco biscuits/love drug
methaprylon (Noludar)	noodlelars

D.   Hallucinogens & Psychotomimetics

*lys*ergic acid *d*iethylamide (LSD)	acelerador/animal/battery acid/ black sunshine/blotter cube/blue tab/ California sunshine/candy/contact lens/green dragon/heavenly blue/*L*ucy in the *s*ky with *d*iamonds/purple haze/sugar cubes/wedding bells/white elephant
*m*ethylene-*d*iox*a*mphetamine	MDA
marijuana	Acapulco gold/African black/brick (kilogram of MJ)/gunga/joy stick/ Mary Jane/Mexican locoweed/ Panama gold/ pocket rocket (cig.)/ poke/toke/weed
marijuana cigarette (roach)	jive stick/joint/reefer/roach/stick
marijuana user	doper/pothead/stoner
pipe for smoking marijuana	bong/hit pipe
smoke an MJ cigarette	burn/take a hit/toke
under the influence of MJ	stoned/wasted
hashish	black/chocolate
tetrahydrocannibinol (THC)	baby/black Russian/Thai sticks

marijuana & other drugs

marijuana and opium	OJ/orange juice
marijuana dipped in heroin	dynamite
marijuana dipped in PCP	killer weed/rough stuff/weed/superweed
marijuana with cocaine added	paserolo/pitillo/susuko
mescaline (Peyote cactus)	(bad seed)/beans/big chief/cactus head/moon/peyote/white light

mescaline and other drugs

mescaline and Preludin	bam
mescaline and MDA	love trip
psilocybin, psilocyn	God's flesh/magic mushrooms/silly putty
dimethyltryptamine	businessman's special/45 minute psychosis

methylaphetamine derivatives	DOB/DOM/Adam and Eve/love drug/ecstasy/TMA/utopiates
other hallucinogens	
nutmeg	mace

E. Miscellaneous Drugs

freon	freebies
isoamyl nitrite	boppers/huffing/poppers
isobutyl nitrite	boppers/bullet/climax
nitrous oxide	laughing gas/whippets
phencyclidine (PCP)	angel dust/butt naked/ crystal/horse/ loveboat/super weed

PCP & other drugs

marijuana and PCP	killer weed/rough stuff
inhalation of	
volatile solvent	poor man's pot/sniffing

The PO must also be familiar with work release and furlough programs. These programs should be restricted to include only offenders who have demonstrated that they do not pose a danger to the community. Work release and furlough enable offenders to pursue employment within the community. The probationer or parolee who experiences stable employment will generally be more successful under supervision. Similarly, the PO needs to be aware of the multitude of agencies and organizations in the community that can be of assistance to his clients. The types of programs and agencies which may be of assistance include: child care programs, drug treatment programs, basic education programs, emergency assistance programs, financial assistance programs, food and clothing assistance centers, health programs, job placement programs, job training programs and vocational rehabilitation programs. Finally, some city and state governments compile information on services available for offenders and should be consulted for assistance.

REFERENCES

Administrative Office of the United States (1981, January) *Classification and Supervision Planning System*. Washington, DC: Probation Division.

Administrative Office of the United States Courts (1978). *The Presentence Investigation Report*. Monograph No. 105. Washington, DC: Author.

Carney, L.P. (1977). *Corrections and the Community*. Englewood Cliffs, NJ: Prentice-Hall.

Federal Judicial Center. *An Introduction to the Federal Probation System*. Washington, DC: Author, FJC No. 76-1.

Friday, P.C. & Peterson, D.M. (1973). Shock Imprisonment: Comparative Analysis of Short-term Incarceration as a Treatment Technique. *Canadian Journal of Criminology and Corrections*, 15:3, 287-288.

Government of the District of Columbia (1973). *Offender Services in the Washington Metropolitan Area*. Washington, DC: Author.

Johnson, N.P. (ed.) (1987). *Dictionary of Street Alcohol and Drug Terms*. University of South Carolina School of Medicine. Columbia, SC: University of South Carolina.

Serrill, M. (1974, September). From "Bums" to Businessmen: The Delancy Street Foundation. *Corrections Magazine*, 1, No. 1, 14.

Smith, M.A. (1973). *As a Matter of Fact: An Introduction to Federal Probation*. Washington, DC: Federal Judicial Center.

State and County Probation: System in Crisis. A report to the Congress by the Comptroller General of the United States, May 27, 1976.

Thalmeier, D.J. (1975) *Cost Analysis of Correctional Standards: Halfway Houses*. Vol. II. Washington, DC: U.S. Government Printing Office.

The Society of Alcoholics Anonymous. (1949, November). *American Journal of Psychiatry*, 106, 5.

U.S. Department of Justice (1971). *Terms and Symptoms of Drug Abuse*. Washington, DC: Bureau of Narcotics and Dangerous Drugs.

Chapter 5

COUNSELING TECHNIQUES:
DEVELOPING AN EFFECTIVE STRATEGY

LEARNING OBJECTIVES

*   To promote an understanding of the origins and principles of selected counseling techniques.

*   To demonstrate the need for implementing counseling techniques in probation and parole operations.

*   To explain the operational dynamics of applied counseling techniques.

DISCUSSION QUESTIONS

1. Briefly explain the central ideas underlying selected counseling theories.

2. Give examples of the successful application of counseling techniques by probation or parole officers, utilizing the counseling theories previously described.

3. What benefits may be gained from the successful mastery of these selected counseling approaches by probation and parole officers?

IMPORTANT TERMS

Reality therapy	Career counseling
Rational emotive therapy	Psychodrama
Behavior modification	Client-centered approach
Transactional analysis	Crisis intervention
Group counseling	Art therapy

NAMES TO REMEMBER

William Glasser	Jacob Moreno
Albert Ellis	Carl Rogers
B.F. Skinner	Eric Berne

COUNSELING TECHNIQUES: DEVELOPING AN EFFECTIVE STRATEGY

Perhaps the most overlooked and often ignored responsibility of a probation or parole officer involves his or her counseling responsibilities. Yet, this responsibility probably comprises a critical phase of probation and parole practice, if not in sheer time allotted, then in potential impact on offender behavior. If the offender's problems are to be resolved and the requirements of probation and parole met, counseling becomes a tool for accomplishing these tasks.

The following discussion will detail some of the origins, elements and applications of many of the more successful and pertinent counseling techniques in probation and parole practice. These approaches have sound theoretical foundations and have experienced wide acceptance and success in a variety of settings. Their application to probation and parole supervision appears logical, practical and increasingly important. As the demands placed upon probation and parole functions continue to increase and the available resources decline, innovations which increase effectiveness will become critical. Adding these ten basic counseling approaches to the existing repertoire of supervisory techniques can contribute to the profession's fulfillment of future societal expectations and criminal justice needs.

REALITY THERAPY

Reality therapy attempts to develop in a very short period of time those human qualities and values which should have been established during the normal maturation process of an individual. Reality therapy rejects the classical belief that considers behavior problems as the result of mental illness or severe behavior disorders. In place of such categorizations, the terms *responsible* and *irresponsible* are used and concentration is directed toward the present, not the unchangeable past. The primary goal of the reality therapist is to assist clients in learning better ways to fulfill their emotional and behavioral needs.

Proponent – William Glasser

William Glasser, a renowned psychiatrist, includes among his vast clinical experience work in juvenile institutions and hospital settings. Perhaps Glasser is best known for his popular book, *Reality Therapy: A New Approach to Psychiatry* (1975). Upon completing his psychiatric training, Glasser expressed doubts about some of the fundamental principles of conventional psychiatry which led him to search for new, practical approaches. This inquisitiveness and recognition of the need for new and viable methods of counseling resulted in the formulation of a theoretical approach called *reality therapy*.

Principles and Application

There are at least 14 principles of reality therapy which can be applied to probation or parole work. The following illustrations relate these principles in a probation setting.

Principle 1: Get involved. the effective PO attempts to develop a warm, friendly and personal relationship with the offender. Involvement takes place between two people much like the development of friendship. Without involvement, significant behavioral and attitudinal changes in offenders are difficult.

Principle 2: The PO should reveal his own personality to the offender in an effort to serve as a model for establishing open communication. Through this process, the offender can follow the PO's example and express his or her fears and concerns.

Principle 3: The PO should encourage the offender to use the personal pronouns "I" and "me" as much as possible in conversation. This process will ensure that conversations between the PO and offender are more meaningful. For example, if an unemployed offender spends hours talking *about* the unemployment problem rather than personalizing his or her own job situation, the need for personal action is minimized.

Principle 4: In conversing with the offender, the PO should talk in the "here and now." For instance, hours spent talking about early childhood difficulties will not usually help the offender with his or her current unemployment situation.

Principle 5: The focus of a counseling session with an offender should be on the topic of his actual daily behavior patterns. Spending lengthy periods of time in counseling sessions talking exclusively about feelings is likely to fail to bring about desired behavioral changes.

Principle 6: A PO must ask "what" behavior an offender exhibits, rather than "why" he or she exhibits such behavior. Asking an offender "why" he or she did not find a job may result in needless excuses. The PO must try to determine what behavior the person is demonstrating that has prevented him from gaining employment, and then work to change the undesirable behavior. For example, the offender may be unable to complete a job application form. The PO should assist the person, as much as possible, in gaining the skills needed to complete the job application.

Principle 7: The PO must ask certain key questions of the offender. First, what does the person think of his or her behavior? Second, is the behavior doing him or her any good? Behavior change is not likely to take place unless individuals evaluate their own behavior and its effects, and understand the important influences of their environment. Additionally, the offenders must decide that their behavior is non-productive and they must desire to do something to improve it.

Principle 8: The PO, in his effort to assist an offender, may ask, "What can be done about this problem?" The PO and offender can then engage in a brainstorming session. This involves mobilizing one's creative capacities to work out a reasonable step-by-step resolution of the problem. The PO provides input and makes his or her own suggestions. Together, they seek to formulate a detailed and concrete plan which relies on common sense to remedy the identified problem. The PO and offender may even role-play and rehearse the details of the plan to increase the chances of its successful completion.

Principle 9: The PO should ask the offender additional questions once a plan has been perfected. First, will the person carry out this plan? Second, how can the PO know that the person will? Third, will the person give his or her promise? Fourth, will the person shake hands on it? Fifth, is the person willing to sign a contract? An offender is more likely to live up to a plan if there is a commitment, a contract or a formal agreement.

Principle 10: The PO should verify if the plan has been carried out. If the offender has failed to carry out the plan, the PO should not waste time scolding or arguing with the person. The PO should not spend time listening to excuses provided by the person as to why the plan failed. The PO makes better use of the time with the person by asking: "Is the contract still in force, or is renegotiation needed?"

Principle 11: The PO does not give up on the offender. He continues working with the person by maintaining concern, friendship, and involvement. The PO continues his or her efforts despite failures, broken promises and missed appointments.

Principle 12: The PO should praise as well as encourage the offender to "keep up the good work." The smallest amount of success on the part of the person could be the beginning of a new way of life. Failure oriented people often do not believe others are genuinely interested in them as human beings.

Principle 13: The PO should be aware of the powerful and therapeutic impact of humor. Smiling, laughing, kidding and joking are valuable tools for intensifying involvement and helping the offender.

Principle 14: The PO should use group counseling as much as possible when working with offenders. Through the use of groups, offenders become aware of the successes of others, and can evaluate the plans used by others in overcoming crises.

Summary

Reality Therapy is directed toward achieving involvement in an open and honest human relationship. Offenders may come to realize that someone is actually concerned about them and their progress, and that the PO will provide them with assistance. The critical elements of reality therapy may be summarized as follows: (1) the basic therapeutic job of the PO (reality therapist) is to become involved with the person; (2) when confronted with reality by the PO, the person is forced to decide whether he will opt for the responsible path; (3) reality may be painful and even harsh to the person. It may also be difficult, as reality changes slowly. Persons should struggle to resolve their problems and enjoy the rewards that follow. A final point to remember is that the PO who utilizes reality therapy should not give up on the person. If he fails to complete the plan, an additional opportunity to pursue an alternate course should be provided.

RATIONAL EMOTIVE PSYCHOTHERAPY

Rational emotive psychotherapy, or rational emotive therapy (RET), is based on the assumption that irrational thinking is a major cause of problems for some individuals. These psychological problems arise from faulty perceptions (mistaken cognitions). Frequently, such problems result from severe emotional reactions to normal and unusual stimuli, and from habitually dysfunctional behavior patterns that may cause repetitive and non-adjustive responses (e.g., prolonged periods of depression resulting from stress of unemployment). Rational emotive therapy postulates that perceived emotional responses are caused by the unconscious evaluations and interpretations of events that are experienced. As a result, persons may feel anxious or depressed because they are convinced that failures are terrible, and rejections painful. These individuals typically become very hostile when others are perceived to be acting unfairly toward them. The role of the therapist is to help the individual alter such perceptions and respond to life situations more rationally.

Proponent – Albert Ellis

Albert Ellis, a leading clinical psychologist, has enjoyed a reputation for being a distinguished academician and practitioner. He has authored hundreds of articles and the well-known book, *A New Guide to Rational Living* (1973). Ellis describes rational emotive psychotherapy as a comprehensive approach to psychological treatment that deals not only with the emotional and behavioral aspects of human disturbance, but places a great deal of emphasis on its "thinking" components (the human mind). Ellis believes that human beings are complex and do not generally become emotionally disturbed for the same reasons. Similarly, there is no single way to help persons who are disturbed.

Principles and Application

The PO using RET should begin the first session by identifying a few central irrational philosophies of life held by the offender. The PO can suggest to the person how these ideas may lead to his emotional problems by demonstrating clinical symptoms, and by helping the person to question and challenge his irrational ideas. Often the PO induces the offender to replace existing negative perceptions with improved feelings about the world, which may prevent future emotional difficulties.

The technique utilized in RET follows an A-B-C format. According to Ellis' view of emotions, point A is the situation (the activating event), point B is the belief system (attitudes, values and philosophies of an individual), point C is the consequences (one's feelings and behavior), point D is the disputation of the irrational beliefs, and finally, point E is the new emotional consequence. An example of the A-B-C theory of emotional disturbance in a probation or parole setting will assist in understanding its potential use. For instance, the activating event (point A) would occur when a girlfriend or boyfriend breaks the news to a person that he/she is going with another, and therefore wishes to break off the relationship. Point B involves the belief or interpretation of the event or fact, which might result in the person thinking, "I really must be a worthless person; or, "I'll never find another great woman like her;" or, "she doesn't want me, therefore, no one could possibly want me;" or, "she shouldn't be that way, I can't stand the world being so unfair." Each illustrates a belief system that is not very rational. Point C involves the upsetting emotional consequence. In such a case, one feels depressed or hostile, or both. The reaction is the product of the belief system. Point D consists of the PO disputing the irrational beliefs. What evidence is there that the person who wishes to end a relationship is worthless? Is the breaking up proof that the person will never be able to have a satisfying relationship with anyone else, or that he or she will not be happy alone? In addition, why should one not expect the world to have injustices and fallible human beings? Point E represents the "new" emotional consequence. It relies on the assumption that one should be sad and annoyed rather than depressed and hostile. An expression of sadness for the probationer might be: "Well, we did have a nice relationship and I'm sorry to see it end, but it did have some problems, and now I can go out and find someone else." Or an annoyed remark might be: "It is frustrating to find out that she was seeing someone, but it isn't the end of the world."

The view of the ABC approach is that probationers, and no one else, created their emotional feelings. No matter how inappropriate others' behavior, it is not the activating behavior but rather the probationer's "belief" about that behavior which proves upsetting. When the probationer feels upset, depressed, or fearful and hostile, he may be reacting to both a rational and irrational belief. The rational belief may be: "I don't like this, it is unfortunate, and I wish I could change it." The irrational belief may take the following form: "This is awful! I can't stand it! It shouldn't exist! I'm a rotten person for allowing it to exist!"

If the probationer consistently and persistently disputes, challenges and questions his irrational beliefs, those beliefs may eventually be minimized or eliminated. If one continues this kind of disputing behavior whenever one feels upset, a different, less demanding and productive philosophy of life can be achieved which prevents constant frustrations.

The following is another example of the ABC approach to emotions and how it might be used successfully. Activating event A occurs when the person in a group counseling session states, "I worked all night and the pay is low. I've also got an unfair boss!" The activating event results in B, the belief about the event. The person in this case is likely to believe: "It's too bad! Things should go better for me!" B leads to C (a resulting emotion) in which the person feels rotten, as shown by his or her response: "I'm depressed, angry!" The next step is D which involves disputing and challenging the attitudes and beliefs of the person by the PO. The PO is likely to comment: "First, you don't work all night. You work just part of the night." The person answers, "That's correct." The PO then replies, "And you say the pay is low, only $5.00 an hour. That is substantially above minimum wage. In addition, you know you could be out of work." Disputing leads to step E, a new emotional consequence. The PO asks how the person feels. The person remarks, "You know, maybe the job is not all that bad."

Rational emotive therapy is a short-term process. Probationers and parolees are educated with the ABCs and given homework assignments. These assignments involve risks, putting themselves in uncomfortable or anxiety-producing situations, and learning to dispute irrational beliefs about these situations. Homework assignments are frequently given to the clients. For example, the person who is frightened of subway trains is instructed to ride several of them. In the next counseling session, the PO obtains the person's written thoughts about this activity.

Rational emotive psychotherapy can also be used to work with groups who are having difficulties with alcoholism. Alcoholics frequently consider themselves *bad* persons who are unreliable, insincere, or dishonest. Such persons may feel that everyone is looking down on them. The alcoholic who believes that everyone feels this way is engaging in irrational, nonproductive thinking. This thinking may seriously hamper his or her attempts to make a successful adjustment in the community.

Using RET in alcoholic groups enables the group members to confront and challenge each other about their irrational beliefs. For example, if one of the members of the alcoholic group states that he or she is angry because someone referred to him or her as a rotten person, the group may help this person examine this reaction. The group would help the person dispute such beliefs and aid in the formulation of a new emotional response. A group leader could also assist alcoholic members of the group in formulating individual homework assignments. The leader could then challenge, along with the other members of the group, the irrational beliefs expressed by different members of the group.

These techniques have been utilized in numerous settings. For instance, a federal probation office in Dallas, Texas established a group counseling program to assist probationers and parolees with their problems on an experimental basis. The director of the program used the ABC model to work with persons in group counseling sessions. It proved very successful (Ruhnow, 1975).

RET assumes that the essential basis for improvement or change in the individual is not removal of his present symptoms, but rather a significant, deep-seated and lasting change in one's basic philosophy of life. RET stresses that certain core irrational ideas are at the root of most emotional disturbances. Ellis describes the following twelve common irrational ideas:

1. It is irrational to believe that it is a dire necessity to be loved for everything one does;

2. It is irrational to consider people as bad, wicked and in need of punishment;

3. It is irrational to consider past experiences and events as total determinants;

4. It is an irrational idea that one must be a perfectionist in order to be considered important;

5. It is irrational to feel that unwanted events are necessarily catastrophic;

6. It is irrational to feel that unhappiness is caused by outside circumstances over which the probationer has no control;

7. It is irrational to allow minor things to become major and continued worries;

8. It is irrational to assume that it is easier to avoid certain difficulties and self-responsibilities than to face them;

9. It is irrational to be extremely upset over other people's problems and disturbances;

10. It is irrational to believe that one should be overly dependent on others;

11. It is irrational to believe that there is always a right or perfect solution to every problem and it must be found or the results will be terrible; and

12. It is irrational to dictate that the world, and especially other people, must be totally fair and just, to make life worthwhile.

Summary

RET demonstrates that no matter what the offender's basic irrational philosophy of life is, or how he acquired it, the person is presently disturbed because he believes the world is self-defeating. In RET, the offender comes to recognize his thoughts. This individual will challenge and question these beliefs and will usually improve significantly. POs should recognize that RET is a comprehensive counseling technique that particularly lends itself to application in the probation and parole setting. Its complexity can be overcome through a proper understanding of its critical elements and the effective use of its simply stated principles. As stated by Epictetus in the first century A.D.: "Men are disturbed not by things, but the views they take of them" (Patterson, 1973: 51).

GROUP COUNSELING

Group counseling in a probation and parole setting provides the offender with the tools for exploring and understanding one's self by examining personal values and norms of behavior. It requires a person to express his problems in a group setting where participants can react to the individual's concerns.

Proponent – George M. Gazda

Group counseling has become widely accepted and applied in diverse settings to the extent that no single proponent should be given primary credit for the development and success it has experienced. The research on group counseling has grown rapidly with increasingly positive results. George M. Gazda, author of *Group Counseling: A Development Approach* (1971), has become known as a leading developer of group counseling, providing ideas and techniques for conducting group counseling that can have immediate benefits for probation and parole professionals.

Principles and Application

A group provides an economical use of a PO's time. While a PO may be able to work with 15 offenders in a group in an hour's time, he or she can only see two or three persons in the same period of time on a one-to-one basis.

The group counseling process facilitates an effective use of peer group pressure. As an illustration: If there are 13 persons in the group, one of whom is talking about drinking difficulties and the others are questioning the person about his or her drinking habits, this peer interaction will probably have a greater effect on changing the person's view toward drinking than simply a PO's advice.

Another advantage of group counseling concerns training new POs as group leaders. For example, federal probation officers in the United States Court for the District of Columbia have been given the opportunity to act as observers in group counseling sessions. By observing the group process, they gain insight into processes for conducting their own groups in the future.

One type of group counseling that can take place in a probation or parole office setting involves employment groups. Probationers or parolees selected for this type of group are those who are having problems in securing and maintaining steady employment. The group may focus on employment questions such as: What type of job am I best equipped for? How do I approach someone for a job? Where do I seek this type of work? If I do get a job, how do I get along with my fellow employees? How may my employer help me once I get the job? The goals of this group are to aid and assist probationers and parolees having problems in the employment area to bring their problems into the open and express them in a group setting. Furthermore, it is possible to have role-playing activities to teach them how to obtain jobs and how to succeed in employer-employee relationships.

A PO who runs a group counseling session has a great deal of impact on the success or failure of the group. He must be sure each person in the group has an opportunity to be heard. In addition, the PO must frequently focus the attention of the group on what is happening within the group. For example, he might say, "Were you aware that only two persons in this group voiced an opinion?" This type of comment should facilitate further discussion. Giving simple directions is also the responsibility of the PO in a group setting. For example, he may structure the group by having the participants complete name tags or suggest exercises in which the group should participate. Sullivan (1952) advised that the group atmosphere should be as friendly, informal and democratic as possible.

The group leader may have to intervene to keep group members from overexposure. Overexposure involves sharing personal feelings that may not facilitate the group or the group goals, or feelings which create a situation where neither the offenders nor the group leader are capable of properly functioning. The PO as group leader may decide to protect a group member if he or she feels remarks from the group are ill-timed or unnecessarily severe. A group leader may at times help a person maintain his views despite group pressure to change the person's views.

It is often advantageous to have two POs act as group co-leaders. Jones and Pheiffer (1975) have long advocated the use of co-leaders in a group. One leader can work with persons experiencing significant emotional problems while the other leader assists remaining group members in dealing with their reactions to the situation. By working as a team, the two officers are able to monitor and facilitate individual and group development better than either could alone.

There are many roles that may be played by group leaders and participants. For example, an *information seeker* assumes the role of trying to clarify problems being discussed in the group. The *information giver*, on the other hand, relates his or her own experience to the group problem. The *encourager* praises, agrees with, and accepts the contributions of others in the group.

The PO counseling a group generally finds it helpful to establish ground rules. One ground rule might be that each group member tries to be as honest as possible in the expression of his or her views. Another ground rule may promote realism. Experience has shown that if group members know the group will be candid and reality-oriented, they do not pretend.

The PO should realize that no two members of a group will derive the same benefit from the group experience. The value of the group to the individual will depend in large measure upon the degree of prevailing acceptance, the quality of the interaction, individual self-perception and interest in other group members, and the group process that is utilized.

Some POs have found that it is effective to label groups according to their goals. For example, an employment group would have the goal of achieving employment for each group member. A family group on the other hand would have as its primary goal the discussion of problems facing offenders and their families.

An additional important consideration relates to the incentive of the offender in participating in the counseling process. This means that a probationer who fails to take part in the probation office group counseling program is subject to a possible revocation of probation.

The ultimate goal of any group counseling session in a probation and parole setting is to increase an offender's chances of succeeding. Kelman (1963) lists the following goals which he considers to be benefits achieved by the group process:

1. to help an individual overcome feelings of isolation;

2. to enhance self-esteem and increase acceptance of self;

3. the group should help develop hope for improved adjustment;

4. to help each individual learn to be himself/herself and to express his or her real feelings;

5. a group should help an individual accept responsibility for himself/herself and for solving his or her problems;

6. a group process should help an individual develop, practice and maintain new relationship skills;

7. a group should help an individual enhance his commitment to change his attitude and behavior;

8. a group should enable an individual to operationalize his or her insights and skills by applying them to daily life.

Summary

Group counseling seeks human learning and problem-solving through social interaction. It improves the social learning process by highlighting the dynamics of the group and not environmental factors. Group members, guided by a leader, are encouraged to share individual and interpersonal feelings and perceptions. The atmosphere proves conducive to both independence and interdependence, and stresses the healthy attributes of each. A frequent benefit from group counseling is the assumption of responsibility by the participants and a knowledge of the assistance and support available from their peers in overcoming problems. It also promotes a forum for discovering desirable alternatives for apparently unsolvable dilemmas. Overall, group counseling provides both an environment and a process in which numerous counseling goals can be met (Kratcoski, 1981).

CAREER COUNSELING

Finding a job is not an easy task, particularly during periods of high unemployment and changing economies. It is especially difficult for a probationer or parolee. Since the PO is charged with the responsibility of assisting the unemployed offender in finding a job, career counseling becomes an important task.

Proponent – Eli Ginzberg

Eli Ginzberg (1972) is one among many students and proponents of career counseling. Ginzberg's research confirmed that a job choice is a continuing process. In this process, the individual typically seeks a job which fits his or her career preparation and goals, as well as the realities of the work world. Especially pertinent in recent years, these realities are frequently changing and result in constant reappraisals of job options and continuing needs for career counseling.

Principles and Application

How does the PO discover the employment potential and career goals of the offender? The answer basically lies in the interviewing process and the pre-sentence investigation report (PSI). The PSI will usually contain information on the person's work history over recent years. It will report the individual's earnings, whether the person was promoted or fired, and reasons for any change in jobs. By reading the PSI, the PO will formulate realistic ideas regarding job possibilities for the person.

The "interview" also provides the PO with the opportunity to ask pertinent questions about the person's work background. This interview typically takes place in the office. For example, does the person still have an interest in the welding trade? The PSI may indicate that the person worked as a welder for ten years prior to arrest and conviction, leading the PO to try to discover whether the interest in that occupation continues. If this person desires a career change, what options are available? A testing of the person's interests and abilities may be required. The Kuder General Interest Survey (KGIS), the Strong Vocational Interest Blank (1974) and the Ohio Vocational Interest Survey (1970) are tests that may reveal vocational interest areas of the person. The KGIS has numerous interest scales which include: outdoor, mechanical, computational, scientific, persuasive, artistic, literary, musical, social service and clerical areas (Kuder, 1965).

Federal and state publications also assist the PO in identifying specific qualities required of particular jobs. One publication, *Dictionary of Occupational Titles* (1965), provides an index of industries and jobs. For instance, if the person wants to be a truck driver, what requirements are demanded? Does the applicant need a diploma from a truck driving school? Such information can provide valuable in assisting the person in a job search.

Once the person has identified a job that appears interesting and has attainable application requirements, the next step may involve education and training. If there are indications that a high school diploma (or GED) is required for the particular job, the person without a high school diploma should consider enrolling in an adult education program.

After the person has completed the required education or training he or she then begins the difficult task of exploring job opportunities. Newspaper ads, state employment office job listings, and industry job announcements are several sources of information which identify available jobs. The PO can also offer substantial assistance in preparing the person for the actual job interview. Through the use of role-playing, the person can learn the art of successful expression for job interviews. The person must learn that punctuality as well as neat appearance is very important in any job interview.

Once the person gains employment, the role of the PO as job counselor does not end. He or she must reinforce positive work progress made by the person and confront the person when he or she fails at job tasks. The PO who assists persons in their quest for employment will find that those who are employed are generally more successful in fulfilling the conditions of probation or parole.

Summary

Career counseling is a tremendous responsibility of the PO and can be performed with relative ease if undertaken with care and determination, although some variables (e.g., economy and employment opportunities) remain beyond the officer's control. The primary tasks of the officer become those of advisement, and identifying and reinforcing the desires and abilities of the job seeker to the existing job market. By developing and applying the proven techniques of successful career counseling, this job becomes both attainable and personally rewarding.

PSYCHODRAMA

Psychodrama attempts to provide an accurate portrayal of a person's present, past, and future actions through a variety of techniques. The person's self-expression and freedom of communication leads to improved self-understanding and personality reorientation.

Psychodrama requires the reenactment of life situations in which the individual's relationships (real or imagined) are acted out in the form of a role which he or she chooses to portray. Other actors may portray persons with whom the person is experiencing difficulty.

Proponent – Jacob L. Moreno

Jacob Moreno, a researcher, began developing the counseling theory of psychodrama after his arrival in the United States in 1925. Moreno's endeavors included the following: dramatist, theologian, poet, philosopher, inventor, psychiatrist, sociodramatist, sociometrist and educator. With such an array of talents and skills, it was not surprising that he became the leading scholar on the concepts of psychodrama. Moreno wrote extensively on the topic and dedicated himself to the training of practitioners.

Principles and Application

Psychodrama normally requires persons to enact important phases of their lives in a group setting. A person may also play the role of an absent person in conflict reenactments. The group (or audience) participants may also serve as a sounding board for expressions of difficulty. They provide the person with corrective and reality oriented advice. Their reactions and advice should contain plausible solutions to the problems. Furthermore, persons in the group can identify and share in the displayed feelings and emotions.

One technique used in psychodrama is that of role playing. This process helps persons to intensely express their feelings. In addition, individuals can express feelings which they perceive others have toward them. Role playing is an effective procedure with unemployed persons. The PO can role play as a prospective employer. The unemployed person then undergoes the "employment" interview. By practicing the job interview, the unemployed person increases his or her chances of being successful during the actual process. Some POs videotape the practice job interview. This videotape session is then shown to the unemployed person. This enables the person to observe how he or she performed during the job interview.

Roles in psychodrama vary depending upon the person's age, sex, social situation and personality make-up. Also, the nature of one's peers, siblings and marital relationships impact the formation of roles. The PO may enact the behavior of a person with whom the offender is having problems. As the person sees how his actions appear to others, a new insight of desired behavior is gained. The PO, for example, can act as a father, boss, teacher, police officer or other authority figure who causes difficulty for the person. Thus, a person can discover new relationships based on a better understanding of his or her interactions with role play figures.

Another psychodrama process is called mirror technique. In this procedure, another person plays the role of the person who is experiencing problems but has difficulty expressing them. The person who is having the problem observes from the outside. Using this technique, he or she can see himself orherself, as if in a mirror.

Future projection is a psychodrama technique which helps the person to realize the anxiety he has concerning the future. In the psychodramatic presentation of the future, the person is required to portray two areas. First, he must portray his wishes and desires, which may be entirely unrealistic. Second, he must portray the realistic perceptions of his future. It is important for the person to portray what he or she feels will actually take place in the future. The person should be encouraged to portray as completely as possible the places, the persons and the events of the future. The more clearly future events are envisioned, the better the person's chances will be to confront them. In such psychodramatic sessions, the person performs as his or her own "prophet." The person is not only tested for the future, but is prepared for it.

Summary

Psychodrama enables the offender to act out problems (Nikelly, 1971). Consequently, he or she can deal more effectively with interpersonal situations. Through role playing, the person reveals his or her current lifestyle. Then, after constructive reorientation, the person is able to originate alternative solutions to present situations. Persons are able to convey feelings and information that otherwise would have been difficult to communicate (Ohlsen, 1970). From this information, the persons are able to understand the sources of their difficulties, and thereby devise strategies for effectively dealing with them. The simplicity with which roles may be enacted allows this technique to be successfully applied to a wide range of individuals.

CLIENT-CENTERED THERAPY

Client-centered therapy is based on the assumption that an individual has the capacity to solve his or her own problems (Shertzer, 1971). It is referred to by many as a *person-centered* approach in counseling. It has been shown effective in a variety of settings, including the following: education, marriage, leadership, organizational development, conflict resolution and the facilitation of large group processes (*International Encyclopedia of the Social Sciences*, 1979).

Proponent – Carl R. Rogers

Dr. Carl Rogers is considered to be the founder of client-centered psychotherapy. In 1951, he authored *Client-Centered Therapy: Its Current Practice, Implications and Theory*. Since his original work, Rogers generalized and extended his research to new settings, including school systems and the probation and parole professions.

Principles and Application

The basic philosophy of the client-centered PO is represented by the counselor's attitude of respect for the person and the right of the person to self-direction. The nature of probation and parole work makes it essential that the PO and client have a relatively close relationship. The client-centered approach should assist the client in experiencing a feeling of safety. The person will find that his or her attitudes are understood by the PO, and not summarily rejected as being without merit. The client is then able to explore and evaluate his or her feelings and to gradually recognize possible remedies. In a safe and secure counseling relationship, the person can perceive for the first time the hostile meaning and purpose of certain types of behavior. In addition, the person can understand why he or she has felt guilty about the behavior and why it has been necessary to deny the basis for the behavior.

The person with these new perceptions should find that the PO also shares similar perceptions, but with an accepting attitude. Generally, this acceptance is embraced by the person as well. The person, in essence, views his or her experiences more in terms of their effect on his or her personal development. Once the person has gained new insight and confidence, he or she can develop strategies to deal with particular problem situations.

In order for the PO to be effective as a client-centered counselor, he or she must have numerous qualities. The first quality is that of *acceptance*. The PO should be accepting of the probationer as an individual. The PO accepts the person with his or her faults, including personality and behavior problems. Such an attitude is more than mutual acceptance; it is respect for the individual as a person of worth.

The second trait of a client-centered counselor is that of *congruence* (Ohlsen, 1970). This term implies that the PO is a real person who lacks phony or superficial qualities. The PO is not just playing a role but is consistent in his/her actions and advice.

The third characteristic which is desirable for the PO using the client-centered approach is that of *understanding*. The PO tries to sense the person's private world as if it were his or her own. Such understanding enables the person to explore feelings freely and deeply, and with greater comprehension. This understanding does not simply involve traditional diagnosis or evaluation, which are external in nature. The desire of the PO "to understand" is more readily accepted by the person, and is generally conducive to progress.

The fourth trait a client-centered counselor should possess is the ability to *communicate* the qualities of acceptance, congruence and understanding. It is of no value for the PO to be accepting, congruent and understanding, if the person does not perceive it. Therefore, it is very important that acceptance, congruence and understanding be effectively communicated to the person. The PO who has these attitudes or characteristics should express them as naturally and spontaneously as possible. The choice of words used by the PO is important, because it sets the tone of the counseling relationship with the person (Cuttle, 1980). Both verbal and non- verbal communication should be employed by the PO. The PO may wish to embrace as well as commend the person for his or her success. The effective use of this approach may ensure that a favorable relationship develops (Rogers, 1951). This relationship is perceived by the person as safe, secure, free from threats and supporting. Likewise, the PO is perceived as dependable, trustworthy and consistent. The resulting relationship between the PO and probationer is one in which positive change can occur. Persons experience new feelings of openness which lead to a deeper understanding of themselves and restore the path to self-improvement.

Yalom (1975) states that in the ideal counselor-client relationship, the following results should take place when the client-centered therapy approach is correctly used:

1.   The person is increasingly free in expressing his or her feelings.

2.   The person begins to test reality. He or she develops discriminatory feelings and perceptions of the environment, other persons and new experiences.

3. The person increasingly becomes aware of the incongruity between his or her experiences and self-concept.

4. The person becomes aware of feelings which have been previously denied or distorted.

5. The person's self-concept becomes more realistic and genuine because of his or her counseling experience.

6. The person becomes increasingly able to experience, without threat, the PO's unconditional, positive attitude toward him or her.

7. The person increasingly evaluates his or her behavior.

8. The person reacts less to evaluations by others and more to the effect of events on his or her own development.

Summary

Client-centered therapy hypothesizes that individuals have within themselves the necessary intrinsic forces for orderly growth, which may at times be hindered. Related to this central organizing tendency is a drive for achieving self-actualization. By developing the proper conditions and using the appropriate techniques, the desired actualizing forces may be released. As a result, the PO may assist the person in freeing these important capacities.

CRISIS INTERVENTION

Crisis and probation/parole work may often seem synonymous. Crisis intervention techniques enable the PO to deal with critical problems and crises that may arise doing field investigations. Most early works in this field dealt with crisis in family situations, but the principles may be more broadly applied (Harper, 1975).

Proponents – Jeffrey A. Schwartz and David A. Liebman

Schwartz and Liebman (1975) developed a crisis intervention training course for criminal justice personnel which provides the average probation officer with those skills necessary for dealing effectively with dispute situations which he encounters in day-to-day activities. Problems addressed by this crisis intervention training model are diverse: general street violence, black and white fights, disputes between parents and a probationer, arguments caused by alcohol or drugs and other problems that arise among people in domestic situations or field investigations.

Principles and Application

Approaching the location of a field investigation or conducting a home visit can be dangerous for a PO (Erickson, 1972). The PO should check the streets around the location of his visit for problems (e.g., loiterers or juvenile gangs). If the PO notices suspicious groups "hanging out," he or she should attempt to avoid them or postpone the visit until the problem conditions improve.

Crisis intervention includes the application of measures to avoid creating or enlarging crisis situations. Defusing techniques assist a PO in restoring order in potentially violent situations. The *request* approach is often effective. For example, a person who is hysterically crying is likely to respond to trivial requests, which may channel concentration away from the emotional ordeal being experienced. In the process, the person is more likely to become less emotional and start to communicate in a calm manner. The *Columbo* approach is another defusing technique. For example, although the PO can clearly see what the person is arguing about, he or she can pretend to be unaware of the conflict which is taking place, forcing the participants to explain the crisis rather than continue it.

Another element in crisis intervention is *mediation*, which may include the process of resolving a person's family feud. The PO attempts to work out something constructive with the disputants, rather than making an arrest or some more drastic measure. The goal of mediation is to help the person and his or her family agree to a specific course of action and to leave them with a positive feeling about their decision. The final agreement reached may be the idea of one of the disputants, but more frequently it will be a compromise which represents the interests of both parties.

There are certain things a PO should avoid when mediating a domestic quarrel. He or she should avoid warning or threatening statements. For example, "Mr. and Mrs. Smith, if you continue to fight, I will have your child taken away from you." Another behavior to avoid is judging or criticizing. For example, "Mr. Smith, you're being pretty disgusting right now." Such comments will likely raise the level of tension and provide an additional obstacle to resolving the dispute.

An important feature of crisis intervention is *referral*. Referral is the process of getting a commitment from the disputants that they will seek a community resource for help in managing specific problems. An example would be the individual who is experiencing a drinking problem. In this instance, a referral might be made to an Alcoholics Anonymous (AA) group for the person and his or her relatives.

A crisis may be encountered by an individual at several points in the criminal justice process. Situations of particular concern are: (1) the arrest and initial detention stage, (2) the presentence phase, (3) the revocation of probation phase, and (4) release from an institution and return to the community. The attitude and verbal as well as non-verbal communication of the PO can greatly increase or decrease the anxiety level of the person during these periods. With most defendants, discussions with the PO can be positive. Defendants can be motivated by the PO to use their time to find jobs, enroll in training or treatment programs, or begin working on interpersonal relationship problems.

The new parolee is a prime candidate for the application of crisis intervention theory. He or she may face crisis problems of unemployment, lack of housing, or new family responsibilities. With such problems, it is important for a PO to keep in mind the crisis concept of breaking down the total problem into smaller, more manageable parts. The unemployed parolee, for example, may need to first learn the proper method of completing a job application, before actually applying and interviewing for a job. Hence, crisis intervention may be considered to include crisis prevention.

Summary

Crisis intervention principles enable a PO to handle problems in a more sensible and controlled manner. They also increase the chances for offenders to become productive members of society. The PO must be aware that while not every probationer is in a state of crisis, many may face potential crisis situations. Although persons may not desire or be responsive to crisis intervention techniques, they still may be needed. Crisis intervention theory can certainly be an important tool to use when a crisis arises in the course of one's job as a probation or parole officer.

ART THERAPY

Art therapy with clients is a recent development available to modern probation and parole. Art therapy may be defined as the process of using art as a way for a person to communicate his or her thoughts, feelings and anxieties to others.

Proponent – Margaret Naumberg

Art therapy, like group counseling, has experienced a gradual and progressive development in the United States. One of the primary developers of modern art therapy concepts has been Margaret Naumberg, a New York psychologist and author of numerous texts on art therapy techniques. One of her most widely acclaimed books, *An Introduction to Art Therapy* (1973), has served as a guide for practitioners in diagnosing and treating behavior problems in children. These same techniques have been refined and applied in the adult setting with similar success. The basic techniques of art therapy involve the participant producing a series of drawings and then rendering interpretations of them. The therapist generally asks questions, offers interpretations, and encourages more drawing. This process gradually results in a more trusting relationship between the therapist and person, and opens a line of communication conducive to a productive interchange of thoughts and ideas. Within such an atmosphere, probation and parole duties may be performed with increased ease and effectiveness.

Principles and Application

How does a PO use art therapy in an office setting? The answer lies in the *Before, Now and After* art therapy technique. This process can be used with an individual or group. The application of art therapy is not difficult and can be performed in a straightforward fashion. For example, the person is given three pieces of blank poster paper and a drawing marker. He is instructed by the PO to write the word *before* on the top of the first poster, *now* on the second poster, and *after* on the third. The PO then instructs the person or persons (if in a group setting), to think about the words *before*, *now* and *after* in terms of their probation or parole status. In other words, what was their life like before they received a criminal sentence? Second, what is their life like now? Third, what do they see in the future for themselves after their conditions are completed? They are told to draw what their life was like before, what it is like now, and what they see for themselves in the future. They are typically given 30 to 45 minutes to complete this task. Once they have completed the task of "drawing their lives" they are asked to present their "drawings" to the group. Each must explain the meaning of his drawings to the group. For example, the person with all "Before" pictures of money and needles explains that before receiving probation, he spent his money on the purchase of heroin. This art therapy technique has been used with new probationers/parolees in group counseling sessions in the U.S. Probation Office in Washington, D.C. where it proved beneficial. The *Before, Now, and After* art technique forced offenders to reflect on their lives and to provide the PO with indicators of their thoughts.

An example of a common "before" drawing is the picture of a stick figure surrounded by other stick figures. The interpretation of such a picture may reveal that before probation the person had many friends. The second picture in such a series might be a stick figure standing alone. The interpretation would be that the probationer has lost his or her friends while on probation. A third picture would generally be a picture of a stick figure surrounded by other stick figures. The interpretation would be that the probationer anticipates finding new friends after the probation period has ended.

Using the art therapy technique of *Before, Now and After* participants learn that their problems are not unique. They learn that others have faced similar problems and have common hopes for the future. This technique has many advantages for the PO. The PO learns of the common problems faced by offenders. It may be discovered that a problem of a new probationer is one of unemployment. As a result, an employment counseling group can be created so that unemployed probationers can regularly meet to make plans to combat their common problems. The PO, in time, is likely to have increased communications with them.

Various researchers have successfully utilized art therapy in their research. Dr. Hanscarl Leuner (1969) concludes that art therapy enables an individual to express his or her emotions with less anxiety. By reducing the anxiety the individual improves his or her ability to communicate. Art therapist Reyher (1963) found that art therapy gives a person a unique opportunity to explore topics meaningful to his or her future behavior. Similarly, another leading therapist, Landgarten (1981), discovered that the process of art therapy enables one to explore in greater depth an individual's strengths as well as faults. Further research is bound to reveal even more benefits.

Summary

Art therapy, like many additional counseling approaches, can be important in discovering the true feelings and fears of probationers and parolees. While many offenders may be unable or hesitant to verbally express their feelings to a supervisory official, these same individuals may be able to communicate their thoughts through art therapy. This process can improve the probation officer/probationer relationship by opening up the channels of communication in a relatively unobtrusive manner. The information gained from this therapy can be used in numerous ways, including: the improvement of one's self-concept; the remedying of present obstacles to reform; and the selection of realistic future goals which will serve present probation or parole needs.

TRANSACTIONAL ANALYSIS

Transactional analysis (TA) enables a PO to assist a probationer through effective communication. TA assumes that a person generally communicates on one of three basic levels: adult, parent, or child. These three levels provide working indicators of the person's mental processes and behavior. By understanding the communication process more precisely, the PO is better able to undertake the counseling that is needed, and to gather the information necessary for supervision.

Proponent – Eric Berne

Eric Berne is considered by many to be the father of transactional analysis. He established the conceptual framework for his communication model in his bestseller, *Games People Play* (1964). Although the work of Berne was embraced and expanded by others, the most significant contributions to his model were perhaps made by Thomas Harris in his book, *I'm OK -- You're OK* (1967). Harris soon gained recognition as a pioneer in the application of transactional analysis to the treatment of psychiatric patients. In the field of criminal justice, articles relating transactional analysis to the problems of probation and parole officers have appeared in the professional journal *Federal Probation* (Nicholson, 1970; Frazier, 1972).

While transactional analysis has been widely read and accepted as an important technique for defining and analyzing communication interactions in the business community (Robbins, 1980), investigations of its applications to the criminal justice system's operations have been limited. Although certain aspects of transactional analysis are used intuitively, it can be helpful for probation and parole professionals to better understand and more effectively implement this technique in their supervision and management practices.

Principles and Application

While the intricacies of TA theory can be examined in great detail and its several components woven into a pattern of complex relationships, the basic elements can be explained in a straightforward fashion and their benefits easily recognized. According to Berne and Harris, one's personality and behavior can be categorized into one of the following ego states: parent, adult and child. Each of these ego states reflects modes of behavior and communication patterns typical of the parent, adult, or child stages of growth and development. In simple terms, the *parent* within a person reflects feelings and behavior similar to those demonstrated by one's mother and father. A parent can be critical, or helping, or both. The *adult* in a person serves to examine facts objectively and to seek reasonable and calculated solutions. An appropriate analogy to this ego state is the information processing and decision-making capability of a computer. The *child* in a person operates in a manner much like that of an actual child. The feelings and behavior appear impulsive and reflect immaturity and childlike reasoning.

Each of these three ego states can be used to describe communications which frequently occur in the probation or parole setting. For example, a PO acts in the parent mode when he or she lectures a person on arriving late for their scheduled appointment. A PO may act in the adult mode when he or she reasons with a person on the best occupational alternatives for his or her newly acquired job skills. Finally, persons may fit into the child mode when they become convinced that society is "out to get them." These three ego states provide essential elements in analyzing levels or modes of communication which can occur between two or more individuals.

The dynamics of transactional analysis involve more than merely categorizing ego states. TA also involves the identification of repetitive sets of social maneuvers (Starling, 1980). These maneuvers are commonly referred to as *pastimes*, *games* and *scripts*.

Pastimes involve interactions which occur in almost ritualistic ways. For instance, a probationer and PO frequently engage in an exchange of pleasantries upon first meeting in order to "break the ice" or as a prelude to establishing a working rapport. The interactions are typically comfortable to the participants, but yield little factual or specific information.

Games refer to a sequence of transactions which occur with a definite pattern. Of special importance to the game situation is the realization that such a transaction has significance at two different levels: it has both a surface and a hidden meaning. More clearly stated, games are a series of human moves with a "gimmick." Games have two chief characteristics: (1) their ulterior quality, and (2) the payoff. While games are certainly frequently played among probationers and parolees, they are not unique to these persons and can also be exhibited by probation and parole officers. For example, a PO may simultaneously attempt to help a person while making fun of the person. Thus, the officer's child state enjoys the game while his adult state considers the exercise productive.

Scripts, according to TA theory, are composed of even larger, more complex sets of transactions which are reflected in a person's behavior and feelings. Everyone is considered to have a "life script" or life plan, which evolves during his or her early formative years, whether the person is aware of it or not. The script can be either healthy or un-healthy. For example, some persons may have decided early in life that they should not trust or confide in others, since others will undoubtedly utilize the information against them. Such life scripts of distrust and self-reliance can have enormous repercussions in trying to effectively counsel persons in coping within a cooperative setting.

An integral part of games and scripts is the concept of *stroking*. A stroke refers to a payoff and can be either verbal or nonverbal, and positive (producing good feelings) or negative (producing bad feelings). People are inclined to seek strokes to which they are accustomed, or which dominated their early personal development. Recognizing and learning to cope with the "stroking" needs of probationers and parolees is of special concern to POs in counseling settings where they must be properly applied.

Finally, in analyzing communication transactions, the existence and importance of complementary, crossed and ulterior transactions must be understood. Examples of each type of transaction will assist in an understanding of each.

A transaction is considered *complementary* when the initiator of the transaction receives a response from the target ego state in the other person. In other words, if a parole officer speaks from a parent state to the parolee in a child state and the parolee responds as anticipated (as a child to a parent), then the transaction is predicted, and some information is gained.

A *crossed* transaction occurs when the stimulus fails to get the anticipated response. Crossed transactions usually precipitate interpersonal conflicts and result in a breakdown of communication, although they also have potential for being used productively by alert and knowledgeable participants. A typical crossed transaction is exemplified by a PO (speaking from a parent state) who admonishes a person to "go to work," but the person (speaking from an adult state) inquires as to the availability of gainful employment for a person with his or her skill (or lack of skills) and a criminal record. In this instance, the unexpected or crossed response might serve to promote a more beneficial dialogue.

An *ulterior* transaction is more complex in nature and involves the activity of two ego states simultaneously, thus frequently providing a basis for games. A transaction which appears to be occurring on the adult-to-adult level may, in fact, reflect a psychological transaction taking place on a different level. For instance, a PO may comment to a person that he may eventually be incarcerated due to a lack of initiative in finding employment. The person may respond from an apparently adult perspective, while secretly harboring child state feelings of resentment which will ultimately determine his or her course of action.

The building blocks of TA theory are not necessarily complex and can provide valuable tools for describing, analyzing and controlling transactions between criminal justice professionals and offenders. In the probation and parole setting, the techniques are especially useful and relatively easy to command. By further examining these transactions in relation to probation and parole practices, an improved understanding of their nature should evolve, which can result in greater competency and higher levels of performance.

Examples of transactions which can occur in the probation and parole settings are briefly analyzed below. While these exact scenarios may not be typical of the experiences found in any given organization, they are presented to illustrate the types and nature of transactions with which a probation or parole officer may well be acquainted.

Complementary transactions are characterized by an absence of conflict. The sender receives the intended type of response and the lines of communication are parallel. A complementary *parent*-to-*parent* exchange, for example, would be one where a PO (in the parent state) says to another PO (in the parent state): "Frank, that Joe Powers ought to know better than that!" Frank responds, "You are absolutely right." This might reflect preexisting negative feelings toward Joe by the two officers. An example of a complementary *adult*-to-*adult* exchange is evidenced by the following exchange between a PO and a secretary. Frank says, "Sally, do you have the file?" Sally responds, "Yes, here it is." This is a complementary *adult*-to-*adult* transaction, as a concise and valuable exchange of information occurs.

Another complementary transaction would be a *child*-to-*child* exchange of feelings. For example: Mark (in his child state) says, "I cannot believe how stupid the probation officers are around here!" Frank responds, "Yeah, I am really fed up with them, and this whole lousy place!" In this case, the exchange of feelings concerns a topic they are both interested in, but little in the way of productive information is exchanged.

Cross-transactions can also be important to the parole and probation function. A crossed-transaction is a transaction in which the stimulus fails to get the anticipated response. Crossed-transactions usually precipitate interpersonal conflicts and can result in a breakdown of communication. An example of crossed-transaction may be a PO talking to his probationer. The PO (speaking from an adult state) states uncritically, "You look tired." The person might be expected to reply in an adult fashion: "No, I'm really not" or "Yes, I am." Instead, he responds from a child state, "Why are you always criticizing me?" The transaction is crossed and the PO's attempt at a productive dialogue is jeopardized. A similar result may occur from the following crossed-transaction: the PO says, "Don't talk to me like that!" This is a parent-to-child transaction. The person responds, "You shouldn't yell at me either." This is a parent-to-child response, and the potential for communication problems emerges.

Ulterior transactions have hidden messages in them. In an ulterior transaction, two messages are sent. One is the obvious message. The other message is a secret message that carries the real meaning of a transaction (sometimes intentionally and sometimes not). Ulterior messages often lead to bad feelings. The PO, for example, says "Since you have never held a job very long, why don't you seek temporary employment?" The conversation appears to be on an adult-to-adult level. However, on a psychological level, the meaning is parent-to-child. The true desire is to entice the person into obtaining full-time employment.

According to transactional analysis theory, everyone occasionally needs "strokes." A stroke may be as simple as a pat on the back or a word of recognition. If the PO greets a probationer with a smile and a handshake, it can constitute a stroke. Similarly, a PO who states to his probationer, "I'm proud that you went out and applied for the job I told you about," is giving the person a *positive stroke* because the person did something desired by the officer.

Here are some positive stroking techniques for a probation or parole officer to consider:

1. Find and reward any good performance, however slight;

2. Reward frequently on a scheduled basis so that the person becomes accustomed to, and comfortable with, receiving positive strokes;

3. Shape behavior gradually, so that person's needs coincide with overall probation and parole goals;

4. Use verbal and non-verbal rewards (e.g., smile or show expressions of pleasure when a person accomplishes something desired); and

5. Develop the ability to give unconditional (spontaneous) strokes as well as conditional (earned) strokes, so that no ulterior motive or sense of bribery surfaces.

Transactional analysis also indicates that individuals may use *rituals*, *pastimes* and *games* because of their inability to become intimate with others.

A *ritual* for a PO is commonly evidenced by greeting a person in a way that reveals a lack of true concern. If the PO says, "How are you doing? How is work?", the person may give pat answers and, as a result, meaningful communication will not be achieved.

A *pastime* for a probation or parole officer may involve simply discussing a casual interest such as professional football with offenders. This might take place for an extended period before actually engaging in a serious discussion of the problems faced by them.

Games are different from rituals, pastimes, activities, and withdrawals, as demonstrated by their characteristics: (1) their ulterior quality, and (2) the payoff. Elements of drama and dishonesty are typically present. A person does not "come on straight" when his or her message to another person is ulterior and secret. He or she is in a sense playing a game. Robert Heise (1974) refers to a game titled *Bum Beef* (or "I'm here on a bummer"). Heise states that parole violators are prime material to play this game due to their past experiences in both sending and receiving verbal communications dealing with their criminal activities. Anyone, however, is a potential candidate. The players in this game are senders or receivers. The active player is the sender and he or she is crying "bum beef." The one listening to the cry about the "bum beef" is the receiver. More than 80 percent of all parole violators (according to Heise) play "bum beef" for at least the first month or two after being caught. Hopefully, they are playing this game with knowledgeable receivers. The PO is usually the first receiver the violator plays this game with after being rearrested. Next, the violator or sender attempts to play this game with his or her family, friends, employer, and then anyone who listens or may be used as an agent to intervene on his or her behalf. For the violator, there is a motivation that goes deeper than that of saving face, or salvaging some kind of false pride. If he or she can win the game by convincing enough people of his or her innocence, he or she may be granted continued freedom.

Heise was previously an inmate and admits to observing caseworkers who become willing receivers in some of the phoniest "bum beef" games ever played. Sometimes a PO who has gone out on limb, or taken a special interest in a parolee, will once again become receptive to the parolee's "bum beef" game when he or she returns.

Another area of importance in transactional analysis involves life scripts and decisions. Everyone has a "life script" or life plan usually formulated in his or her early years. The PO can help persons discover their life scripts and change their way of behaving by following these steps:

1. Learn to recognize the child within: its fears, its fun, and its abilities;

2. Recognize the parent state: its reasoning and decision-making processes;

3. Recognize the child, parent and adult states in other persons in order to promote improved social skills and interdependence;

4. Sort out the parent and child states from reality in order to foster rational behavior; and

5. Work out a system of values which is desirable and rehabilitative.

From these examples of common exchanges confronting probation and parole professionals, methods for improving the communication process and achieving tangible, significant results in probation and parole functions are outlined. The usefulness of this approach to overcoming dysfunctional responses to a variety of situations has become widely accepted and advocated in literature on the social psychology of work behavior (Eddy, 1981) and motivation theory (Lee, 1979).

Summary

With a knowledge of the elementary features of TA, and experience in their application, probation and parole officers can increase their effectiveness in supervision and management. The benefits of using TA in the work environment have proven effective in their application to private and corporate business settings, and also many areas within the public sector. Among the most important benefits derived are: (1) game avoidance, (2) effective communication, (3) improved personal relationships, and (4) enhanced job satisfaction.

The first benefit, *game avoidance*, demonstrates that games can frequently be avoided once they are recognized and remedial actions taken. By refusing to go along with another's game, or to offer the expected payoff, attention can be focused more directly on the source of an offender's problem and his or her most pressing needs. Similarly, the person (probationer or parolee) who attempts to engage in nonproductive or destructive games can benefit from having the negative behavior called to his attention and learn how to avoid future repetitions.

The second benefit, *effective communication*, is promoted by TA through diagnosing the ego states involved in the transactions and providing remedial measure to overcome obstacles to productive and rational communication. An awareness of actions outside the adult ego state can also serve administrators in selecting the most effective action level, considering existing constraints. If an individual is unable to engage in an adult-to-adult transaction, perhaps an adult-to-child approach is necessary. Usually, however, the achievement of an adult-to-adult transaction will render more valuable information, more rational decision-making and greater effectiveness in the communication process.

The third benefit, *improved personal relationships*, results primarily from the recognition and utilization of stroking techniques. Persons intent on harming themselves through negative strokes can be taught to react to positive strokes, often leading them to adopt improved self-images, overcoming their games and recreating their life scripts. Stroking needs are usually evidenced by negative self-perceptions (or lack of self-assurance). By recognizing these underlying needs and overcoming such negative perceptions, the person is more likely to benefit in his future personal transactions, over which he will be able to exercise greater control.

A fourth benefit of *increased job satisfaction* is likely to evolve from an appreciation of the previous results. Probation and parole officers are called upon to deal with increasing numbers of offenders who have very complex problems. TA can help these officers better understand and more effectively cope with the perspectives and reasoning abilities of these persons, resulting in more effective treatment and their reintegration into the mainstream of society.

BEHAVIOR MODIFICATION AND THERAPY

Behavior therapy or modification must be explained in terms of the broader concept of behavior influence (Kratcoski, 1981). Behavior influence refers to the exertion of control by one person over another and varies in magnitude. Common examples of behavior influence include public education, political campaigning, television viewing and a multitude of interpersonal interactions. Behavior modification is one form of behavior influence involving the application of experimental psychology research findings to individuals for purposes of alleviating suffering or improving behavior. It requires close monitoring and evaluation of modification efforts, and it generally attempts to improve self-control by increasing a person's independence and analytical abilities. Behavior therapy, frequently used synonymously with behavior modification, refers to clinical intervention (i.e., therapist-patient relationship).

Proponent – B.F. Skinner

B.F. Skinner is regarded by most counseling theorists and practitioners as one of the greatest contributors to the scientific study of human behavior. He also developed a reputation as perhaps the most influential, controversial and visible American psychologist (*International Encyclopedia of the Social Sciences*, 1979). Skinner (1938; 1953; 1971) contributed much to the literature of behavior theory. Regarding the human condition, Skinner states:

> The struggle to avoid aversive situations is a legitimate struggle for freedom. We are certainly not beyond this. This kind of 'struggle for freedom' is mainly directed toward intentional controllers -- toward those who treat others aversively in order to induce them to behave in particular ways. Thus, a child may stand up to his parents, a citizen may overthrow a government, a communicant may reform a religion, a student may attack a teacher or vandalize a school, and a dropout may work to destroy a culture (Skinner, 1972: 27).

Principles and Application

Behavior modification techniques rely on the general principle that individuals are influenced by the consequences of their actions, and that their current environments are more relevant than other factors (e.g., early life experiences, personality characteristics) in determining their present behavior. As a result, counselors direct their attention to observable behavior and the person's environment, rather than the person's feelings or internal processes. A technique that frequently may be used in behavior modification involves a negotiated contractual agreement (behavioral contract) with definite goals and procedures. In addition, the therapist must be able to objectively define the desired goals and to ensure that they are attainable. If the person suffers from an internal crisis of identity, then another mode of treatment, such as psychotherapy, may be desired.

In the probation and parole setting, the officer must perform the role of the therapist, which may not be as difficult as one might believe. To a large extent, the application of behavior treatment principles emphasizes what is commonly regarded as "common sense," although the technique strives to add organization and structure to the process. By examining some examples of behavior therapy which can be utilized by a PO, one should be able to realize the many opportunities in which this technique may prove beneficial.

For example, if the PO smiles upon receiving the monthly report from the probationer and also shakes the individual's hand, indicating a *positive* reaction to his behavior, there is a good chance the person will be more inclined to bring the report in the following month as required. This subtle form of positive reinforcement increases the probability of desirable behavior.

Time Projection is also a behavior modification technique. Time projection enables clients to imagine themselves functioning happily and effectively at a future date. Using this technique, the person can establish productive goals which can provide guidance for his actions upon completion of probation or parole conditions.

Another behavior change technique is *thought control*. Many persons may experience persistent and intrusive patterns of negative thoughts. Persons who experience a high degree of anxiety resulting from harmful negative thoughts may be asked to close their eyes and dwell on the destructive thoughts in the presence of the PO. The PO then voices the command, "Stop!", and draws the person's attention to the fact that the thoughts actually do stop. This is practiced several times, and the person is told to interrupt his or her own negative thoughts by mentally saying "Stop!" The person is then encouraged to practice this control technique outside the confines of the office.

The *blow-up* technique is a behavior modification technique that attempts to control or eliminate obsessive thinking. This technique requires having the person "blow-up" the distressing habit to a degree where it becomes absurd and funny. For example, a person who is afraid of stuttering because of simple nervousness would be instructed to try to stutter as much as possible. When people encourage their anticipatory anxieties to erupt, they frequently find the opposite reaction coming about. Their fears often subside and after using this method several times, the behavior they dread may eventually disappear.

The *as if* behavior therapy technique is useful for persons who complain about the negative aspects of their past life, (e.g., hostile siblings; domineering or unaffectionate parents). This procedure takes them back in time (through concentrated thought) and allows them to fantasize in a manner which is inconsistent with their present thinking. In other words, the hostile brother would be imagined as being kind, supportive and considerate. This experience then serves to replace directed anger with general feelings of ambivalence, serving to alleviate accumulated aggressions.

In carrying out behavior treatment, there are nine principles that a PO should remember (Lazarus, 1971):

1. He or she must decide what is solvable and what is not. This dictates what can be changed and what cannot be changed in the behavior of probationers and parolees.

2. The PO should screen out those persons for whom behavior modification or therapy is inappropriate.

3. The PO must focus on the life-role and self-esteem of the individual.

4. The PO seeks out the offender's reinforcers, those things which the person considers valuable. The PO must utilize these incentives in working out the person's treatment plan or behavior contract.

5. The PO must discover the person's behavioral expectations. Does he or she desire to change his or her behavior? Or does the individual believe he or she does not need to change?

6. The PO should specify target behaviors. Should work be done on the person's job problem or drinking problem?

7. The PO should identify the goals most beneficial to the person and the behavior necessary to achieve them.

8.   The PO should shape the behavior of the person by providing constant direction and advice as the person pursues his goals.

9.   The PO should build on success by reinforcing positive behavior.

It is possible, and frequently desirable, to apply behavior modification to more than one person.   The approach may be used with a probationer's or parolee's family (Erickson, 1972).   Desired behaviors in the family are also typically in need of reinforcement.   For instance, families prone to problems involving alcohol can deal more effectively with an alcoholic probationer or parolee if they are taught the behavior modification technique of desensitization.   Desensitization involves the process of teaching family members how to relax or to get the individual to relax when a tense situation erupts (*The Workbook for Alcoholic Patients*, 1975).   For example, family members may be instructed in methods of focusing attention to more relaxing images (e.g., sailing), rather than immediate problems.   This technique forces tempers to cool and promotes more reflective, rational reactions.

Summary

Behavior modification or therapy, in essence, is counseling which offers the probationer or parolee a new opportunity for learning more appropriate behavior. The therapy process creates a situation in which the probationer's or parolee's undesirable responses are extinguished and better responses are learned.   This technique can be readily applied and successfully adapted to many of the demands of probation and parole counseling. Noted authorities in this field, however, offer the following cautionary advice which must be heeded when dealing with offenders in nearly all settings (Alonzo and Braswell, 1977):

Of course, there is no one behavioral approach which is suited to all inmates. Just as offenders bring a variety of problems to the correctional professional, so the correctional professional must also bring a variety of prevention strategies to the helping process.

Certainly, over-reliance upon behavior modification therapy may be ineffective and even detrimental.   Yet, as a counseling approach in the probation and parole setting, it is at times invaluable.   As a result, it seems incumbent upon professionals to attempt to master, improve and expand the many techniques of behavior modification, only a few of which are explained herein.

REALITY THERAPY

References

Glasser, W. (1975). *Reality Therapy -- A New Approach to Psychiatry*. New York: Harper and Row.

Sandu, H.S. (1974). *Modern Corrections: The Offenders, Therapies, and Community Reintegration*. Springfield, IL: Charles C Thomas.

Selected Readings

Ackerman, J.R. (1969). *Reality Therapy Approach to Probation and Parole Supervision*. Probation and Parole.

Blum, G.S. (1953). *Psychoanalytic Theories of Personality*. New York: McGraw- Hill.

Coleman, B.I. & Schmideberg, M. (1970). Reality Therapy with Offenders: Practice and Principle. *International Journal of Offender Therapy*, 14 (1).

Evans, D.B. (1983). What Are You Doing? An interview with William Glasser. *Personnel and Guidance Journal*, 60, (8), 460-465.

RATIONAL EMOTIVE THERAPY

References

Ellis, A. (1974). *Rational Emotive Psychotherapy*. NY: Institute for Rational Living -- Publisher.

Ellis, A. (1974). *The Essence of Rational Psychotherapy: A Comprehensive Approach to Treatment*. NY: Institute for Rational Living, Publisher.

Ellis, A. (1969). *How to Live with a Neurotic*. NY: Universal Publishing.

Ellis, A. (1962). *Reason and Emotion in Psychotherapy*. NY: Lyle Stuart.

Patterson, C.H. (1973). *Theories of Counseling and Psychotherapy*. NY: Harper and Row.

Ruhnow, M.E. (1975). *Supervision of Group Counseling*. Dallas, TX: Federal Probation Office Publication.

Selected Readings

Ellis, A. & Harper, R.A. (1973). *A New Guide to Rational Living*. Hollywood, CA: Wilshire.

Ellis, A. (1981). Science, Religiousity, and Rational Emotive Psychology. *Psychotherapy: Theory, Research and Practice*, 18 (2), 155-158.

Ellis, A. (1974). *Techniques for Disputing Irrational Beliefs*. NY: Institute for Rational Living, Publisher.

Ellis, A. & Maultsby, M.C. (1974). *Techniques for Using Rational Emotive Imagery*. NY: Institute for Rational Living, Publisher.

GROUP THERAPY

References

Gazda, G.M. (1971). *Group Counseling: A Developmental Approach*. Boston, MA: Allyn and Bacon.

Jones, J.E. & Pfeiffer, J.W. (1975). Co-facilitating. *The 1974 Annual Handbook for Group Facilitators*. La Jolla, CA: University Associates Publishers.

Kelman, H.C. (1963). The Role of the Group in the Induction of Therapeutic Change. *International Journal of Group Psychotherapy*, 13, 299-432.

Kratcoski, P.C. (1981). *Correctional Counseling and Treatment*. Belmont, CA. Duxbury Press.

Sullivan, D.F. (Ed.) (1952). *Readings in Group Work*. NY: Association Press.

Selected Readings

Beene, K. & Sheats, P. (1948). Functional Roles of Group Members. *The Journal of Social Issues*, 4 (2).

Dyer, W.G. (1969). An Inventory of Trainer Intervention. *Human Relations Training News*, 41-44.

Frank, J.D. (1974). Some Determinates, Manifestations and Efforts of Cohesiveness in Therapy Groups. In G. Gazda, *Basic Approaches to Group Psychotherapy and Group Counseling*. Springfield, IL: Charles C Thomas.

Gendlin, E. *Ground Rules for Group Sessions*, unpublished handout.

Gibb, C.A. (1954). Leadership. In Lindzeg, *Handbook of Social Psychology* (Vol. II). Reading, MA: Addison-Wesley. Hotfelder, P. & Saches, A.D. (1979, June).

Intake group counseling. *Federal Probation*.

Jones, J.E. & Pfeiffer, J.W. (1975). Styles of Influence. *The 1975 Annual Handbook for Group Facilitators*. La Jolla, CA: University Associates Publishers.

Kemp, C.G. (1964). *Perspectives on the Group Process*. Boston, MA: The Riverside Press Cambridge Houghton Mifflin Company.

Phillips, H. (1957). *Essentials of Social Work Skills*. NY: The Association Press.

Rest, W.G. & Ryan, E.J. (1970, June). Group Vocational Counseling for the Probationer and Parolee. *Federal Probation*.

Schwartz, W. & Zalba, S.R. (1971). *The Practice of Group Work*. NY: Columbia University Press.

Wallen, J.L. (1975, February). How to Recognize an Effective Group. *Probation Officers Group Training Seminar*, 134-138.

Zastowny, T.R., Janosik, E., Trimborn, S., & Milanese, E. (1982, April). Cognitive Orientation, Identified Curative Factors and Depression as Predictors for Treatment Outcomes in Group Therapy Programs for Alcoholism. *Psychological Reports*, 50 (2), 477-478.

CAREER COUNSELING

References

Campbell, D.P. (1974). *Manual for Strong-Campbell Interest Inventory*. Stanford, CA: Stanford University Press.

D'Costa, A.G., Winefordner, D.W., Odgers, J.G., & Koons, P.B., Jr. (1970). *Ohio Vocational Interest Survey: Manual for Interpreting*. NY: Harcourt.

Department of Labor, U.S. Employment Service. (1965). *Dictionary of Occupational Titles*. (Vol. 1). Washington, DC: U.S. Government Printing Office.

Kuder, G.F. (1965). *Kuder General Interest Survey*. Chicago: Science Research Associates.

Ginzberg, E. (1972). Toward a Theory of Occupational Choice: A Restatement. *Vocational Guidance Quarterly*, 20, 169-176.

Selected Readings

Butcher, E. (1982). Changing by Choice: A Process Model for Group Career Counseling. *Vocational Guidance Quarterly*, 30, (3), 200-209.

Byron, W.J. (1970). Needed: A Special Employment Clearinghouse for Ex-Offenders. *Federal Probation*.

Kelley, H. (1970). Work Hard and Hope for a Miracle, Too. *Federal Probation*.

Miller, J.V. (1982). Lifelong Career Development for Disadvantaged Youth and Adults. *Vocational Guidance Quarterly*, 30, (4), 359-366.

Nakamura, S.S. (1982). An Experimental Focus on the Development of Employment for Ex-Offenders. *Federal Probation*.

Norris, W. (1972). *The Information Service in Guidance*. Chicago: Rand McNally College Publishing.

U.S. Department of Labor, Bureau of Employment Security. (1965). *Training and Reference Manual for Job Analysis*. Washington, DC: U.S. Government Printing Office.

PSYCHODRAMA

References

Enneis, J.M. & Moreno, J.L. (1950). *Hypodrama and Psychodrama*. Beacon, NY: Beacon House.

Gazda, G.M. (1968). *Basic Approaches to Group Psychotherapy and Group Counseling*. Springfield, IL: Charles C Thomas.

NiKelly, A.G. (1971). *Techniques for Behavior Change*. Springfield, IL: Charles C Thomas.

Ohlsen, M.M. (1970). *Group Counseling*. New York: Holt, Rinehart and Winston.

Selected Readings

Blajan-Marcus, S. (1968). Psychodrama and Its Diverse Uses. *International Mental Health Research Newsletter*, 10, (2).

Buchanan, D.R. (1980). The Central Control Model Framework for Structuring Psychodramatic Production. *Group Psychotherapy, Psychodrama and Sociometry*, 33, 47-62.

CLIENT-CENTERED THERAPY

References

Cottle, W.C. & Downie, N.M. (1960). *Procedures and Preparation for Counseling*. Englewood Cliffs, NJ: Prentice-Hall.

Kemp, C.G. (1964). *Perspectives on the Group Process*. Boston, MA: Houghton Mifflin Company, the Riverside Press.

Ohlsen, M.M. (1970). *Group Counseling*. NY: Holt, Rinehart and Winston.

Patterson, C.H. (1973). *Theories of Counseling and Psychotherapy* (2nd ed.). NY: Harper and Row.

Rogers, C.R. (1951). *Client Centered Therapy*. Boston, MA: Houghton Mifflin   Company, The Riverside Press.

Shertzer, B. & Stone, S.C. (1971). *Fundamentals of Counseling*. Boston, MA: Houghton Mifflin Company, The Riverside Press.

Yalom, I.D. (1975). *The Theory and Practice of Group Psychotherapy*. NY: Basic Books.

Selected Readings

Patterson, C.H. & Watkins, C.E. (1982). Some Essentials of a Client-Centered Approach to Assessment. *Measurement and Evaluation in Guidance*, 15, (1), 103-106.

CRISIS INTERVENTION

References

Cunningham, G. (1973, December). Crisis Intervention in a Probation Setting. *Federal Probation*.

Erickson, G.D. & Hogan, T.P. (1972). *Family Therapy -- An Introduction to Theory and Technique*. Monterey, CA: Brooks-Cole.

Harper, R.A. (1975). *The New Psychotherapies*. Englewood Cliffs, NJ: Prentice-Hall.

Schwartz, J.A., Liebman, D.A., & Schwartz, C.A. (1975). *Correctional Crisis Intervention Training Court*.

Selected Readings

Crow, G.A. (1977). *Crisis Intervention*. New York: Association Press.

Goldstein, A.P.; Minti, P.J.; Sardino, T.J.; & Green, D.J. (1977). Police Crisis Intervention. *Kalamazoo, MI: Behaviordelia, Inc.*

Hill, R. (1958). Generic Features of Families Under Stress. *Social Casework*, 39, 32 - 52.

Lukton, R.C. (1982). Myths and Realities of Crisis Intervention. *Social Casework*, 63, 276-285.

Pasewark, R.A. & Albers, D.A. (1972, March). Crisis Intervention: Theory in Search of a Program. *Social Work*, 17, 70-77.

Reid, W.J. & Shyne, A.W. (1969). *Brief and Extended Casework*. New York: Columbia University Press.

Schwartz, M.C. & Weintraub, J.F. (1974, December). The Prisoner's Wife: A Study in Crisis. *Federal Probation*, 38, 20-26.

Wade, T.C., Morton, T.L, Lind, J.E. & Ferris, N.R. (1977). A Family Crisis Intervention Approach to Diversion from the Juvenile Justice System. *Juvenile Justice*, 28, (3), 43-51.

ART THERAPY

References

Landgarten, H.B. (1981). *Clinical Art Therapy*. New York: Branner/Mazel.

Leuner, H. (1969). Guided Affective Imagery (GAI). A Method of Intensive Psychotherapy. *American Journal of Psychotherapy*, 23, 4-22.

Naumberg, M. (1966). *Dynamically Oriented Art Therapy: Its Principle and Practice*. New York: Gune and Stratton.

Reyher, J. (1963). Free Imagery: An Uncovering Procedure. *Journal of Clinical Psychology*, 19, 454-459.

Selected Readings

Hays, R.E. & Lyons, S.J. (1981). The Bridge Drawing: A Projective Technique for Assessment in Art Therapy. *Arts in Psychotherapy*, 8, (3-4), 207-217.

Horowitz, M. (1970). *Image Formation and Cognition*. New York: Appleton-Century-Crofts.

Horowitz, M. (1963). Graphic Communication: A Study of Interaction Painting with Schizophrenics. *American Journal of Psychotherapy*, 17, 320-327.

Kramer, E. (1965, October). Art Therapy and the Severely Disturbed Gifted Child. *Bulletin of Art Therapy*, 3-20.

Kwiatowska, N. (1967, January). The Use of Families' Art Productions for Psychiatric Evaluation. *Bulletin of Art Therapy*, 52-69.

Naumberg, M. (1966). *Psychoneurotic Art: Its Function in Psychotherapy*. NY: Grune and Stratton.

Pickford, R. (1967). *Studies in Psychiatric Art*. Springfield, IL: Charles C Thomas.

Pickford, R.W. (1972). *Psychology and Visual Aesthetics*. London, England: Anchor Press.

TRANSACTIONAL ANALYSIS

References

Albano, C. (1974). *Transactional Analysis on the Job*. NY: AMACOM.

Berne, E. (1964). *Games People Play*. NY: Grove Press.

Harris, T.A. (1969). *I'm OK -- You're OK*. NY: Harper and Row.

Heise, R.E. (1974). *Games Convicts Play*. WA: McNeil Island Penitentiary.

Selected Readings

Eddy, W.B. (1981). *Public Organization Behaivor and Development*. Cambridge, MA: Winthrop.

Frazier, T.L. (1972, September). Transactional Analysis Training and Treatment of Staff in a Correctional School. *Federal Probation*.

Huff, V.E. (1978). Creativity and Transactional Analysis. *Journal of Creative Behavior*, 12, (3), 202-208.

James, M. (1975). *The O.K. Boss*. Reading, MA: Addison Wesley.

Lee, R.D., Jr. (1979). *Public Personnel Systems*. Baltimore: University Park Press.

Nicholson, R.C. (1970, September). Transactional Analysis: A New Method for Helping Offenders. *Federal Probation*.

BEHAVIOR MODIFICATION AND THERAPY

References

Alonzo, T.M. & Brasswell, M.C. (1977, March). Behavior Modification and Corrections: An Analysis. *Lambda Alpha Epsilon: American Criminal Justice Association*, 40, 10-15.

Erickson, G.D. & Hogan, T.P. (1972). *Family Therapy: An Introduction to Theory and Technique*. Monterey, CA: Brooks-Cole.

International Encyclopedia of the Social Sciences. (1972). NY: Macmillan.

New Jersey Neuro-Psychiatric Institute. (1975). *The Workbook for Alcoholic Patients.* Princeton, NJ: Author.

Kratcoski, P.C. (1981). *Correctional Counseling and Treatment.*   Belmont, CA: Wadsworth.

Lazarus, A.A. (1971). *Behavior Therapy and Beyond.* NY: McGraw-Hill.

Skinner, B.F. (1972). *Beyond Freedom and Dignity.* NY: Bantam Books.

Skinner, B.F. (1953). *Science and Human Behavior.* NY: Macmillan.

Thorne, G.L., Tharp, R.G., & Wetzel, R.J. (1967, June). Behavior Modification Techniques: New Tools for Probation Officers. *Federal Probation.*

Selected Readings

Bandura, A. (1962). Punishment Revised. *Journal of Consulting Psychology*, 26, 298 - 301.

Gazda, G.M. (1968). *Basic Approaches to Group Psychotherapy and Group Counseling.* Springfield, IL: Charles C Thomas.

Harper, R.A. (1975). *The New Psychotherapies.* Englewood Cliffs, NJ: Prentice-Hall.

Jamieson, R.B. (1965). Can Conditioning Principles be Applied to Probation? *Trial Judges Journal*, 4, (1).

Shah, S. (1966, June). Treatment of Offenders! Some Behavior Principles and Approaches. *Federal Probation.*

Wardlaw, G. (1981). Applied Behavior Analysis and Crime Prevention: Some Cautions. *Australian Psychologist*, 16, (3), 391-397.

Wolpe, J., Salter, A., & Reyna, L.J. (1964). *The Conditioning Therapies: The Challenge in Psychotherapy.* NY: Holt, Rinehart and Winston.

Yates, A.J. (1981). Behavior Therapy: Past, Present, Future-Imperfect? *Clinical Psychology Review*, 1, (3), 269-291.

Chapter 6

FUTURE TRENDS AND ISSUES
IN PROBATION AND PAROLE

LEARNING OBJECTIVES

* Knowledge of major trends impacting probation and parole services.

* Understanding the forces underlying future trends.

* Recognition of major issues accompanying future trends.

* Ability to anticipate future needs of probation and parole and to react to change.

DISCUSSION TOPICS AND QUESTIONS

1. Identify major trends impacting future probation and parole services.

2. What important issues are likely to arise from the continuance of these trends?

3. Discuss several primary factors underlying each of the future trends and the policy considerations with which probation and parole officers must be familiar.

4. Will probation and parole officials be able to accommodate each of these trends in their future delivery of services? Explain.

5. What additional issues impacting the future of probation and parole do you foresee?

FUTURE TRENDS AND ISSUES

While the future of probation and parole is by no means certain, the following selected trends should provide some indication of future issues and areas of concern to the probation and parole profession.

VICTIM RIGHTS, COMPENSATION AND ASSISTANCE

According to prevailing public opinion, victims have been the forgotten persons by the criminal justice system for too long. At present, there is growing interest in victim compensation programs, and most states have implemented or expanded existing programs in recent years. The first state to formally institute a victim compensation program was California in 1965. Since then, benefits totalling many millions of dollars have been paid to hundreds of thousands of crime victims nationally.

In 1984, the U.S. Department of Justice established the Office for Victims of Crime to provide federal leadership, assistance and compensation to states for improving the treatment of crime victims. In addition, the Federal Victim and Witness Protection Act of 1982 guarantees broad protection for victims of federal crime. Also at the federal level, in 1984 the Victions of Crime Act established a program of federal financial assistance supported by fines from federal criminals.

The operations of victim compensation programs differ among the states, although certain key elements are common to most. Generally, victims must file claims for any damages not covered by insurance. A governing board typically evaluates the claims and directs payment according to legislatively established guidelines. Understandably, most states have set ceilings on individual claims. Many states allow limited compensation for both personal injury and property.

The role of probation and parole officers in dealing with victim assistance programs is central. An officer is likely to be asked to develop an assessment of the effects of the offender's crime upon the victim in the form of a Victim Impact Statement (VIS). Such a report is generally included in the presentence investigation report and may become crucial to the sentencing process. The following guidelines (used in the training of POs) should illustrate the nature of a VIS and serve as a model for completing the reports:

The victim impact statement should include the following information when pertinent: first-hand statements of complainants, witnesses, and victims in relation to understanding the defendant and the offense. When applicable, include an assessment of the nature and extent of the victim's loss (i.e., victim impact statement).

This statement should contain: information concerning any harm, including financial and social, psychological, and physical harm done to or loss suffered by any victim of the offense; and any other information that may aid the court in sentencing, including the restitution needs of the victim. All parties making such statements to a probation officer should be aware that the court must disclose all such information to the defendant and the attorney for the government.

In writing a VIS, special attention should be directed to ensuring clarity and conciseness, yet including all important details. The following hypothetical case illustrates a typical VIS (see Illustration 6-A).

ILLUSTRATION 6-A

VICTIM IMPACT STATEMENT

Mr. Ray Reed of Washington, DC was the victim of the instant offense in which the defendant hit him over the head and stole his wallet. The wallet had $50, his driver's license, credit cards, and car keys. The defendant also stole his car. The offense occurred at gunpoint outside Mr. Reed's apartment. Mr. Reed's 1989 Chrysler was discovered by local police four weeks later in a damaged condition in Charlotte, North Carolina.

Although Mr. Reed was covered by insurance against loss, he was not compensated for the damage to his car by his insurance company because his car was recovered. Damages to the car included a broken windshield, two flat tires, and a smashed right front fender. Further, he had to travel to Charlotte, North Carolina, at his own expense, in order to pick up his car. Mr. Reed was also hospitalized for a slight concussion, and as a result, lost two weeks' work. Mr. Reed certified by way of receipts that his total loss, because of the defendant's offense, was as follows:

Hospital bill (deductible costs):	$ 200.00
Plane ticket to North Carolina:	235.00
Gasoline return trip:	20.00
Loss of 2 weeks' work at $10.00 per hour:	800.00
Two tires at $80 each:	160.00
Windshield:	250.00
New right fender/paint job:	200.00
Cost of new driver's license:	20.00
Cash lost:	50.00
	$1,935.00

Mr. Reed also stated that he now suffers from anxiety attacks when he considers leaving his apartment at night. He would like to attend counseling for this problem but presently does not have any money for this expense. It would not be covered by health insurance. An estimate of the cost of such counseling is $90 per session. Mr. Reed thought he might need as many as 20 counseling sessions to clear up this anxiety problem.

RESTITUTION ALTERNATIVES

While the public seems to direct much of its attention and interest to the restitution of victims, citizens are also showing increased concern for additional or alternative forms of restitution. Restitution, according to recent research (Galaway, 1977), may be categorized as four separate types:

(1) MONETARY: Victim Restitution (the defendant pays the victim to compensate for his or her loss);

(2) MONETARY: Community Restitution (the defendant pays for a service to the community);

(3) SERVICE: Victim Restitution (the defendant performs services to help the victim);

(4) SERVICE: Community Restitution (defendant performs a useful service for the community).

For many of the same reasons which support victim compensation, community monetary restitution and compulsory services are being used more frequently as conditions of probation or parole. An additional rationale, however, includes reimbursing governmental or community resources to alleviate increasing economic burdens. As demonstrated in the following examples, there is a growing reliance upon new forms of restitution, particularly in juvenile settings.

Restitution alternatives are especially receiving acceptance in the juvenile setting. The implementation of a restitution program is typified by the provisions of a program established in the state of South Carolina. This program requires juvenile offenders to repay victims for losses, damages or injuries involving either persons or property. The benefits of this program are perceived to accrue to all involved: the community, the victim and the juvenile (South Carolina Department of Youth Services, 1980). Restitution may be in the form of reparations, monetary payments or community service labors. Reparation generally involves ordering the offender to make restitution through direct service to the victim. Monetary payment typically includes reimbursing the victim payment for the actual damages experienced. The amount of repayment is usually established by the court and may have ceiling. If current employment opportunities are not available, the responsibility may fall upon the probation and parole officer to promote vocational training or job placement in efforts to enhance restitution possibilities. Community service alternatives are usually restricted to non-violent offenders and involve working with volunteers. An added benefit of restitution involves development of more responsibility and socially desirable behavior patterns by the offender. For numerous and often compelling reasons, restitution will probably continue to be emphasized in the search for alternatives to traditional incarceration practices.

COMPUTERIZATION

The "information" age has arrived in America, according to social analyst John Naisbitt (1982). The transformation from an industrial society to an information society is now underway and computer technology appears to be the focus to this transition. While courts and the criminal justice system have resisted innovation or change, increasing reliance on computers is inevitable. Management information systems will become increasingly critical to probation and parole services. For instance, recent experience demonstrates the benefits of microcomputers in the supervision process. Computers can be utilized in a variety of ways, including the administration of questionnaires, psychological instruments and educational tests. They can also provide for the analysis of family data and the completion of required reports. These benefits can free officers from many of the traditionally mundane duties and increase their time for more important supervision and treatment responsibilities.

DECENTRALIZATION

A currently felt trend in many governmental programs and agencies is one of decentralization. The movement to decentralize government programs has grown out of an awareness of the limitations of past centralized programs, many of which came to be perceived as failures. Sometimes this attitude is communicated in terms of "distrust of big government," or a "state and local government emphasis" approach to Federalism. Within the criminal justice system, this rekindled concern for "community corrections" and decentralized services appears to have evolved for a very similar reason: the perceived ineffectiveness of some centralized programs, particularly large state institutions. A movement has now begun to place offenders back into community facilities and programs both for purposes of punishment and treatment.

Since PO responsibilities often center upon treatment, officers must continue to match community resources and opportunities with deserving and appropriate offenders. Past research has indicated that parolees are far more likely to be successfully reintegrated into the community if they are released from institutional environments to the care of a Community Treatment Center (CTC), followed by intensive supervision and monitoring. The potential for success in finding employment is also greater for those re-entering the community from a local treatment center than from a traditional isolated institution (Beck, 1981). If reformation of carefully screened offenders is to have any chance for success, a decentralized approach to treatment may be conducive to its attainment. Still, centralization of certain functions (e.g., data collection and analysis) will continue to be important, as will state compacts for tracking offenders.

DIVERSION

Related to decentralization trends concerning increased reliance upon community corrections and treatment is the growing acceptance of pretrial diversion programs for appropriate non-violent offenders. These programs are gaining popularity for a variety of reasons, the foremost of which is generally considered to be the financial savings over incarceration. Such programs should continue to be limited to offenders who are charged with non-violent types of crimes, or otherwise pose no danger to the community. Requirements for entry into pre-trial programs are exemplified by those recently established in a state setting (South Carolina):

(1) The offender is 17 years of age or older;

(2) There is substantial likelihood that justice will be served if the offender is placed in an intervention program;

(3) It is determined that the needs of the offender can be better met outside of the traditional criminal justice process;

(4) It is apparent that the offender poses no threat to the community;

(5) It appears that the offender is unlikely to be involved in further criminal activity;

(6) The offender is likely to respond quickly to rehabilitative treatment; and

(7) The offender has no significant history of prior delinquency or criminal activity.

With mounting concern for the structural and procedural inadequacies of the current criminal justice system in handling its workload, movement toward diversionary programs will probably continue out of necessity. It is one option to be considered in light of overloaded systems, but it must incorporate stringent screening requirements if it is to operate safely and effectively.

SPECIALIZATION

In a world of increasing complexity, specialization is a trend felt by nearly all professions: the legal community, the medical profession and certainly, the criminal justice profession. This specialization is particularly felt in the probation and parole professions. A recent indicator of this trend is a recognized emphasis on "workload" as opposed to "caseload" in supervision practices. The National Advisory Commission on Criminal Justice Standards and Goals (1973) advocated the assignment of offenders on the basis of their particular problems. For instance, offenders with specific problems (e.g., unemployment) should be assigned to an officer with expertise in that area of specialization (e.g., job placement). This desire to match the special needs of an offender to a resource person with the requisite skills should continue to evolve, especially as more time-saving and cost-effective methods of supervision and treatment are sought.

PREDICTION MODELS

Prediction models should continue to have a major impact on the criminal justice system although such models are often controversial in nature (e.g., predicting violence). For example, in recent years a PO using the salient factor score (SFS) and guidelines developed by the United States Parole Commission could inform a Federal judge what the average amount of time a defendant would serve if placed in a correctional institution with a specified sentence length. Sentencing guidelines now perform a similar function. These scientifically derived models also serve as mechanisms for guiding judicial discretion through reliance upon acceptable factors in considering appropriate and alternative sentences. Past studies indicate that judges place great importance on the probation and parole recommendations which utilize prediction models. With the public's concern regarding the problems of sentencing variation and perceived leniency in sentencing, it seems likely that new types of sentencing will be attempted among the states.

EXPERIMENTATION AND INNOVATION

Experimentation and innovation in the delivery of probation and parole services will inevitably increase as the service environment continues to change. New problems will surface and new ways for resolving them will have to be discovered. For instance, in recent years, both nutrition and drugs have been found in some instances to have influences on the behavior of persons with specific psychological and physiological characteristics or ailments. In addition, new counseling and psychiatric treatment programs are proving to be successful in assisting with certain behavior difficulties (e.g., group counseling for job stress related disorders). As both the physical and behavioral sciences continue to study human behavior and mechanisms of control and treatment, new treatment or behavior modification programs will be tested.

Among the experiments that have been attempted within the probation and parole setting are the *scared straight* program (introduction to the "hardened" prison environment), *shock probation* (temporary incarceration prior to probation) and *boot camp* incarceration (a form of shock incarceration involving a military-type "boot camp" program). Such programs share the philosophy of ensuring that an offender's first experience within the correctional environment will dissuade the individual from future criminal activity (Gatz, 1975). Preliminary results from several of these programs have been mixed but are potentially promising, with recognition that further research is needed.

An experiment that has been attempted for improving the delivery of probation and parole within given communities is that of *satellite offices*. A satellite office is one located within a community setting, rather than a courthouse. This permits a probationer or parolee to gain easier access to his or her supervising officer and improves his or her adherence to conditions of release.

Because experimentation and innovation have proven beneficial to probation and parole services, it seems certain that the need and desire for improvements will continue. Experimentation and innovation are necessary steps in resolving these demands, and exploring new punishment and treatment options.

ORGANIZATIONAL DEVELOPMENT AND MANAGEMENT

Probation and parole services, like the services of most public agencies, will experience new internal and external influences on their modes of operation and the future delivery of their services. An analysis of how these influences can have an impact on the management of probation services was the focus of an article by David Cochran (1982), a supervisor of probation services. Cochran's article applies contemporary ideas and principles of organizational development to probation systems and concludes that new approaches to management are needed.

Unlike the traditional surveillance and rehabilitation orientations of most POs, future officers will need to better understand and manage the mission and functions of their organizations. This function may involve restructuring the administration of programs whenever necessary to accomplish primary goals. It will also involve the redefinition of organizational tasks and goals. These changes will occur in an evolving environment, one which is subject to such phenomena as the cyclical baby boom, fluctuating economies, constrained resources, new political orientation, and new technologies. As a result of these trends, long-term forecasting and planning capabilities will be essential.

Once management learns to appreciate and understand the forces of change upon the probation system, it will become management's duty to create an organizational climate supportive of innovation and experimentation. This climate must simultaneously attempt to support principles of fairness and equity as a part of the organization's service delivery mission while ensuring community safety.

Probation and parole management will demand bold leadership and the ability to develop organizational plans. Management will have to deal effectively with the problems of human motivation, and to apply the concepts and principles developed by modern behavioral sciences. Not only will managers need to meet these immediate internal organizational challenges, but they will also need to pursue them while experiencing considerable external pressures (e.g., fiscal, demographic and correctional philosophy changes). Consequently, managers will need the emotional and intellectual skills necessary for the rational and effective delivery of services in an extremely volatile environment.

Donald Cochran (1982) very succinctly summarizes the talents and strengths required of future probation and parole administrators:

If probation is to survive and flourish, the administrators within the system are going to have to have strong technical, human relations and conceptual skills. Managers of probation systems during the 1980s are going to have to be persons of strong convictions, openmindedness, courage, and a strong sense of fair play.

PROBATION AND PAROLE OFFICER STRESS

Juvenile and adult probation and parole officers play significant roles in the monitoring, supervision and treatment of offenders. In meeting the challenges of the profession, the officers are often burdened with enormous case loads and are responsible for offenders of all types: violent offenders, drug addicts, alienated clients and the mentally ill. To understand the impact of these and other factors in causing occupational stress among probation and parole officers, it is important to review past research on the topic of stress and to examine whether the factors associated with stress are likely to continue.

The many problems confronting probation and parole officers were identified in 1967 when the President's Commission on Law Enforcement and Administration advised:

> Probation and parole officers have too much to do and too little time in which to do it. Over 76 percent of all misdemeanants and 67 percent of all felons on probation are in case loads of 100 or more, though experience and available research data indicate an average of 35 is about the highest likely to permit effective supervision and assistance. At best, they receive cursory treatment from overworked probation officers who must also spend typically half their time preparing presentence investigations for the court. In addition, their efforts often are held suspect by employers, police, school officials, and other community figures whose help is essential if the offender is to be fitted into legitimate activities. (President's Commission, 1967: 4-5).

Since the 1960s, research has begun to focus on the problem of stress and its impact on probation and parole practices. Following is an overview of such research during the 1970s and 1980s.

Fagan (1970) alluded to some of the causes of occupational stress in correctional counseling by concluding that most counselors are engaged by clients who are seeking assistance because they are dissatisfied with certain aspects of their lives. However, probation officers often deal with reluctant and distrustful clients who perceive the therapist as someone who has the ultimate authority to take away their freedom. Similarly, Studt (1972) argued that parole officers are expected to deal with an immense range of human problems far beyond individual capabilities and that the problem of competence contributes to the stressful nature of probation work. In attempting to clarify the multiple problems inherent in probation counseling, Arcaya (1973) described some of the causes of occupational stress in juvenile and adult probation officers as follows:

> Inherent in the job of a probation officer is this tension of perspectives. It localizes itself between the officer and the court (how closely to abide by its for-

mal rules of supervision), the officer and the client (how many breaks to give an offender), and between the officer and himself (what kind of officer to be). (Arcaya, 1973: 58).

Finally, Blumberg (1979), writing on the unique problems of probation work in a court-dominated bureaucracy, noted that negative outcomes should be expected:

> Frustrated as professionals, stripped of real decision-making power, lacking a genuine motif, and assigned relatively low status by the community, it is not surprising that probation workers often develop a high degree of cynicism. (Blumberg, 1979: 283).

Blumberg also observed that the role of the probation officer was relatively minor in the court bureaucracy where plea bargaining and other negotiations predominated over other concerns. He observed: "[Probation officers'] lack of genuine professional status in the court is a constant source of personal anxiety, role alienation, and general dissatisfaction." (Blumberg, 1979: 281).

A survey by Thomson and Fogel (1980) on perceived training needs of probation officers found that problems mentioned included large case loads and an emphasis on paperwork. Although stress was not specifically addressed, many of the complaints were similar to those raised by police officers as factors contributing to occupational stress. Ohlin (1956) alluded to the inherent stress in the field of probation for those individuals who frequently had to compromise their counseling or social work orientation in order to perform the role of a law enforcement officer.

Kahn (1978), while studying the prevention of job burnout, found that occupational stress was often caused by role conflict, the difficulty of the assigned tasks and the overload of assigned duties. He noted that the continued presence of job stress led to inappropriate attitudes toward clients and self, uncomfortable physical and emotional symptoms, and a deterioration of performance.

Chavaria and Faria (1981) noted the need for research in occupational stress in observing that the feelings and attitudes of those employed in the field of probation had been virtually ignored by the literature:

> Since individual and collective attitudes produce the grease and sand which ease or foul the workings of an agency attempting to accomplish its purpose, it is necessary to look at the feelings and resultant moods of those employed in a unique profession wherein confusion abounds, contradictions arise and personal rewards are dubious. (Chavaria & Faria, 1981: 55).

Whitehead (1981) pointed out that different conceptions of what the term "job stress" means and how it can be managed continue to exist for probation and parole officers. He further wrote that additional research is needed in order to explore the nature and scope of this problem and how this issue impacts on juvenile and adult probation officers.

Walker and Beaumont (1982), writing on occupational problems encountered by probation officers, pointed out that the job involves attempting to solve problems that often lack solutions. They note that probation officers, when confronted with the overwhelming social and economic limitations of their clients, often feel ineffective and powerless.

Bartollas (1985) found that some of the pressures that contribute to occupational stress among probation officers stem from the fact that officers have insufficient time for individualized treatment and are confronted with both quantitative and qualitative overload. He states:

> Probation and parole officers simply lack the time to provide individualized treatment of clients. First, case loads are typically too large. The average case load is usually 80 or more for federal probation and parole officers, 100 or more for state officers, and even larger for county probation officers. Such large case loads make it difficult enough for officers to know the names of their clients, much less to develop rapport and a working relationship with them. (Bartollas, 1985: 204).

Studies have shown that probation officers are often frustrated in their attempts at rehabilitating clients due to inadequate community resources and the frequent reluctance of potential employers to hire ex-offenders. (Taggart, 1972; Waller, 1974).

In researching this problem, Beck (1981) studied the employment status of parolees released from incarceration during 1978-1979, discovering a 25 percent unemployment rate among offenders during a 12-month period. During the same time, the national unemployment rate for all members of the labor force was six percent.

Tomaino (1975) identified a major source of stress among juvenile and adult probation officers as role conflict. Tomaino considered control and rehabilitation to be in conflict with one another. Role conflict occurs when a probation officer is confronted by conflicting job demands of being both a rehabilitation counselor and a controlling agent. Petronio (1982) investigated this problem in terms of the rehabilitative and controlling styles utilized by juvenile probation officers and found that probation officers did not always accept the roles which had been communicated to them by management or the courts. The study suggested that those officers who encountered role conflict due to what they perceived as conflicting job demands were likely to reflect higher levels of work stress.

Lawrence (1984) pointed to stress in probation work when he found that probation officers were expected to solve many of the problems facing corrections despite the fact that many probation offices were underfunded and lacked adequate staffing. He concluded:

> Probation is increasingly being looked to for helping in alleviating the serious problems of overcrowding in jails and prisons. A greater percentage of convicted offenders are being placed on probation -- the foremost agency of community corrections -- as an alternative to incarceration. This increase neces-

sarily results in a greater workload on probation officers: more presentence investigations, larger case loads, and more paperwork to complete. The increased pressure on probation often adversely affects the quality of the officers' reports and the supervision provided. (Lawrence, 1984: 14).

Supervising hostile and mentally ill clients is another factor which contributes to stress in probation work. More often than not, probation officers have little choice in determining what types of cases they will supervise. Yet, they are confronted on a daily basis with the realization that they must manage probationers and parolees with histories of violent and unpredictable behavior. In discussing this problem, Prins (1983) opined:

It is a sad truism that there are no statistical or actuarial measures available that offer the prediction of dangerousness with any degree of certainty, although useful beginnings have been made in this area by various workers. Despite the fact that much research has been carried out into the prediction of antisocial behavior generally, the research merely seems to suggest that although actuarial techniques can discriminate between high-risk groups and low-risk groups, there will always be a residual majority in the middle-risk groups whose re-offending rates are too near "fifty-fifty" to be of much use prognostically. (Prins, 1983: 46).

Thomas (1983) noted that the probation profession lacks a special body of technical knowledge and has neither a local or national constituency. His observation implies that the failure of probation to convey a positive image contributes to occupational stress and raises the question of effectiveness:

Probation lacks the forceful imagery which other occupations in criminal justice can claim. Police catch criminals, prosecutors try to get them locked up, judges put them in prison, guards and wardens keep them there, but, probation in the public view, offers crime and the criminal a second chance. (Thomas, 1983: 3).

Fogel (1981) suggests that the probation profession is often under stress because of its difficulty in agreeing upon those factors that reflect success and failure rates. Gendreau and Ross (1981), in a similar vein, state that probation officers are becoming demoralized as a result of an emerging public opinion that nothing works in terms of offender rehabilitation. They observe:

Correctional workers have been repeatedly told that their efforts at offender rehabilitation are unlikely to be profitable. The pundits have stated that correctional rehabilitation programs have been tried, tested, and found wanting. They have been advised that research has demonstrated that treatment of delinquent and adult offenders is an ineffective response to criminal behavior. (Gendreau and Ross, 1981: 45).

Cunningham (1980) alludes to the stressful nature of probation work when pointing out that professionals employed in the social fields often succumb to finger- pointing when their efforts at rehabilitating clients meet with failure:

> In frustration we are inclined to look for someone or something to blame for our failures to predict with accuracy how thousands of unique individuals in unique environments will respond to our helping effort. Sometimes we blame the clients and declare them "untreatable". We blame our theoretical forbear-ers: Freud, Skinner, or Mary Richmond or our methodologies. More often we blame one another for not having all the right answers, and our professional name-calling makes us vulnerable to attacks from others, especially in light of the escalating competition for dwindling funding [of] resources. (Cunningham, 1980: 64).

Tabor (1987) found that some of the variables closely associated with occupational stress among juvenile and adult probation officers included: types of offenders super-vised, percentage of clients treated as "impersonal objects," length of employment, per-centage of clients trusted, salary and marital status.

Bartollas (1985) notes that legislators have historically underfunded probation oper-ations when funding correctional programs and implies that this has impacted on the stress experienced by juvenile and adult probation officers. He writes:

> More commonly, probation, the most widely used judicial sentence, receives the smallest share of the correctional dollar. Consequently, too few probation officers are hired, resulting in large case loads and overworked officers. Inade-quate funding also means officers are both underpaid and inadequately trained. (Bartollas, 1985: 205).

It may be concluded that stress is a phenomenon that is found in many occupations. Its ultimate impact on individual workers may be reflected in feelings of helplessness, physical and psychological fatigue, and a sapping of the spirit. Much research has been conducted in recent years on job stress and this topic continues to receive close attention as stresses and demands placed on our criminal justice systems continue.

As shown, the problem of stress in our criminal justice system has received intense scrutiny by researchers in the last decade, even though the topic of occupational stress is not of recent origin. Most of the research has focused primarily on the problem of job stress among police officers and correctional personnel, despite the fact that probation officers play a significant role in our criminal justice system. As shown, probation and parole officers must engage in competing roles such as surveillance and treatment, and often operate with limited authority and with limited resources. Hence, it is important that research be continued on the problems of occupational stress among juvenile and adult probation officers in order to clarify the scope and nature of this problem, and to assist in the development of measures or programs that will contribute to its solution.

REFERENCES

Allen, E. (1982). *Critical Issues in Adult Probation*. Washington, DC: U.S. Government Printing Office.

Arcaya, J. (1973). The Multiple Realities Inherent in Probation Counseling. *Federal Probation*, 12, 58-63.

Bartollas, C. (1985). *Correctional Treatment -- Theory and Practice*. Englewood Cliffs, NJ: Prentice-Hall.

Beck, J. (1981). Employment, Community Treatment Center Placement, and Recidivism: A Study of Released Federal Offenders. *Federal Probation*, 45, 3-8.

Blumberg, A. (1979). *Criminal Justice: Issues and Ironies* (2nd ed.). New Viewpoints.

Chavaria, F. & Faria, D. (1981). Toward an Effective Integration of It with Us and Them. *Federal Probation*, 45, 55-57.

Cochran, D. (1982). The 1980s. In G. Stephens (Ed.), *The Future of Criminal Justice*. Cincinnati, OH: Anderson Publishing Co.

Cunningham, G. (1980). *Offender Rehabilitation: The Appeal of Success*. Federal Probation, 44, 64-69.

Eskridge, C.W. (1980). Issues in VIP Management: A National Synthesis. *Federal Probation*, September.

Fagan, J. (1970). *The Tasks of the Therapist*. Palo Alto, CA: Science and Behavior Books.

Fogel, D. (1981). Probation in Search of an Advocate. Paper presented at the meeting of the 13th Annual John Jay Criminal Justice Institute, New York.

Galaway, B. (1977). The Use of Restitution. *Crime and Delinquency*.

Gatz, N. (1975). First Shock Probation: Now Shock Parole. *American Journal of Corrections*, January-February, 37.

Gendreau, P. & Ross, R. (1981). Offender Rehabilitation: The Appeal of Success. *Federal Probation*, 45, 45-47.

Healion, J.V. (1982, April 2). United Press International. *For the Victims, Money Won't Erase the Memory, but it Helps*. The (Columbia, SC) State.

Hurd, J.L. & Miller, K.D. (1981). Community Service: What, Why, and How. *Federal Probation*.

Kahn, R.L. (1978). Job Burnout: Prevention and Remedies. *Public Welfare*, 36, 61-63.

Lawrence, R.l. (1984). Professional or Judicial Civil Servants? An Examination of the Probation Officers Role. *Federal Probation*, 4, 14-21.

Naisbitt, J. (1982). *Megatrends: Ten New Directions Transforming Our Lives*. New York: Warner Books, Inc.

National Advisory Commission on Criminal Justice Standards and Goals. (1973). *Report on Corrections*. Washington, DC: U.S. Government Printing Office.

Petronio, R.J. (1982). Role Socialization of Juvenile Court Probation Officers. *Criminal Justice and Behavior*, 9, 143-158.

President's Commission of Law Enforcement and Administration of Justice (1967). *Task Force Report: Corrections*. Washington, DC: U.S. Government Printing Office.

Prins, H.A. (1983). Counseling the Mentally Abnormal (Dangerous) Offender. *Federal Probation*, 47, 3-9.

South Carolina Department of Youth Services. (1980). *Juvenile Restitution: A Working Alternative*. Columbia, SC: Author.

South Carolina Office of Pretrial Intervention. (1980). *Pretrial Intervention: A Guide for South Carolina Officers*. Columbia, SC: Author.

Studt, E. (1972). *Surveillance and Service in Parole*. Washington, DC: U.S. Government Printing Office.

Tabor, R. (1987). *A Comparison Study of Occupational Stress Among Juvenile and Adult Probation Officers*. Unpublished doctoral dissertation. Blacksburg, VA: Virginia Polytechnic Institute.

Taggart, R. (1972). *The Prison of Unemployment*. Baltimore: Johns Hopkins University.

Thomas, R.L. (1983). Professionalism in Federal Probation: Illusion or Reality? *Federal Probation*, 47, 3-9.

Thomson, D. & Fogel, D. (1980). *Probation Work in Small Agencies: A National Study Training Provisions and Needs*. Chicago: University of Illinois, Center for Research in Criminal Justice.

Tomaino, L. (1975). The Five Faces of Probation. *Federal Probation*, 12, 42-45.

United States Department of Justice (1977). Federal Parole Guidelines. *Federal Register*, 42 (121), 31786.

Waldron, J., Sutton, C. & Buss, T. (1981). Professional's Use of a Microcomputer in a Court Setting. *Federal Probation*, December.

Walker, H. & Baumont, B. (1981). *Probation Work*. London, England: Billing & Sons, Limited.

Waller, J. (1974). *Men Released from Prison*. Toronto, Canada: University of Toronto.

Whitehead, J. (1981). Management of Job Stress in Probation and Parole. *Journal of Probation and Parole*, 13, 29-33.

Epilogue

RECENT REFORMS

Although probation and parole principles had their origins centuries ago, federal and state probation and parole practices are now experiencing dramatic changes. As illustrated in the preceding discussion, much of the change experienced in recent years has resulted from the increasing pressures and expanding workloads impacting a strained criminal justice system. In general, probation and parole caseloads have increased, as have prison populations. Increasing numbers of problems are being experienced, ranging from prison riots to stress-related "burnout" among professionals. Despite these growing problems, the criminal justice system must operate with a degree of efficiency, fairness and safety that is acceptable to the American public. This task is not easily accomplished. It has been, and continues to be, the impetus for further reform.

The reforms that are now being instituted, while continuing to be shaped by the aforementioned trends and issues, must be analyzed in the context of additional forces that serve to shape public policies. These forces, typically viewed as being "external" influences on probation and parole policies and practices, include: politics, technology, fiscal constraints and legal change. Obviously, these forces (or factors) are interrelated. For instance, political attitudes favoring increased emphasis on crime control (as opposed to "due process") have resulted in legal changes that promote the crime control goal. Similarly, fiscal constraints on federal, state and local government have forced those entities to seek alternatives and supplements to the increasingly expensive practices of institutionalization. The combination of these "external" influences and existing trends that favor policy changes have recently resulted in dramatic reforms in probation and parole practices.

The following discussion will outline selected major reforms at both the federal and state levels that may profoundly influence the direction and substance of probation and parole practices in America. Some of the reforms will prove temporary, others will be of lasting importance.

THE UNITED STATES SENTENCING COMMISSION

The U.S. Sentencing Commission was created by Congress as part of the far-reaching legislation known as the Federal Crime Control Act of 1984, which was signed into law October 12, 1984. The Sentencing Commission is an independent body in the Judicial branch of government composed of seven voting members, two non-voting members and staff. The Commissioners were appointed by the President and confirmed by the Senate. They were sworn into office on October 29, 1985 by Chief Justice of the United States Supreme Court, Warren Burger. At least three voting commission members are required to be federal judges. The judges are not required to resign their appointments to the bench while serving on the Commission.

As defined by statute, the purposes of the Commission are to establish sentencing policies and practices for the federal criminal justice system that:

(a) assure the meeting of the purposes of sentencing set forth in Title 18, United States Code (e.g., just punishment, deterrence, incapacitation and rehabilitation);

(b) provide certainty and fairness in meeting the purposes of sentencing, avoiding unwarranted sentencing disparities among defendants with similar criminal conduct while maintaining sufficient flexibility to permit individualized sentencing when warranted by mitigating or aggravating factors not taken into account in the establishment of general sentencing practices;

(c) reflect, to the extent practicable, advancements in knowledge of human behavior as it relates to the criminal justice process; and

(d) develop means of measuring the degree to which sentencing, penal and correctional practices are effective in meeting the purposes of sentencing as set forth in Title 18 of the United States Code.

The statute further requires that, after the Sentencing Commission submits its initial guidelines to Congress, it must, by Congressional mandate, report to the General Accounting Office, the Department of Justice, and Congress, detailing the operation of the sentencing guidelines system and identifying any problems which need correcting. This report is due four years after the guidelines are enacted. The Commission will periodically review and revise the guidelines. In addition to serving as a national clearinghouse for sentencing information, the Commission will:

(1) monitor the performance of probation officers with regard to sentencing recommendations;

(2) conduct seminars and workshops across the country for those involved in the sentencing process;

(3) study the feasibility of developing guidelines for juvenile cases; and

(4) make recommendations to Congress concerning modification or enactment of statutes relating to sentencing, penal and correctional matters that the Commission finds necessary to carry out an effective, humane and rational sentencing policy.

The Comprehensive Crime Control Act not only mandates sentencing guidelines, but it also abolishes parole for offenders sentenced under the guideline's determinate sentences. The Act was the result of an 11-year bipartisan effort to make major revisions in the criminal justice system. Under the determinate sentencing guidelines system, parole is abolished and the U.S. Parole Commission will disband after guidelines are successfully implemented. Prior to its dissolution, the Parole Commission will assign a parole release date for every inmate under its jurisdiction who was sentenced to prison prior to enactment of the guidelines.

Determinate sentencing, stripped to its essence, means that the sentence imposed in court by the judge is the actual sentence the offender will serve, minus a small consideration for good behavior. The sentencing guidelines reflect a move from an indeterminate sentencing system to a determinate (or "truth in sentencing") system. Under the old system, the uncertainty introduced into sentencing (through parole eligibility dates, good time, and other variables) significantly reduced the actual prison time served. Under sentencing guidelines, the only reduction in a judge's sentence will be a maximum number of days per year for good behavior.

As described, the Sentencing Commission will attempt to reform the federal sentencing system while promoting the goals of fairness (to the public and defendant) and uniformity in sentencing. This will be attempted by:

(1) providing a comprehensive and consistent statement of the purposes of the sentencing;

(2) mandating (or recommending) the imposition of sentences within specific guidelines, except in very unusual cases;

(3) allowing defense appeals for sentences above the guidelines and government appeals for sentences below; and

(4) abolishing parole for offenders sentenced under the guidelines' determinate sentences.

In September 1986, the Commission published a preliminary draft of sentencing guidelines. In January 1987, a significantly revised draft was issued. Public hearings on the revised draft followed. In the revised draft, the Commission adopted offense levels (from 1 to 43) corresponding to potential sentencing ranges. In general, the application of the sentencing guidelines involves: (a) computing the defendant's criminal history; (b) selecting the statute of conviction and applying specific offense characteristics from the appropriate offense section of the guidelines; and (c) making appropriate adjustments to the offense level.

In arriving at numbers for determining sentence length, the Commission reviewed hundreds of presentence investigation reports; examined the guideline ranges used by the U.S. Parole Commission; utilized data from the Federal Judicial Center, the Administrative Office of the U.S. Courts, and law enforcement agencies; and obtained testimony from judges, prosecutors, defense attorneys, and victim's advocates. The Commission considered all this information in making its decisions with respect to the relative severity of offenses and the appropriate levels of punishment. In determining the proper sentence, the system required that all conduct, circumstances, and injuries relevant to the offense of conviction and all relevant offenders characteristics be taken into account.

On the statutory deadlines for its recommendations to Congress, April 13, 1987, the Sentencing Commission arrived at still another set of proposed guidelines. By a 6-to-1 vote, the Commission approved a set of guidelines less far-reaching than the earlier versions. The proposals will leave greater discretion in sentencing to judges. Existing plea-bargaining practices will largely remain unchanged.

In submitting its recommendations to Congress for purposes of meeting the November 1, 1987 implementation deadline, the Commission reported:

> For now, the Commission has sought to solve both the practical and philosophical problems of developing a coherent sentencing system by taking an empirical approach that uses data estimating the existing sentencing system as a starting point...This empirical approach has helped the Commission resolve its practical problem by defining a list of relevant distinctions that, although of considerable length, is short enough to create a manageable set of guidelines...The Commission's empirical approach has also helped resolve its philosophical dilemma...The guidelines will not please those who wish the Commission to adopt a simple philosophical theory and then work deductively to establish a simple and perfect set of categorizations and distinctions. The guidelines may prove acceptable, however; to those who seek more modest, incremental improvements in the status quo, who believe the best is often the enemy of the good, and who recognize that these initial guidelines are but the first step in an evolutionary process. After spending considerable time and resources exploring alternative approaches, the Commission has developed these guidelines as a practical effort toward the achievement of a more honest, uniform, equitable, and therefore effective, sentencing system.

> Source: United States Sentencing Commission, Sentencing Guidelines and Policy Statements for the Federal Courts, April 13, 1987, 1.4.

On October 5, 1988, the United States Supreme Court heard arguments concerning the constitutionality of the U.S. Sentencing Commission and the federal guidelines in *Mistretta v. United States*, No. 87-7028. One of the central arguments involved whether the Commission and the guidelines violated the Constitutional requirement of separation of powers. On January 18, 1989, the U.S. Supreme Court held by an 8-1 vote in *Mistretta v. United States* that, although the United States Sentencing Commission is "an unusual hybrid in structure and authority," its guidelines withstand constitution challenge on the grounds that Congress delegated excessive legislative power to the Commission or that the placement and structure of the Commission violates the principle of separation of powers. As a result, the U.S. Sentencing Commission will continue to promulgate binding guidelines for use in sentencing federal defendants. (57 LW 4102)

NATIONAL DRUG CONTROL INITIATIVES

In the 1980s, drug control efforts developed as major initiatives for the federal government. The Comprehensive Crime Control Act of 1984 (Pub. L. 98-473), the Anti-Drug Abuse Act of 1986 (Pub. L. 99-570) and the Anti-Drug Abuse Act of 1988 (Pub. L. 100-690) are major initiatives that strengthened the nation's drug laws and established or enhanced federal drug control programs.

The 1984 Act included a major revision of federal criminal statutes and generally enhanced criminal penalties. It further provided for the establishment of the Office of Justice Programs (OJP) within the U.S. Department of Justice to coordinate and manage five program bureaus that work with state and local law enforcement and the criminal justice community. The OJP Bureaus and Offices are: The Bureau of Justice Assistance (BJA), the Bureau of Justice Statistics (BJS), the National Institute of Justice (NIJ), the Office of Juvenile Justice and Delinquency Prevention (OJJDP), and the Office for Victims of Crime (OVC). Among its many responsibilities, BJA funds demonstration projects and administers grants to state and local units of government for demand reduction programs and programs that improve the apprehension, prosecution, adjudication, incarceration and treatment of drug offenders. In addition to maintaining the national Drug Data Center and Clearinghouse, BJS collects, analyzes, publishes and disseminates statistical information on crime, offenders, victims and other criminal justice system topics. NIJ funds and conducts a national research program that emphasizes drug-related issues. OJJDP assists states and local units of government to improve their juvenile justice systems and to prevent delinquency, emphasizing programs for youth at high- risk for drug abuse. OVC provides federal assistance and compensation to states for improving the treatment of crime victims and supports various victim initiatives.

The 1986 Act enacted new drug crimes and penalties and provided increased federal funds and resources for drug abuse control. Federal funds for drug abuse control climbed from $1.2 billion in 1981 to almost $4 billion in 1987, reflecting the heightened national concern over the problems of drug abuse and drug trafficking. The Act also established a White House Conference for a Drug-Free America to serve the following purposes:

* To share information and experiences in order to vigorously and directly attack drug abuse at all levels, local, state, federal and international;

* To bring public attention to those approaches to drug abuse education and prevention which have been successful in curbing drug abuse and those methods of treatment which have enabled drug abusers to become drug free;

* To highlight the dimensions of the drug abuse crisis, to examine the progress made in dealing with such a crisis, and to assist in formulating a national strategy to thwart sale and solicitation of illicit drugs and to prevent and treat drug abuse; and

* To examine the essential role of parents and family members in preventing the basic causes of drug abuse and in successful treatment efforts. (Section 1933).

In 1987, President Ronald Reagan issued Executive Order No. 12595, which added as a purpose: "to focus public attention on the importance of fostering a widespread attitude of intolerance for illegal drugs and their use throughout all segments of society." The conference issued a Final Report in June 1988.

The Anti-Drug Abuse Act (ADAA) of 1988 represents the most significant legislative enactment to date for combating the nation's drug problem. This comprehensive Act represents a multifaceted approach; it establishes the Office of National Drug Control Policy (ONDCP), increases drug treatment and prevention programs, authorizes funding for expanded criminal justice system anti-drug activities, broadens federal interdiction efforts, supports drug abuse education and user accountability, and strengthens criminal laws and penalties.

The new office, ONDCP, is established in the Executive Office of the President and is headed by a Presidential appointee (commonly referred to as the "Drug Czar") with Cabinet-level responsibilities. Two deputy director positions (one for demand reduction and the other for supply reduction) were created, as was the position of associate director for state and local affairs. The ADAA of 1988 terminated the National Drug Enforcement Policy Board, the National Narcotics Border Interdiction System and the White House Drug Abuse Policy Office. The director of ONDCP is to prepare a national drug-control strategy and submit recommendations to the President regarding changes in the budgets, management and organizations of federal departments and agencies involved in drug activities and programs.

The ADAA of 1988 authorized more than $2 billion for anti-drug activities and programs. While approximately $500 million was appropriated by Congress in 1988 for Fiscal Year 1989, the authorization provides a mechanism for increased funding in a number of continuing and new program areas. In the treatment and prevention areas, increased funding levels were authorized for alcohol, drug abuse and mental health services formula grants. Similarly, the "Edward Byrne Memorial State and Local Law Enforcement Assistance Programs" were assigned to BJA to encourage the targeting of state and local resources to reduce drug crimes. Authorizations for increased funding were provided to operational agencies, such as the Drug Enforcement Administration (DEA), and a special asset forfeiture fund was established within the Treasury Department to fund future drug enforcement activities.

New federal crimes and penalties were defined by the ADAA of 1988, including a death penalty provision. Among the penalties are: up to 10 years imprisonment for illegally manufacturing a controlled substance; up to 20 years for possessing crack, a cocaine derivative; up to 15 years for operating a locomotive while under the influence; and life in prison without parole for third time felony drug convictions. The death penalty is provided for the killing of a person while one is engaged in a drug-related felony offense. Of special importance to probation and parole officers, the Act requires the revocation of probation, parole or supervised release of anyone found to possess a controlled substance. Furthermore, the Act provides for establishing pilot drug testing projects to detect the illegal use of drugs, and to report the results of the project to Congress for determining whether the drug testing of probationers should become a permanent program.

Obviously, the "war on drugs" will continue as the impacts of drug abuse in America become increasingly apparent. Evidence of the scope of this problem and why it continues to impact probation and parole systems is described in the following findings of Congress in the ADAA of 1988, which are cited in support of the goal for a drug-free America by 1995:

(1) approximately 37 million Americans used an illegal drug in the past year and more than 23 million Americans use illicit drugs at least monthly, including more than 6 million who use cocaine;

(2) half of all high school seniors have used illegal drugs at least once, and over 25 percent use drugs at least monthly;

(3) illicit drug use adds enormously to the national cost of health care and rehabilitation services;

(4) illegal drug use can result in a wide spectrum of extremely serious health problems, including disruption of normal heart rhythm, small lesions of the heart, high blood pressure, leaks of blood vessels in the brain, bleeding and destruction of brain cells, permanent memory loss, infertility, impotency, immune system impairment, kidney failure and pulmonary damage, and in the most serious instances, heart attack, stroke and sudden death;

(5) approximately 25 percent of all victims of AIDS acquired the disease through intravenous drug use;

(6)   over 30,000 people were admitted to emergency rooms in 1986 with drug-related health problems, including nearly 10,000 for cocaine alone;

(7)   there is a strong link between teenage suicide and use of illegal drugs;

(8)   10 to 15 percent of all highway fatalities involve drug use;

(9)   illegal drug use is prevalent in the workplace and endangers fellow workers, national security, public safety, company morale and production;

(10) it is estimated that 1 of every 10 American workers have their productivity impaired by substance abuse;

(11) it is estimated that drug users are 3 times as likely to be involved in on-the-job accidents, are absent from work twice as often and incur 3 times the average level of sickness costs as non-users;

(12) the total cost to the economy of drug use is estimated to be over $100,000,000,000 annually;

(13) the connection between drugs and crime is also well-proven;

(14) the use of illicit drugs affects moods and emotions, chemically alters the brain, and causes loss of control, paranoia, reduction of inhibitions and unprovoked anger;

(15) drug-related homicides are increasing dramatically across the nation;

(16) 8 of 10 men arrested for serious crimes in New York City test positive for cocaine use;

(17) illicit drug use is responsible for a substantially higher tax rate to pay for local law enforcement protection, interdiction, border control, and the cost of investigation, prosecution, confinement and treatment;

(18) substantial increases in funding and resources have been made available in recent years to combat the drug problem, with spending for interdiction, law enforcement, and prevention programs up by 100 to 400 percent and these programs are producing results:

(A)   seizures of cocaine are up from 1.7 tons in 1981 to 70 tons in 1987;

(B)   seizures of heroin are up from 460 pounds in 1981 to 1,400 pounds in 1987;

(C)   Drug Enforcement Administration drug convictions doubled between 1982 and 1986; and

(D)   the average sentence for federal cocaine convictions rose by 35 percent during this same period;

(19) despite the impressive rise in law enforcement efforts, the supply of illegal drugs has increased in recent years;

(20) the demand for drugs creates and sustains the illegal drug trade; and

(21) winning the drug war not only requires that we do more to limit supply, but that we focus our efforts to reduce demand.

(Pub. L. 100-690; 102 STAT. 4309; SEC. 5251(a))

On September 5, 1989, President Bush announced the release of his *National Drug Control Strategy* as the initial comprehensive blueprint for national anti-drug efforts. (The Executive Summary of the strategy is presented in the Appendix of this text.)

STATE REFORMS: INTERMEDIATE PUNISHMENTS

In 1982, President Reagan's Task Force on Violent Crime proclaimed "...the problem of available bed space in our state prisons is the single most significant criminal justice issue in the country today." Research findings reveal that approximately 600,000 men and women are now incarcerated in America's prisons. Stemming from this crisis of crowded prisons and the need to devise additional appropriate sanctions to supplement imprisonment, intermediate punishments and innovative alternative sentencing options are being sought and implemented for offenders who are suitable for such options and will not pose dangers to society.

Electronic Monitoring

One sentencing option and surveillance mechanism is electronic monitoring. An electronic monitoring system generally consists of three parts: a control computer located at the controlling agency; a receiver unit located in the offender's home; and a transmitter device worn by the offender. Various types and styles of transmitters may be worn, typically on the offender's ankle, wrist or neck. If the transmitter is removed or tampered with, an alarm is sent to the receiving unit.

This surveillance method is not used for violent offenders. It is best used with offenders who are evaluated and considered not to pose a serious risk to the public. These individuals are able to adapt to the normal responsibilities of work and family life. For them, the system becomes a curfew device rather than a method of physical control.

Electronic monitoring can be used effectively in supervising both probationers and parolees. The method also has been suggested for use with some pretrial releasees. It has the obvious benefits of permitting individuals to maintain their family units and to engage in productive employment. Offenders who break the conditions of this supervision remain subject to the same probation and parole revocation practices as others.

States recently experimenting with (or actively considering) electronic monitoring include: New Mexico, Florida, Idaho, Kentucky, Michigan, Oregon, Utah, Indiana, South Carolina and New Jersey. In South Carolina, legislation has recently been passed to abolish a prohibition to surveillance of probationers by electronic means, and to permit electronic monitoring under controlled circumstances.

House Arrest

A second innovative program is house arrest. At the time of sentencing, a judge may decide that house arrest is an appropriate option. Under house arrest, an individual is restricted to his or her home (or the immediate vicinity), except for travel with an approved official or when specifically approved by the court. Travel to and from work is generally permitted.

Probation officers remain responsible for the supervision of probationers under house arrest. This normally requires periodic and random checks by telephone to ensure that the individuals are indeed at their assigned locations. To date, the states of Florida, California and Illinois have pioneered effective house arrest programs. Careful screening and close monitoring have been critical to the success of these programs.

Intensive Probation Supervision (IPS) and Drug Testing/Recognition

A program of intensive probation supervision is a third innovative approach for monitoring and supervising offenders. Generally, the concept of intensive supervision involves a reduced caseload for a probation officer with a rigid surveillance plan for those individuals assigned to the officer. For example, an intensive supervision program in the state of Georgia requires strict compliance with the following rules:

(1) five face-to-face contacts by the individual with the probation officer each week, once in the probation office, once at the person's workplace, and three home visits (including one weekend visit);

(2) weekly verification of continued employment;

(3) nightly curfew (e.g., 8:00 p.m.), unless the work schedule of the individual conflicts with the time restriction;

(4) a coordinated record check with pertinent law enforcement officials each week; and

(5) drug testing.

Evaluation findings strongly suggest that intensive supervision has significantly reduced the flow of offenders to prison in those jurisdictions where such programs have been strongly supported. Preliminary estimates indicate that a state will save more than $7,000 for each offender who is placed under the program. A survey by the Rand Corporation revealed that at least 28 states have adopted formal intensive probation supervision programs.

As recognized by the National Drug Control Strategy announced by President Bush in September 1989:

> Drug tests should be a part of every stage of the criminal justice process--at the time of arrest and throughout the period of probation or incarceration, and parole--because they are the most effective way of keeping offenders off drugs both in and out of detention. (p. 26)

Similarly, probation officers are in need of tools for systematically examining offenders under their supervision for the presence of drug or alcohol impairments. thus, rigorous drug testing and drug recognition programs should be incorporated into intensive supervision activities.

Shock Incarceration ("Boot Camps")

Shock incarceration is a relatively new intermediate sanction which provides an option between traditional prison incarceration and release. Typically, it is designed for the young, non-violent, first offender, age 18-25, who has a short sentence. It differs from shock probation, which was designed to show offenders how terrible imprisonment could be through a brief exposure to prison life followed by a supervised release. Ohio first instituted a form of shock probation in the 1960s, followed by Texas, Kentucky, and Illinois.

More recently, states have experimented with shock incarceration (or prison "boot camps"). By 1989, eleven states had adopted forms of shock incarceration in their correctional systems. The specific components of these programs vary including activities such as work, community service, education and counseling. Some programs require intensive supervision upon release. However, one similarity among programs is a highly structured, military-type environment where offenders are required to participate in drills and physical training, all of which is directed by staff in a military, or boot camp, atmosphere. The sentence lengths are usually shorter than traditional detention. Among the benefits cited by proponents of these programs are the following:

* *Alternative sentencing options.* Boot camps should be considered as intermediate sanctions for offenders who pose risks too high for supervised release alone. This option reinforces "user accountability" and promotes effective drug testing programs for those on release.

* *Enhanced public safety through incapacitation.* Offenders in boot camps are, in fact, incapacitated for a period of time, preventing an immediate threat or opportunity for continued drug abuse.

* *Deterrence and punishment.* the rigors of boot camp discipline, the appearance of punishment, and the threat of more serious sanctions provide a potential deterrent and the perception of punishment for some offenders.

* *Rehabilitation and treatment.* The system of discipline and structured rewards demonstrates the relationships of wrongful behavior and undesired consequences. the curriculum typically includes structured physical drills, life skills improvement, self-esteem enhancement, educational and vocational training, confidence building, personal hygiene improvement, and substance abuse treatment.

* *Reduced costs and implementation advantages.* Boot camps may utilize surplus property and have shortened start-up time requirements. While costs are dependent upon design features, boot camps offer potential cost-savings over prisons and experience less community resistance because they pose significantly reduced threats to the communities.

SUMMARY

New and innovative programs continue to be studied and tested in the fields of probation and parole, and within the criminal justice system as a whole. As shown, major changes are being sought in the legal environment practices as we know them today. In fact, the federal parole system is to be abolished under new sentencing guidelines. Whether this will have lasting effects has yet to be seen. As with many policy issues of this type, opinions are susceptible to change over time, and policies may shift as a result of such forces as resource constraints, technological advancements, and other contingencies.

Finally, a variety of innovative programs are now being instituted across the nation. Electronic monitoring, house arrest, intensive supervision, shock incarceration, and various combinations or hybrids of each can be expected in the future.

Are further reforms and innovations to be expected in the next few years? The answer is undoubtedly "yes." Just as the past decade has been marked by radical changes in the nation's prison systems and probation and parole programs, the next decade will face additional complex problems and societal demands. For example, the rapidly spreading illness of Acquired Immune Deficiency Syndrome (AIDS) has already become a major issue and concern for criminal justice professionals. A substantial number of inmates have been stricken by the illness, and a significant number of offenders fall within the high-risk group for AIDS (e.g., drug users). It is certain that the criminal justice system will respond with new programs and measures to combat this serious problem and to alleviate public concerns. Similarly, drug abuse has emerged as an issue of growing concern and debate that will undoubtedly result in policy changes that will impact existing probation, parole and correctional practices.

As demonstrated by shifting public opinion (e.g., concerning the death penalty), federal, state and local governments can be expected to respond to continuing problems and new crises in various ways. In many situations, the response selected will not meet with everyone's approval, nor will it provide a perfect remedy. Additional future concerns may include such issues as privatization of various criminal justice programs, new methods of behavior modification and control, and improved scientific techniques for physical control.

Whether future probation and parole professionals will be able to successfully adapt to the many complex and demanding issues that confront them may depend upon how well informed they are regarding probation and parole practices that have been employed to date, and how prepared they will be to use this knowledge in designing and implementing programs for the future. A firm understanding of probation and parole practices should be a prerequisite to accomplishing this important goal. It is incumbent upon professionals in this field to build upon an expanding body of knowledge concerning probation and parole practices, and to apply this knowledge in their work. Dedication to this goal will provide the essential foundation for progress in this critical field and, hopefully, the cornerstone to continued professional success.

APPENDIX

National Drug Control Strategy

Executive Summary
September 1989

Most Americans believe that illegal drugs represent the gravest present threat to our national well-being. The evidence reinforces this concern:

Crime. Fear of drugs and attendant crime are at an all-time high. Rates of drug-related homicide continue to rise — sometimes alarmingly — in cities across the country.

Health. The number of drug-related emergency hospital admissions increased by 121 percent between 1985 and 1988, as many as 100,000 babies are born each year to mothers who use drugs, and intravenous drug use is now the single largest source of new AIDS virus infections.

The Economy. A U.S. Chamber of Commerce estimate puts annual gross illegal drug sales at $110 billion — more than our total gross agricultural income, and more than double the profits enjoyed by the Fortune 500 companies combined.

Overseas. In many foreign nations the drug trade and drug inspired violence and corruption are causing serious social, economic, and political disruption. Trafficking threatens stability and democratic institutions.

However, there is also some positive news. Recently, the National Institute of Drug Abuse (NIDA) released the results of its National Household Survey on Drug Abuse — the first such national study since 1985. The survey found the number of Americans using any illegal drug on a "current" basis (i.e., at least once in the 30-day period preceding the survey) has dropped 37 percent: from 23 million in 1985 to 14.5 million last year.

The survey tells us that, despite the persistent widespread availability of illegal drugs, millions of Americans who once used them regularly appear to have given them up altogether. This and other surveys indicate that many others — young people for the most part — have chosen not to try drugs in the first place.

But the NIDA survey also found that "frequent" use of cocaine in any form (i.e., the number of respondents who report ingesting the drug one or more times each week) is up a shocking 33 percent since 1985. One word probably explains much of the intensifying drug-related chaos that we see every day: **crack**.

There are really two drug wars to be fought. The first is against "casual" use of drugs, and that is being won. The other, much more difficult war is against addiction to cocaine, by far the most common dangerous drug of abuse. On this second front, increasingly located in our cities, the war is being lost — badly.

To win the drug war it is important first to come to terms with the drug problem in its essence: drug use. Drug use must be reduced, but it is necessary to be scrupulously honest about the difficulties that are faced and set reasonable goals and objectives. In addition, there must be created something that has never existed before: a comprehensive, fully integrated national drug control strategy — a strategy with particular emphasis on attacking the use of crack cocaine.

The Strategy lays out a coordinated plan of attack involving all basic anti-drug initiatives and agencies. Following the Introduction, seven chapters examine the "fronts" on which the drug war must be waged: Criminal Justice; Treatment; Education, Community Action, and the Workplace; International Initiatives; Interdiction; Research; and Intelligence. Each chapter is preceded by a summary of the recommendations contained therein.

Several Appendices are included within the Strategy. Quantified goals and measures of success, as required by Section 1005(b) of the Anti-Drug Abuse Act of 1988, are set forth in Appendix A. Also included are implementation plans (Appendix B), recommended State anti-drug legislation (Appendix C), high-intensity drug trafficking areas (Appendix D), a plan for improved automatic data processing and management among Federal drug agencies (Appendix E), and a list of individuals consulted in writing the Strategy (Appendix F).

Several fundamental themes underlie the Strategy, including:

- society has been too permissive of drug use;

- better coordination and management of government efforts is needed;

- State and local governments should adopt Federal principles of accountability as a model in developing their anti-drug strategies; and

- efforts should focus heavily on certain aspects of the problem, such as cocaine.

This is a truly national strategy. It calls upon all sectors of American society — private (individuals, educators, philanthropic organizations, businesses, the media, and religious, cultural, and community organizations) and public (Federal, State, and local governments) — to combat the drug problem.

What follows is a summary of the key priorities of the National Drug Control Strategy.

I. CRIMINAL JUSTICE

Overview

The absence of a significant risk of punishment for illegal drug activity is perhaps the single greatest hindrance to drug reduction efforts. More predictable, severe sanctions provided by the criminal justice system will be one of the most powerful forms of drug prevention. They will make it increasingly difficult to engage in any drug activity with impunity.

In order to be an effective deterrent, the criminal justice system must expand to accommodate more people at every point, from arrest through prosecution, release, and final supervision. This means more law enforcement officers, prosecutors, judges, courtrooms, and jails.

Priorities

- Increased Federal funding to States and localities for street-level drug law enforcement.

- Federal funding to States for planning, developing, and implementing alternative sentencing programs for nonviolent drug offenders, including house arrest and boot camps.

- Increased Federal funding for Federal law enforcement activities (including courts, prisons, prosecutors, and law enforcement officers); and additional resources targeted on Federal money laundering investigations.

- Vigorous prosecution of and increased fines for all misdemeanor State drug offenses.

- Expanded programs to eradicate the domestic marijuana crop.

- Adoption by the States of drug-testing programs throughout their criminal justice systems: for arrestees, prisoners, parolees, and those out on bail. Adoption of such programs will be a condition for receipt of Federal criminal justice funds.

- Funding through the Department of Housing and Urban Development to establish security systems for public housing projects, including tenant identification cards, guards, and security fences.

- Establishment of a Supply Reduction Working Group, chaired by the Office of National Drug Control Policy, to carry out the statutory requirement to "coordinate and oversee the implementation by National Drug Control Program agencies of the policies, objectives, and priorities" defined in the National Drug Control Strategy. This group will consider supply-related drug policy issues that are interdepartmental in nature. It will not deal with operational decisions or have line authority or responsibility.

- Revision of Federal drug agency personnel evaluation systems, where appropriate, to add a criterion for career advancement and reward that emphasizes cooperation among employees within and across various agencies.

- Strong encouragement for States to adopt policies revoking the drivers licenses of those convicted of a drug offense and recommendation of model drivers license revocation legislation to the States.

II. DRUG TREATMENT

Overview

Effective treatment is an important part of the overall strategy to reduce drug use. Millions of Americans need help to stop using drugs. Responsible and compassionate public policy requires that our nation's drug treatment capacity be increased.

Priorities

- Increased Federal funds for treatment in order to expand the number of treatment slots and the range of treatment methods available.

- Greater State, local, and individual treatment program accountability for effectiveness. Submission of State plans for treatment resource allocation and systemic improvements will be a condition for receipt of Federal treatment funds.

- Improved coordination among local treatment facilities so that treatment resources and availability match community needs, and so that drug users are referred to the most appropriate treatment provider.

- Improved coordination between treatment facilities and social, health, and employment agencies in order better to assist those drug-dependent persons who need services in addition to treatment. Under some circumstances, treatment facilities will be assisted in the development of their own programs in these areas.

- Increased funding of outreach programs and early treatment for expectant mothers who use drugs.

- State and private insurance company coverage of outpatient and other less intensive forms of treatment for drug use. A thorough review of Federal policy will be conducted to determine whether changes in Federal coverage are necessary.

- Exploration of ways to increase the use of civil commitment as a means to bring more drug dependent persons into the treatment system.

- Expanded and improved Federal information collection and research. Priority will be given to describing our current treatment capacities and needs; evaluating treatment effectiveness for specific populations; and developing methods of treatment for cocaine and crack dependency, cocaine in combination with other substances, and individuals with both psychiatric and drug problems.

III. EDUCATION, COMMUNITY ACTION, AND THE WORKPLACE

Overview

The principal goal of prevention is to see that Americans, especially children, never start taking drugs. Prevention begins at the local level: at homes, in schools, and in the community.

The Federal government should galvanize public opinion to make it clear that illegal use of drugs is wrong and harmful. This includes support for community drug prevention efforts. Activities should be targeted at youth; in addition, individuals, parents, and employers must become involved in drug prevention and education.

Priorities

- Implementation of firm drug prevention programs and policies in schools, colleges, and universities. Such programs and policies will be a condition of eligibility for receipt of Federal funds.

- Development of model alternative school programs for youths with drug problems. Federal assistance to local education agencies will promote such development.

- Federal support for community-wide drug prevention efforts.

- Federal support for development of anti-drug media outreach activities that deal with the dangers of using illegal drugs — particularly crack — and with drug-impaired pregnancies.

- Creation of a national program to mobilize volunteer efforts to prevent the illegal use of drugs.

- Implementation of Executive Order 12564 to ensure a drug-free Federal workforce.

- Drug-free workplace policies in the private sector and State and local government, including clear penalties for drug use, and drug testing where appropriate.

- Establishment of a Demand-Reduction Working Group, chaired by the Office of National Drug Control Policy, to carry out the statutory requirement to "coordinate and oversee the implementation by National Drug Control Program agencies of the policies, objectives, and priorities" defined in the National Drug Control Strategy. This group will consider demand-related drug policy issues that are interdepartmental in nature. It will not deal with operational decisions or have line authority or responsibility.

IV. INTERNATIONAL

Overview

The international drug trade poses a serious threat to the welfare, economy, and national security of the United States. The principal foreign drug threats are cocaine, heroin, and marijuana. Programs are needed to deter and incapacitate international production and the trafficking organizations responsible for bringing these drugs into the United States. Other nations must be motivated to engage their resources and efforts to defeat international narcotics trafficking.

Priorities

- Disruption and dismantlement of drug-trafficking organizations.

- Reduced cocaine supply. Law enforcement, military, and economic assistance will be provided to the three Andean cocaine-producing countries to isolate major coca-growing areas; to block delivery of chemicals used for cocaine processing; to destroy cocaine hydrochloride processing labs; and to dismantle the trafficking organizations. Efforts in transit areas will be improved and Joint Intelligence Collection Centers will be created in the Caribbean Basin.

- Reduced heroin supply through efforts to convince other countries to exert influence on opium growers and reduce heroin processing and distribution.

- Reduced marijuana supply through strengthened foreign law enforcement and eradication, and through efforts to discourage minor producing nations from becoming major producers.

- U.S. assistance and encouragement for European community and multi-lateral efforts aimed at source country and transit country production and distribution, and at European consumption. European community support against international and regional drug organizations will be enlisted.

- Other international objectives:

  - Elevation of drugs as a bilateral foreign policy issue.

  - U.S. ratification of the United Nations Convention Against Illicit Traffic in Narcotic Drugs and Psychotropic Substances, along with other pending Mutual Legal Assistance Treaties. Other nations will be urged to ratify the Convention.

  - Support for the U.S. foreign aid certification process in order to achieve more effective supply- and transit-country compliance with American drug control objectives.

  - Bilateral and multi-lateral efforts against international money-laundering activities.

V. INTERDICTION

Overview

Effective interdiction is critical in the effort to reduce the flow of drugs. Interdicting illegal drug shipments and intercepting other resources is an important method of attacking the drug trade at home and abroad. Interdiction should focus not only on drug seizures, but also on creating serious personal and financial risk for trafficking organizations and their top level personnel.

Priorities

- Development of a comprehensive information-based approach to Federal air, maritime, land, and Port-of-Entry interdiction.

  - Upgraded intelligence support to interdiction, through intensified interdiction-specific investigations and undercover operations.

- Enhanced computer support to interdiction through acceleration of machine readable documentation programs; installation of document machine readers at appropriate Ports of Entry; and development of the International Border Interdiction System (IBIS) and other computerized border information systems.

- Creation of interagency/interdisciplinary teams to analyze and target smuggling modes, methods, and routes.

• Concentration on high-value individuals and shipments.

- Review of existing methods for deterring air smugglers.

- Improved operations aimed at money couriers and shipments.

- Improved container inspection techniques and intelligence.

• Enhanced border systems, operations, and activities.

- Dramatically reduced document fraud, especially fraudulent use of U.S. birth certificates and other "breeder documents."

- Expanded use of drug detection dogs, anti-vehicle barriers, and container inspections.

- Provision of automatic exclusion authority and general arrest authority to Immigration and Naturalization Service officers.

- Improved detection and monitoring systems and secure operations procedures.

- Expanded secure communications systems.

VI. RESEARCH

Overview

The quality of information, research, and technological capabilities available to implement drug control policies and programs must be improved. A more up-to-date and flexible data base is needed to refine and target drug control efforts. Technology must be developed and adapted to aid in law enforcement. More medical research is also needed into the causes of and treatment for drug addiction.

Priorities

- Establishment of a Drug Control Research and Development Committee involving directors of research and evaluation, and chief technology advisers to all appropriate drug supply and demand reduction agencies. This committee will:

  - Recommend to the Office of National Drug Control Policy policies and priorities for drug-related research and development;

  - Review, monitor, and coordinate Federal research, data collection, and evaluation activities;

  - Eliminate duplication and gaps in current data collection, and generate accurate and useful information on which to base national drug control policies; and

  - Assist agencies in effectively acquiring and using new technologies to prevent and treat drug use and to detect and suppress the flow of illegal drugs and related commodities.

- Better and more frequent data collection and analysis, including flexible, quick-response data collection instruments.

- Increased basic and clinical research on drug use and addiction.

- Development of new technologies or innovative adaptation of existing technologies for use against illegal drugs.

- Development of a comprehensive information base about "what works" in controlling drug use through support for public and private evaluation of drug enforcement, drug prevention, and drug treatment programs.

- Archived and disseminated information, research, and evaluation results through an appropriate mechanism that combines prevention, treatment, and criminal justice data.

VII. INTELLIGENCE

Overview

The war against drugs cannot be fought without comprehensive collection, analysis, and dissemination of critical information on drug production and trafficking. To target the traffickers' most vulnerable points, more information about the enemy must be obtained.

Priorities

- Increased intelligence efforts to concentrate on the infrastructure of trafficking organizations and their allied enterprises, particularly money laundering.

- Improved drug automation and information systems to allow swifter, better, and more cost-effective drug law enforcement, prosecutions, and interdictions.

- Sharing of intelligence developed in the course of investigations and intelligence operations, and dissemination of finished, analyzed intelligence to appropriate Federal law enforcement and intelligence agencies.

- Establishment of an interagency working group chaired by the Office of National Drug Control Policy to develop plans for an intelligence center to unite U.S. drug-related analytical capabilities, and to improve intelligence capabilities. Results will be presented to the appropriate Cabinet Council.

GOALS AND OBJECTIVES (APPENDIX A)

The Strategy includes comprehensive, research-based, long-range goals for reducing drug use as well as short-term measurable objectives. There are nine goals for reducing drug use in two stages of measurement: during the next two years and over the next ten years. Specific percentage reductions are proposed in the nine categories, including overall drug use, use of specific drugs, use by certain age groups, and overall supply reductions.

FEDERAL IMPLEMENTATION and RESOURCE REQUIREMENTS (APPENDIX B)

Overview

The National Drug Control Strategy recommends the largest dollar increase in the history of the drug war — nearly $2.2 billion, 39 percent above the Fiscal 1989 level. Key funding priorities for Fiscal Year 1990 are to:

- Increase assistance to State and local law enforcement;

- Expand resources for treatment and prevention programs;

- Initiate a major anti-drug campaign in the cocaine source countries;

- Establish order in the nation's public housing projects;

- Build more Federal prisons, expand Federal and State courts and correctional systems, and add more prosecutors;

- Step up efforts against money laundering operations;

- Expand our knowledge base about drugs and how to fight them through more research, data collection, and information sharing; and

- Provide sufficient resources to operate and maintain our border interdiction system.

The following priorities will be added in 1991 and 1992:

- Expand inter-agency drug task force operations;

- Augment drug intelligence capabilities;

- Strengthen the presence of the Border Patrol along the Southwest border;

- Help the police get people who are driving while under the influence of drugs off the highways; and

- Reduce the amount of marijuana cultivated on American soil.

Major changes over FY 1989 are:

Drug Resources, Fiscal Year 1990

Budget Authority (Millions of Dollars)

	FY1989 Enacted	Feb 9 Budget FY1990*	Feb 9 Budget Plus Drug Portion of Crime Bill**	Drug Strategy Sep FY1990**	FY89-FY90 % Increase	FY89-FY90 $ Increase
Corrections	734	894	1,601	1,601	118%	867
International	250	306	306	449	80%	199
State and Local Grants	150	150	156	350	133%	200
Judiciary	209	242	250	250	20%	41
Other Law Enforcement	2,779	3,018	3,058	3,113	12%	334
Prevention/Education	943	1,041	1,041	1,176	25%	233
Treatment	604	735	735	925	53%	321
Total	5,669	6,386	7,147	7,864	39%	2,195

* These columns include resources for the U.S. Court and make other minor adjustments to the figures presented in the "Building a Better America" document issued in February, 1989.

** These columns include the "drug portion" ($0.8 billion) of the President's $1.2 billion crime initiative announced in May, 1989. The Administration supports enactment of the crime initiative (The Comprehensive Crime Control Act of 1989) in its entirety.

The drug portion of prison construction is based on the projected share of drug offenders in Federal prison at the time the construction is completed. This new methodology reflects more accurately the likely impact of drug offenses. For consistency with prior years, the historical prison construction numbers have been adjusted to reflect this new methodology.

EXAMPLES

A. EXAMPLE PRESENTENCE WORKSHEET (TRADITIONAL)

PROB 1 (Rev. 11/78) UNITED STATES DISTRICT COURT Federal Probation System **WORKSHEET FOR PRESENCE REPORT** *(See Publication 105 for Instructions)*	DISTRICT of Mass.	DOCKET NUMBER
	SENTENCING JUDGE Montgomery	SENTENCING DATE Oct. 14, 19__

1. IDENTIFYING DATA

COURT NAME (Last, first, middle) AKA Doe, John Mark		DATE OF FIRST INTERVIEW Oct. 19__
		REPORT DUE as assigned
TRUE NAME (Last, first, middle)		RECORDED BY probation officer
CURRENT ADDRESS (Directions, how long) Hampden County House of Corrections	LEGAL ADDRESS (if different) 71 Lee Avenue Holyoke, Mass.	CONSENT FORMS SIGNED ☒ YES ☐ NO
		RACE Caucasian
		CITIZENSHIP U.S.

PHONE NO. 782-4003	AGE 28	BIRTHDATE 11-15-__	BIRTHPLACE Boston, Mass.	SEX M	MARITAL STATUS Divorced
NO. OF DEPENDENTS one (child)	SOC. SEC. NO. 987-65-4321		FBI NO. 999 888 H		OTHER IDENTIFYING NO.

2. OFFENSE

OFFENSE AND DATE OCCURRED Viol.Title 21 USC 841(a) & 846 (attempt & conspiracy)	DATE, BY WHOM AND WHERE ARRESTED
PLEA OR VERDICT Guilty to Mass.Indict.on 9-29-__ Will plead guilty under Rule 20 to W.Dt.Tx. Indict.	CUSTODIAL STATUS IN CUSTODY IN LIEU OF &1,000,000 SURETY BOND SINCE 8-15-__

PENALTY
Imprisonment 5 to 40 yrs/$2,000,000 & Supervised Release of at least 4 yrs.

ASST. U.S. ATTORNEY David Crawford	DEFENSE COUNSEL (Name, address, & phone no.) Richard Pratt 981 Maine St., Springfield, Mass. ☐ APPOINTED ☒ RETAINED

3. DEFENDANT'S VERSION (Summary of offense and arrest by defendant/explanation and reasons for involvement)

Defendant going to Mexico on vacation along with co-defendant,
Nancy Rooney. A guy she met wanted some heroin. He shows up in El Paso
and demands to know where the stuff is. Nancy agreed to get him some and
asked the defendant to come along. Defendant states he was there so he
guesses he is guilty. Defendant arrested by Mexican police but released
him. States he doesn't deserve to go to jail.

4. OTHER DEFENDANT INFORMATION (Relative culpability of all the defendants)

Co-defendant, Nancy Rooney, in custody in Mexico awating trial.

EXAMPLE WORKSHEET (TRADITIONAL) *(continued)*

DATE Juvenile	AGE	OFFENSE	REASON FOR INVOLVEMENT	COURT OF CONVICTION	DISPOSITION	COUNSEL YES	NO	WAIVED
11-5-	14	Using motor veh. w/o authority	joy riding	Springfield, Juv Ct.	1 yr.probation	x		
10-28-	15	Break. & Entering	broke in private res.	Holyoke, Dt.Ct.	committed, youth service board	x		
12-23-	20	shoplifting	stealing jewl. in dept.store	Springf. PD	dismissed		x	
5-11-	20	rec. stolen property	stolen TV set from pawn shop	Holyoke Dt.Ct.	4 mos. county suspen. prob. 2 yrs.	x		
9-15-	21	burglary & enter. in nighttime	arrested in drugstore	Northhampton/ Dt.Ct.	6 mos.county jail	x		
6-27-	25	larceny over $100 & forgery	withdrew $500 w/forged withd.	Hampden /Co.Ct.	2 yrs. susp. to 18 mo. prob.	x		

5. PRIOR RECORD (List below all other arrests whether convicted or not including juvenile adjudication)

6. ADDITIONAL DATA (Detainers or charges pending; previous probation/parole and institutional history, dates, report of adjustment, present release status)

Rule 20, W. Dt. of Texas -- same offense

6. PERSONAL AND FAMILY DATA (If essential, include home and neighborhood, religion, previous addresses, interests and use of leisure time)

Parents -- natives of Austria. Violent arguments between parents. Wife thinks husband drinks excessively. Police called due to domestic quarrels (no arrests). Mrs. Doe had tuberculosis. Children placed in West Mass. home until Mrs. Doe recovered. Defendant remained home.

EXAMPLE WORKSHEET (TRADITIONAL) *(continued)*

6. PERSONAL AND FAMILY DATA (Cont.)

6. Cont. NAMES OF IMMEDIATE FAMILY (List spouse & children under Item 7. MARITAL)

NAME	RELATIONSHIP	AGE	PRESENT ADDRESS	OCCUPATIONAL	PRIOR RECORD YES	NO
Henry Doe	Father	59	Holyoke, MASS	machine opera.		x
Geraldine Ericksen Doe	Mother	58	" "	housewife		x
Stanley Doe	Brother	24	" "	unemployed		x
Audrey Doe	Sister	19	" "	college stud.		x

7. MARITAL (Present and previous marriages, including cohabitation)

NAME OF SPOUSE	AGE	PLACE AND DATE OF MARRIAGE	No. of Children	Outcome of Marriage
Barbara Raymond	20	Hartford, Conn., Nov.22,19	1	Divorced 12/28/
Pregnant at time of marriage				

NAMES OF CHILDREN (Including those from previous marriages)	AGE	ADDRESS, SCHOOL, CUSTODY, SUPPORT
John	8	custody of mother (attends public school)

ATTITUDE OF SPOUSE AND CHILDREN TOWARD DEFENDANT AND HOME ATMOSPHERE

defendant required to pay $50 weekly child support

EXAMPLE WORKSHEET (TRADITIONAL) *(continued)*

8. EDUCATION

HIGHEST GRADE COMPLETED	AGE LEFT SCHOOL	REASON FOR LEAVING
10th	17	older than classmates and wanted to get a job

OTHER TRAINING RECEIVED (Business or trade)

NAME OF SCHOOL (List schools attended; start with last school)	LOCATION	ATTENDED FROM/TO	DEGREE RECEIVED
Baram H.S.	Holyoke, Mass.	Fall __ Nov. __	

SUMMARY OF SCHOOL DATA (Test Results, Academic Rating, Class Standing, Behavior)

9. EMPLOYMENT (Cover last ten years including reasons for periods of unemployment or disability)

DATES	NAME AND ADDRESS OF EMPLOYER	NATURE OF WORK, WEEKLY WAGE, REASON FOR LEAVING
STARTED Nov. __	Unemployed, collected unemployment comp. $200 weekly	
ENDED present		
STARTED Aug. __	Smith Chemical Co.	forklift operator $5.00/hr.
ENDED Nov. __	Northhampton, MASS.	
STARTED March __	United Rug Co.	Warehouse $5.00/hr.
ENDED Dec. __	Easthampton	quit due to disagreement over hours
STARTED 19__	Roofing business	(3-4 mos. in any year)
ENDED 19__		
STARTED Apr. __	Central Bakery, Inc.	worked on delivery truck -- minimum wage
ENDED Oct. __	Holyoke, MASS.	lost job when co. went out of business
STARTED		
ENDED		
STARTED		
ENDED		

OCCUPATIONAL SKILLS, INTERESTS, AND AMBITIONS

EXAMPLE WORKSHEET (TRADITIONAL) *(continued)*

10. HEALTH

PHYSICAL DESCRIPTION (Height, weight, scars, illnesses being treated; health problems, and all past and present treatment and medication)

Good physical conditions

DRUG ABUSE, ALCOHOL, NARCOTICS (Age use began, frequency/cost, type of drug, past and present treatment)

Denial use of narcotics
Urinalysis negative

MENTAL AND EMOTIONAL (Self evaluation, personality traits, disorders, treatment)

I.Q. 102   113

Youth Services Board (19__)

Court Ordered Examination

11. MILITARY SERVICE

SERVICE NUMBER	BRANCH OF SERVICE	DATE OF ENTRY	DATE DISCHARGED	TYPE OF DISCHARGE
HIGHEST RANK HELD	RANK AT SEPARATION	DECORATIONS AND AWARDS		VA CLAIM NUMBER

SUMMARY OF MILITARY DATA

EXAMPLE WORKSHEET (TRADITIONAL) *(continued)*

12. FINANCIAL CONDITION

LIST FINANCIAL ASSETS (Real estate, insurance, real and personal property, stocks, bonds, checking and saving accounts, income from pensions and compensation, rentals, and family income, net worth, ability to pay fine or restitution)	LIST FINANCIAL LIABILITIES (INCLUDING BALANCE DUE AND MONTHLY PAYMENTS FOR home mortgage, rent, utilities, medical, personal property, home repairs, charge accounts, loans, taxes, fines, restitution, pending civil suits)

<u>Confiscated</u>
 	
'__ Cadillac $20,640
Speedboat w/ motor $8,000
 	
Defendant's savings acc't.
  $20,000
	GMAC (loan) for Cadillac $8,200
	              (balance)
	
	(Defendant plans to make no
	 further payments unless car is
	 returned)

13. EVALUATION (the probation officer's professional assessment of the defendant)

14. SENTENCING DATA (Use appropriate forms and charts)

15. ALTERNATIVE PLANS (Provide a statement of realistic sentencing alternatives available to the court and treatment plan)

B. PRESENTENCE REPORT (TRADITIONAL)

PRESENTENCE REPORT

NAME (Last, First, Middle)		DATE
Doe, John Mark		October 14, 19--

ADDRESS	LEGAL ADDRESS	DOCKET NO.
Hampden County House of Correction	71 Lee Avenue Holyoke, Mass.	RACE Caucasian
		CITIZENSHIP U.S.

AGE	DATE OF BIRTH	PLACE OF BIRTH	SEX	EDUCATION
	11-15-__	Boston, Mass.	Male	10th grade

MARITAL STATUS	DEPENDENTS
Divorced	One, in custody of former wife

SOCIAL SECURITY NO.	FBI NO.	OTHER IDENT. NO.
987-65-43231	999 888 H	

OFFENSE
D/Mass. -- Consp. & Dist. heroin, 21 USC 841(a) (1) & 846

PENALTY
5 to 40 years and/or $2,000,000 and supervised release of at least 4 yrs. on each count

CUSTODIAL STATUS
In custody in lieu of $100,000 surety bond since 8-15-__

PLEA
Guilty to Mass. Ind. 9-29-__; will plead guilty under Rule 20 to W. Dt. of Tx. indict

VERDICT

DETAINERS OR CHARGES PENDING
Rule 20, W. Dt. of texas, Violation of 21 USC 841(a) (1), same penalty

OTHER DEFENDANTS
Nancy Rooney, in local custody in Mexico

ASSISTANT U.S. ATTORNEY David Crawford, Esq.	DEFENSE COUNSEL: Phillip Pratt, Esq. 981 Main Street Springfield, Mass.(413)555-4321(Retained

DISPOSITION

SENTENCING JUDGE	DATE

PRESENTENCE REPORT (TRADITIONAL) *(continued)*

PRESENTENCE REPORT

OFFENSE

Official Version.   John Doe is the subject of two separate indictments, one in the District of Massachusetts and one in the Western District of Texas. On August 20, 19__, the Grand Jury in Massachusetts returned an indictment against Doe and Nancy Rooney charging that they conspired between May 28, 19__, and July 30, 19__, to distribute a quantity of heroin and that they distributed that heroin on June 23, 19__.

On August 26, 19__, a grand jury in El Paso, Texas, returned an indictment against Doe and Rooney charging that they imported 101.7 grams of heroin into the United States on or about July 30, 19__, and that they distributed that heroin on the same date at El Paso, Texas. Doe appeared on September 29, 19__, and pled guilty to the Massachusetts indictment. He has indicated his intention to plead guilty to the Texas indictment under Rule 20.

This investigation began in May 19__ when the Drug Enforcement Agency received information that Doe was looking for a buyer for a large quantity of heroin. On May 28, 19__, an undercover agent was introduced to Doe at a bar in Springfield and Doe acknowledged that he was looking for a buyer for a kilo of heroin. He was initially reluctant to deal with a stranger but, after four meetings, he offered to make the agent a partner if the agent agreed to purchase the heroin as soon as it came across the border into Texas. The agent accepted the offer but insisted on first receiving a sample of the heroin.

On June 23, 19__, the agent and Doe met in Springfield and drove to a shopping mall where they met Doe's girlfriend, Nancy Rooney. After receiving instructions from Doe, Rooney went to her car and returned with a sample of 2.70 grams of heroin which she gave to the agent. The latter paid Doe $300. The substance was tested and found to contain 31.7 percent heroin.

On July 21, 19__, the agent informed Doe that the sample was of acceptable quality. On July 24, Doe instructed the agent to meet him in El Paso, Texas, on July 29. The agent flew to El Paso where he met with Doe and Nancy Rooney at the Yellow rose Hotel. At 8:15 a.m., on July 30, Doe and Rooney crossed the border into Juarez. They returned two hours later and Doe told the agent that he was able to obtain only a quarter kilogram of heroin. The agent expressed disappointment but Doe said that the heroin was of very

PRESENTENCE REPORT (TRADITIONAL) *(continued)*

high quality and could be cut many times. Doe then sold the agent the first installment of 101.7 grams for $4,000. Tests determined that this substance contained 44.6 percent heroin. Doe explained that he and Rooney would return to Mexico that afternoon to obtain the balance.

Doe and Rooney crossed into Juarez and were arrested by Mexican police later in the day. Nancy Rooney had 147.3 grams of heroin in her possession. No heroin was found on Doe who was released after two days in custody. Rooney was held for trial. Doe returned to Massachusetts where he was arrested on August 14, 19__.

Defendant's Version. "I was going to Mexico on a vacation and Nancy decided to come with me. This guy she met in Springfield was pestering her to get him some heroin. I had seen him a couple of times in June. All of a sudden he shows up in El Paso and demands to know where the stuff is. She finally agreed to get him some and she asked me to come in case anything happened. I was there so I guess I'm guilty. All of a sudden I was arrested by the Mexican cops but they let me go because they didn't have anything on me. Then, all of a sudden I'm arrested up here. My lawyer says entrapment is hard to prove so I guess I'm guilty. But I didn't say all those things the narc claims. I don't deserve to go to jail.

PRIOR RECORD

Juvenile Adjudications

| 11-05-__ | Using motor vehicle | Springfield, Mass. | 1 year |
| Age 14 | without authority | Juvenile Court | probation |

Mr. Doe was represented by counsel. He and two other juveniles stole a car and went on a "joy ride." Mr. Doe made a good adjustment on probation during the initial months, but became increasingly uncooperative thereafter.

10-28-__	Breaking & Entering	Holyoke	Committed, Youth
Age 15		District	Service Board
		Court	

Mr. Doe was represented by counsel. He and one other juvenile broke into a home in Holyoke. The Youth Service Board sent him to the Industrial School at Shirley, Massachusetts, where he remained until June 19__ when he was paroled. He was discharged one year later. His institutional performance was routine. He participated in a

PRESENTENCE REPORT (TRADITIONAL) *(continued)*

woodworking course and was placed on report on one occasion for fighting in the dining hall.

<u>Adult Record</u>

| 12-23-__
Age 20 | Shoplifting | Springfield | Dismissed, lack
of prosecution |

Doe was arrested after he allegedly attempted to steal several jewelry items from a department store. The store manager declined to press charges.

| 9-13-__
Age 21 | Burglary & Entering
in the nighttime | Northhampton
District Ct. | 6 mos. County
Jail |

Mr. Doe was represented by counsel. He was apprehended at 2:15 a.m., inside a drug store. He had activated a silent alarm when he entered the building. Jail officials recall that Mr. Doe attempted to be reclusive while incarcerated. He voluntarily spent several months in segregation because of his fear of attack by other inmates.

| 6-27-__
Age 25 | Larceny over
$100 and
Forgery | Hampden Cty.
Superior Ct. | 2 yrs. suspended
to 18 mos. prob.
w/ restitution |

Mr. Doe was represented by counsel. He withdrew $500 from a bank account using a stolen passbook and forged withdrawal slips. He was identified through bank photographs. Mr. Doe paid $310 in restitution and the balance was remitted. He performed well under probation supervision.

PERSONAL AND FAMILY DATA

<u>Defendant</u>. Joe Doe was born on October 15, 19___, in Boston, Massachusetts. His parents, natives of Austria, came to the United States as displaced persons after World War II. The family has lived for the last fifteen years at their present residence in Holyoke. The defendant's early years were turbulent because of many violent arguments between his parents. These were caused by Mrs. Doe's belief that her husband was an excessive drinker. She summoned police assistance on several occasions although no arrests were made. Later, Mrs. Doe contracted tuberculosis. She was hospitalized for almost one year and the father was unable to keep the family together. The defendant and his siblings were placed in the Western Massachusetts Home for Children but the family was

PRESENTENCE REPORT (TRADITIONAL) *(continued)*

reunited when Mrs. Doe recovered. The defendant remained with his family until he married at the age of twenty. He returned to the family home after his divorce three years later.

Mr. and Mrs. Doe picture their son as a well-intentioned individual whose difficulties with the law were caused by his unwise selection of associates. They are bitter toward codefendant Nancy Rooney whom they believe was responsible for this offense. They view his previous juvenile and adult transgressions as minor matters which were treated with undue harshness by police and the courts. His parents describe the defendant as an intelligent and ambitious individual who values financial success above all else. They are proud of the fact that, in recent years, the defendant has acquired such material possessions as an expensive automobile and a boat. They also note that he has been especially generous with his younger brother and sister.

<u>Parents and Siblings</u>. The father, Henry Doe, resides with his family and for the last seventeen years has been employed as a machine operator earning a moderate salary. The home atmosphere improved considerably when Mr. Doe stopped drinking approximately five years ago. The mother, Geraldine Ericksen Doe, resides with her husband and is a housewife. Her health is poor due to respiratory ailments.

There are two siblings. Stanley Doe, age 14, resides with his parents and is unemployed. Stanley believes that his brother is the victim of harassment by law enforcement authorities. Audrey Doe, age 19, resides with her parents and is a community college student.

<u>Marital</u>. John Doe married Barbara Raymond in a civil ceremony in Hartford, Connecticut on November 22, 19__. Both parties were 20 years old at the time and she was pregnant. The couple had one child, John Jr., who was born on April 29, 19__. Mrs. Doe reports the marriage was troubled from the start by financial problems since the defendant was unemployed. He turned to illegal means of supporting the family and his subsequent arrests caused even more strain on the couple's relationship. There were several brief separations during 19__ and 19___, and in September of 19__. When he was released, Mrs. Doe found him a "different man" and it was impossible to reconstitute their relationship. The Hampden County Probation Court granted a divorce on December 28, 19__, on grounds of incompatibility and awarded her custody of the child. The defendant was required to pay $20 a week child support. Mrs. Doe is employed as a telephone operator. She reports that her ex-husband's support payments have been sporadic. He often goes for

PRESENTENCE REPORT (TRADITIONAL) *(continued)*

months without visiting the child or making any payments but he will then arrive with lavish gifts for his son and lump sum support payments. Mrs. Doe says that her relationship with the defendant is now amicable but they see each other infrequently.

Mr. Doe asserts that he has no plans to marry again. He stated that Nancy Rooney was merely a friend.

Education. Mr. Doe was educated in local public schools. He left junior high school in October 19__ when he was committed to the Youth Service Board. He returned to Baran High School in Holyoke in the fall of 19___ and dropped out of the eleventh grade in November 19__.

School officials describe Mr. Doe as an intelligent individual who never worked up to his capabilities. His grades were generally Cs and Ds. Mr. Doe left school because he was older than most of his classmates, and wanted to get a job.

Employment. Between November 19__ and the time of his arrest Mr. Doe was unemployed and collected unemployment compensation of $200 a week. From August 19__ to November 19___, he was a forklift operator at the Smith Chemical Company in Northhampton. He earned $5.00 an hour but he was subject to frequent layoffs. Company officials described him as an uncooperative employee with a high degree of tardiness. He would not be considered for reemployment.

Between March 19___ and December 19___, Mr. Doe worked in the warehouse of the United Rug Company in Easthampton, Massachusetts. He earned $6.00 an hour and he quit after a disagreement over hours. Between 19__ and 19__, Mr. Doe was sporadically employed in the roofing business. This work paid well but he seldom was able to get more than 3 or 4 months work in any year.

After he left high school, Mr. Doe worked on a delivery truck for Central Bakery, Inc., of Holyoke. He held this job between April 19__ and October 19__ and earned the minimum wage. He lost this job when the company went out of business.

Mr. Doe said that he would like someday to open his own business. He had no clear ideas about the nature of this business but stressed that he saw himself in a managerial capacity and would hire others to do the menial labor.

PRESENTENCE REPORT (TRADITIONAL) *(continued)*

HEALTH

Physical. Mr. Doe is in good physical condition. He denies having used drugs of any kind and he specifically disclaims the use of heroin. Discussion with family members as well as with law enforcement sources revealed no information that would contradict Mr. Doe's assertions in this respect. A physical examination and urinalysis test performed at the jail were negative for heroin use.

Mental and Emotional. On two occasions, Mr. Doe was tested in public schools and received I.Q. scores of 102 and 113.

Mr. Doe has been examined by mental health professionals on two occasions. The first occurred shortly after Mr. Doe was committed to the Youth Service Board in 19__. A psychologist diagnosed him as "a person whose anxiety is stimulated by a frustrated need for affection. He has developed no healthy conscience. His response to social demands is not based on a close commitment to moral principles."

Mr. Doe was examined once again as a result of this court's pretrial order. Dr. Robert Land administered a battery of psychological tests, the results of which suggested "that he seems to be unusually fearful of being overpowered and destroyed. It is obvious that he has been unable to resolve childhood problems and continues to feel quite rejected. He tends to view threatening environmental forces as coming outside his control."

FINANCIAL CONDITION

Assets. Mr. Doe lists two main assets: one is a 19__ Cadillac purchased in January of that year for $20,640. This automobile was confiscated by the Drug Enforcement Administration. The other asset is a 19-foot fiberglass speedboat with a 115 horsepower Mercury outboard engine worth approximately $8,000.

Mr. Doe's parents displayed to the probation officer a savings account passbook with a present balance of $20,000. The account was listed to Mr. Doe and his mother, but the parents made it clear that the defendant had made the deposits. When questioned about this, Mr. Doe asserted that the account in fact belonged to his mother and that his name was on it only as a matter of convenience. His mother subsequently contacted the probation officer and retracted her earlier statement. She said that she made a mistake and that the money in the account belonged to her.

PRESENTENCE REPORT (TRADITIONAL) *(continued)*

<u>Liabilities</u>.   The only debt Mr. Doe lists is a loan from GMAC to finance the purchase of his Cadillac. The loan balance is presently $8,200 and Mr. Doe plans to make no further payments until such time as his car is returned to him by the Government.

EVALUATION

Although he attempts to shift responsibility to his codefendant, Mr. Doe was the principal figure in the importation and sale of over 100 grams of high quality heroin. Were it not for the intervention of the Mexican authorities, he would have completed the sale of a quarter kilogram to an undercover agent. Mr. Doe is not a user of the drug. He apparently values financial success to the point that he made a calculated decision that heroin trafficking was profitable. His lack of concern about the serious and moral aspects of his decision confirms the observation of mental health professionals that his personality lacks the constraints under which most people operate. For Mr. Doe, participation in this offense, as well as in earlier offenses, was a logical means of satisfying his economic motives.

The members of Mr. Doe's family are intensely loyal to him and they have an unrealistic view of his participation in criminal activities. They do not question the sources of his assets, which are surprisingly large for a person with his employment history. The family cannot be counted upon to exert the pressure that might convince Mr. Doe to conform to law abiding behavior. Mr. Doe himself is unrealistic in his personal goals. Without much education or skill, he expects a high degree of financial compensation, but he has not thus far shown a willingness to work toward that goal. It is unlikely that Mr. Doe will attempt conventional paths to economic success until he is convinced that illegal means are too hazardous.

C. EXAMPLE SENTENCING RECOMMENDATION (TRADITIONAL)

The probation office recommends a five-year commitment for each count, consecutive, to be followed by five years and supervised release. This recommendation considers the quantity and quality of the heroin involved, and the defendant's prior record. The court may also consider recommending commitment to a minimum security institution.

Respectfully submitted,

Matilda Gormally
U.S. Probation Officer

Approved: _____
J. Grant Hogan
Chief, U.S. Probation Officer

D. EXAMPLE SENTENCING GUIDELINES PRESENTENCE REPORT

IN UNITED STATES DISTRICT COURT

FOR THE DISTRICT OF COLUMBIA

UNITED STATES OF AMERICA	)	
	)	
	)	Docket No. 88-0001-01
v.	)	
	)	
JOHN SMITH	)	

_____

PRESENTENCE REPORT

Prepared for:

The Honorable John J. Walker
United States District Judge

Prepared by:

Thomas W. Winchester
United States Probation Officer
(202) 535-3100

Sentencing Date:

July 2, 1988 at 9:00 a.m.

Offense:

21 USC 841(a), Unlawful Possession With Intent to Distribute a Controlled Substance (Heroin), a Class B Felony

Release Status:

In custody since February 26, 1988

Identifying Data:

Date of Birth:
Social Security Number:
Address:

December 23, 1958
007-22-0077
222 Oakmont Avenue, N.W.
Washington, D.C. 20007

Detainers:

Parole violation warrant, Virginia Division of Parole, 158 West Street, Arlington, VA 10732

Codefendants:

None

Assistant U.S. Attorney
Richard Smith
300 U.S. Courthouse
Washington, D.C. 20544
(202) 633-2079

Defense Counsel
James C. Fallon
1914 4th Street, N.W.
Washington, D.C. 20665
(202) 738-4015

Date report prepared: June 1, 1988
Revised: June 14, 1988

EXAMPLE SENTENCING GUIDELINES PRESENTENCE REPORT *(continued)*

PART A.   THE OFFENSE

Charge(s) and Conviction(s)

1.   Mr. John Smith, the defendant, was named in a one-count Indictment on April 14, 1988, in U.S. District Court, Washington, D.C., charging Unlawful Possession With Intent to Distribute a Controlled Substance (Heroin).   On May 25, 1988, Smith pled guilty to the one-count Indictment pursuant to a plea agreement.

2.   Since the offense occurred after November 1, 1987, the Sentencing Reform Act of 1984 is applicable.

Related Cases

3.   None.

The Offense Conduct

4.   On February 26, 1988, members of the Drug Enforcement Administration Task Force and Amtrak officers entered Amtrak Train Two which had arrived from Miami, Florida.   While walking through the car, "Sniff 3", a narcotic dog jumped on a seat where an individual, later identified as John Smith was sitting.   The narcotic dog leaped in the direction of a black suitcase which was placed on the shelf above the defendant.   Upon being asked for his ticket, Mr. Smith produced a one-way ticket from Miami, Florida, to Washington, D.C.   The defendant subsequently acknowledged ownership of the suitcase and gave law-enforcement authorities permission to examine the contents.

Upon opening the suitcase, the officers discovered that it contained 37 wax paper packets of heroin.   Mr. Smith was placed under arrest and advised of his rights.

5.   A chemical analysis confirmed that the 37 packets contained heroin, weighing 18 946 milligrams with a purity at 55 percent.

6.   The street value of the seized heroin was estimated to be $10,480.   According to Sergeant Joseph Charles, Narcotics Unit, D.C. Police Department, the 55 percent purity level indicates that the heroin had a greater purity value than heroin usually sold in the Washington, D.C. area.

7.   Sergeant Charles related that Smith traveled from Miami, Florida, to Washington, D.C., on the day of the offense in order to sell illicit narcotics.   Sergeant Charles further related that Smith was perceived to be a courier of heroin.   He was unable to ascertain whether the subject had previously transported the substance from the Miami, Florida area.

Adjustment for Obstruction of Justice

8.   The probation officer has no information suggesting that the defendant impeded or obstructed justice.

EXAMPLE SENTENCING GUIDELINES PRESENTENCE REPORT *(continued)*

Adjustment for Acceptance of Responsibility

9. Smith readily admitted participating in the instant offense. The subject noted that he had purchased heroin in the Miami area for $5,000. He further noted that he intended to sell the narcotic in Washington, D.C., for a profit.

Offense Level Computation

10. Base Offense Level: The guideline for a 21 USC 841(a) offense is found in Section 2D1.1(a)(3) of the Guidelines. That specific section provides that offense involving 10-19 grams of heroin have a base offense level of 16. Due to the fact that the offense of conviction involved 18946 milligrams of heroin (18.9 grams), the base offense level is 16.   **16**

11. Specific Offense Characteristics: None.   **0**

12. Adjustment for Role in the Offense: None.   **0**

13. Victim Related Adjustment: None.   **0**

14. Adjustment for Obstruction of Justice: None.   **0**

15. Adjusted Offense Level (Subtotal):   **16**

16. Adjustment for Acceptance of Responsibility: The defendant freely admitted his involvement in the instant offense. Based on Section 3E1.1(a), the offense level is reduced two levels.   **-2**

17. **Total Offense Level**   **14**

PART B. THE DEFENDANT'S CRIMINAL HISTORY

Juvenile Adjudications

	Date of Referral	Charge/Agency	Date Sentence Imposed/ Disposition	Guideline/ Score
18.	3-14-73 (Age 14)	Auto Theft Superior Court Washington, DC	7-20-73 Placed on probation. Probation terminated 7-19-74.	4A1.2(d)(2)(B) 4A1.1(c) 1

The subject was represented by counsel. The offense involved Smith stealing a 1972 Corvette in the vicinity of 1000 North Capitol Street, N.W., Washington, D.C. and joyriding in the vehicle.

EXAMPLE SENTENCING GUIDELINES PRESENTENCE REPORT *(continued)*

Criminal Convictions

Date of Arrest	Charge/Agency	Date Sentence Imposed/ Disposition	Guideline/ Score
19. 9-20-74 (Age 15)	Armed Robbery	12-6-74: Convicted as an adult and sentenced from 7 to 21 years. Paroled: 8-5-87. (Parole Term expiration: 12-5-95). Warrant lodged as a detainer.	4A1.1(a) 4A1.2(d)(1)

3

Mr. Smith was represented by counsel. The offense involved the subject participating in the robbery of a citizen at gunpoint in the vicinity of 191 Pennsylvania Avenue, Arlington, VA, on 9-20-74. While Smith was acting as a lookout, his accomplice (Dan Zale) fatally shot the victim.

Criminal History Computation

20. The juvenile adjudication and criminal conviction previously mentioned result in a subtotal criminal history score of 4.

4

21. At the time of the instant offense, Mr. Smith was on parole for the Armed Robbery conviction of 12-6-74. Pursuant to 4A1.1(d), 2 points are added.

2

22. The instant offense was committed less than two years following the subject's release from custody on 8-5-87, for sentence of 12-6-74. Pursuant to Section 4A1.1(e), one point is added.

1

23. The total of the criminal history points is 7. According to the sentencing table (Chapter 5, Part A), 7 to 8 criminal history points establish a criminal history category of IV.

Pending Charges

24. The Virginia Division of Parole has issued a parole violation warrant against Mr. Smith which notes the instant offense as a violation of parole.

PART C. SENTENCING OPTIONS

Custody

25. Statutory Provisions: The maximum term of imprisonment is 20 years. 21 USC 841(b)(a)(c).

26. Guideline provisions: Based on a total offense level of 14 and a criminal history category of IV, the guideline imprisonment range is 27-33 months.

EXAMPLE SENTENCING GUIDELINES PRESENTENCE REPORT *(continued)*

Supervised Release

27.   Statutory Provisions: If a term of imprisonment is imposed, a term of supervised release of at least 3 years must also be imposed. 21 USC 841(b)(1)(c).

28.   Guideline Provisions: The guideline range for a term of supervised release is 3-5 years under Section 5D3.2(a).

Probation

29.   Statutory Provisions: Because the instant offense is a Class B Felony, the defendant is ineligible for probation. 18 USC 3561(a)(1).

PART D: OFFENDER CHARACTERISTICS

Family Ties, Family Responsibilities, and Community Ties

30.   John Smith was born on December 23, 1958, to Tom Watson and Charlene Smith. The parents of the subject never married and Mr. Smith was essentially raised by his mother. The mother of the defendant possessed limited skills and received financial support through public assistance.

31.   The defendant has never been married and has no children. The subject notes that he has been dating a Ms. Joyce Austin, who resides at 3641 Locust Terrace, N.E., Washington, D.C., but reports no marriage plans.

Mental and Emotional Health

32.   The mother of the defendant informed the probation officer that her son encountered behavioral difficulties while in elementary school and underwent a psychological evaluation while in the fifth grade. Information received from D.C. Public Schools reflects that Mr. Smith experienced reading difficulties and was identified as being dyslexic.

Education and Vocational Skills

33.   Smith attended public schools in the Washington, D.C. area but withdrew from the ninth grade in 1972. Educational records reflect that the subject was frequently tardy and received poor grades. The subject was referred to a special class since he was experiencing reading difficulties but failed to attend on a regular basis.

Employment Record

34.   Mr. Smith noted that he has never maintained a full-time job and has worked odd jobs in order to financially support himself.

PART E.   FINES AND RESTITUTION

Statutory Provisions

35.   The maximum fine is $1,000,000. 21 USC 841(b)(1)(C).

EXAMPLE SENTENCING GUIDELINES PRESENTENCE REPORT (continued)

36.   A special assessment of $50 is mandatory. 18 USC 3013.

37.   The Victim and Witness Protection Act does not apply to Title 21 offenses.

Guideline Provisions

38.   The fine range for the instant offense is from $4,000 (Section 5E4.2(c)(3), the fine table) to $1,000,000. Section 5E4.2(c)(4).

39.   Subject to the ability of the defendant to pay, the court shall impose an additional fine amount that is at least sufficient to pay the costs to the government of any imprisonment, probation, or supervised release ordered. Section 5E4.2(i). The most recent advisory from the Administrative Office of the U.S. Courts, dated March 15, 1988, suggests that a monthly cost of $1,221 be used for imprisonment and a monthly cost of $83.33 or $1,000 yearly be used for supervision.

Defendant's Ability to Pay

40.   In addition to the written statement of the defendant regarding his financial situation, the probation officer reviewed the title to the car owned by Smith and interviewed his mother to verify the following:

Assets

    Cash

Cash on hand	$ 60
TOTAL ASSETS	$260

Unemcumbered Assets

1975 Chevrolet Chevette	$200 (Blue Book Value)

Unsecured Debts

Loan from mother	$700
TOTAL UNSECURED DEBTS	

Net Worth	-$440

Monthly Cash Flow

Subject reports that he has no income and relates that he has essentially worked odd jobs in order to support himself.

41.   Based on the financial profile of the defendant and his employment history, it appears that he would be unable to pay a fine.

EXAMPLE SENTENCING GUIDELINES PRESENTENCE REPORT *(continued)*

PART F. FACTORS THAT MAY WARRANT DEPARTURE

42.   Departure may be warranted on the basis of the serious criminal record of the defendant. See Section 4A1.3. The juvenile delinquency adjudication for Auto Theft counts for one point in the criminal history computation, thereby placing him in category IV instead of category III. Had the subject been placed in category III, his guideline range would have been 21–27 months instead of 27–33 months.

PART G. IMPACT OF PLEA AGREEMENT

43.   Under the plea agreement, Mr. Smith has entered a guilty plea to a one-count Indictment charging Unlawful Possession With Intent to Distribute a Controlled Substance (Heroin), a Class B Felony. Accordingly, no additional counts are involved which would affect the offense level or any other guideline computation.

Respectfully submitted,

EUGENE EASTLY
CHIEF PROBATION OFFICER

By:

Thomas W. Winchester
U.S. Probation Officer

TWW/hb

Reviewed & Approved:

DEBORAH HASSON
SUPERVISOR

EXAMPLE SENTENCING GUIDELINES PRESENTENCE REPORT *(continued)*

ADDENDUM TO THE PRESENTENCE REPORT

The probation officer certifies that the presentence report, including any revision thereof, has been disclosed to the defendant, his attorney, and counsel for the Government, and that the content of the addendum has been communicated to counsel. The Addendum fairly states any objections they have made.

OBJECTIONS

By the Government

The Government has no objections.

By the Defendant

Defendant Smith contends that the information presented in paragraph 30 of the report is incorrect and relates that his parents were legally married. The probation officer has checked marital records and has been unable to verify this information.

CERTIFIED BY

EUGENE EASTLY
CHIEF PROBATION OFFICER

By

_____
THOMAS W. WINCHESTER
U.S. Probation Officer

Reviewed & Approved:

_____
DEBORAH HASSON
SUPERVISOR
Date:

E. EXAMPLE GUIDELINES SENTENCING RECOMMENDATION

United States v. Smith, Dkt. No. 88-0001-01
U.S. District Court, District of Columbia

CUSTODY

Statutory maximum:	20 years
Guideline range:	27-33 months
Recommendation:	30 months

Justification:

Due to the fact that Smith has a serious but limited prior arrest record, it appears that a sentence in the middle of the guideline range would appear appropriate in addressing the sentencing objectives of punishment, deterrence, and incapacitation.

SUPERVISED RELEASE

Statutory requirement:	Not less than 3 years
Guideline term:	3-5 years
Recommended term:	5 years

1. That the defendant not commit any crimes, Federal, state, or local.
2. That the defendant abide by the standard conditions of supervised release recommended by the Sentencing Commission.
3. That the defendant participate in a program approved by the probation office of urinalysis testing and, if necessary, treatment of narcotic addiction or drug dependency.
4. That the defendant participate in vocational training and job placement programs recommended by the probation office.

Justification:

John Smith has a sporadic employment history and limited skills. It is noted that the subject withdrew from the ninth grade and his prospects for locating viable employment appear poor. Upon his release to the community, he will need close supervision and monitoring. A special condition for drug testing and possible treatment is recommended in view of the involvement of the defendant with drugs, although it has not been shown that he is an active user of narcotics. A special condition requiring that he participate in a vocational/job placement program is recommended in order that the subject may enhance his ability to locate and maintain employment.

FINE

Statutory maximum:	$1,000,000
Guideline range:	$4,000 plus the costs of incarceration and/or supervision to $1,000,000
Recommendation:	$0

EXAMPLE GUIDELINES SENTENCING RECOMMENDATION *(continued)*

Justification: Based upon his lack of assets and his sparse employment history, it appears that the subject does not have the ability to pay a fine obligation. Subject does not appear to be a candidate for community service work at this time.

SPECIAL ASSESSMENT $50

VOLUNTARY SURRENDER

Since a Virginia parole warrant has been lodged as a detainer, the defendant is ineligible for the voluntary surrender program.

Respectfully submitted,

EUGENE EASTLY
CHIEF PROBATION OFFICER

By _____
Thomas W. Winchester
U.S. Probation Officer

Reviewed and Approved:

_____
DEBORAH HASSON
SUPERVISOR

Date:

F. SENTENCING GUIDELINES TABLE

Criminal History Category

Offense Level	I 0 or 1	II 2 or 3	III 4, 5, 6	IV 7, 8, 9	V 10, 11, 12	VI 13 or more
1	0 - 1	0 - 2	0 - 3	0 - 4	0 - 5	0 - 6
2	0 - 2	0 - 3	0 - 4	0 - 5	0 - 6	1 - 7
3	0 - 3	0 - 4	0 - 5	0 - 6	2 - 8	3 - 9
4	0 - 4	0 - 5	0 - 6	2 - 8	4 - 10	6 - 12
5	0 - 5	0 - 6	1 - 7	4 - 10	6 - 12	9 - 15
6	0 - 6	1 - 7	2 - 8	6 - 12	9 - 15	12 - 18
7	1 - 7	2 - 8	4 - 10	8 - 14	12 - 18	15 - 21
8	2 - 8	4 - 10	6 - 12	10 - 16	15 - 21	18 - 24
9	4 - 10	6 - 12	8 - 14	12 - 18	18 - 24	21 - 27
10	6 - 12	8 - 14	10 - 16	15 - 21	21 - 27	24 - 30
11	8 - 14	10 - 16	12 - 18	18 - 24	24 - 30	27 - 33
12	10 - 16	12 - 18	15 - 21	21 - 27	27 - 33	30 - 37
13	12 - 18	15 - 21	18 - 24	24 - 30	30 - 37	33 - 41
14	15 - 21	18 - 24	21 - 27	27 - 33	33 - 41	37 - 46
15	18 - 24	21 - 27	24 - 30	30 - 37	37 - 46	41 - 51
16	21 - 27	24 - 30	27 - 33	33 - 41	41 - 51	46 - 57
17	24 - 30	27 - 33	30 - 37	37 - 46	46 - 57	51 - 63
18	27 - 33	30 - 37	33 - 41	41 - 51	51 - 63	57 - 71
19	30 - 37	33 - 41	37 - 46	46 - 57	57 - 71	63 - 78
20	33 - 41	37 - 46	41 - 51	51 - 63	63 - 78	70 - 87
21	37 - 46	41 - 51	46 - 57	57 - 71	70 - 87	77 - 96
22	41 - 51	46 - 57	51 - 63	63 - 78	77 - 96	84 - 105
23	46 - 57	51 - 63	57 - 71	70 - 87	84 - 105	92 - 115
24	51 - 63	57 - 71	63 - 78	77 - 96	92 - 115	100 - 125
25	57 - 71	63 - 78	70 - 87	84 - 105	100 - 125	110 - 137
26	63 - 78	70 - 87	78 - 97	92 - 115	110 - 137	120 - 150
27	70 - 87	78 - 97	87 - 108	100 - 125	120 - 150	130 - 162
28	78 - 97	87 - 108	97 - 121	110 - 137	130 - 162	140 - 175
29	87 - 108	97 - 121	108 - 135	121 - 151	140 - 175	151 - 188
30	97 - 121	108 - 135	121 - 151	135 - 168	151 - 188	168 - 210
31	108 - 135	121 - 151	135 - 168	151 - 188	168 - 210	188 - 235
32	121 - 151	135 - 168	151 - 188	168 - 210	188 - 235	210 - 262
33	135 - 168	151 - 188	168 - 210	188 - 235	210 - 262	235 - 293
34	151 - 188	168 - 210	188 - 235	210 - 262	235 - 293	262 - 327
35	168 - 210	188 - 235	210 - 262	235 - 293	262 - 327	292 - 365
36	188 - 235	210 - 262	235 - 293	262 - 327	292 - 365	324 - 405
37	210 - 262	235 - 293	262 - 327	292 - 365	324 - 405	360 - life
38	235 - 293	262 - 327	292 - 365	324 - 405	360 - life	360 - life
39	262 - 327	292 - 365	324 - 405	360 - life	360 - life	360 - life
40	292 - 365	324 - 405	360 - life	360 - life	360 - life	360 - life
41	324 - 405	360 - life	360 - life	360 - life	360 - life	360 - life
42	360 - life	360 - life	360 - life	360 - life	360 - life	360 - life
43	life	life	life	life	life	life

GLOSSARY

ALCOHOLICS ANONYMOUS. An organization founded in 1935 that assists individuals in dealing with problems of alcohol abuse.

ARRAIGNMENT. The post-indictment stage when a court considers information on defendant's alleged crimes and the defendant enters a plea to the charges.

ART THERAPY. A recently developed counseling technique used in developing trust and open communication, that involves interpreting the drawings of clients in analyzing their problems and perceptions.

BAIL. The pre-trial release of a defendant by posting financial security the amounts set by a judicial official, to ensure a later court appearance.

BEHAVIOR MODIFICATION AND THERAPY. Counseling treatment techniques which attempt to modify behavior through the application of principles derived from experimental, psychological research.

BENEFIT OF CLERGY. A practice allowed in early English history that granted clerical exemption from trial and punishment to certain individuals authorized by the church.

CAREER COUNSELING. A form of counseling aimed at obtaining productive employment and desired career goals for clients with occupational needs.

CLIENT-CENTERED THERAPY. An approach in counseling that is based upon the cultivation of a close and trusting relationship between counselor and client that promotes self-actualization and psychological adjustment to problems.

CLIENT MANAGEMENT CLASSIFICATION (CMC). An innovative approach to classifying and managing adult probation and parole clients by the designated authority, through rapid needs assessment and appropriate casework planning.

COMMUNITY CORRECTIONS. Conditions, sentences or programs involving the placement of offenders in the community rather than incarceration.

CONCURRENT SENTENCES. Sentences that are not added together in determining sentence length, but instead run "concurrently" (e.g., two five year terms to be served by five years' incarceration).

CONSECUTIVE SENTENCES. Sentences that are added together in determining the total time to be served (e.g., two five year terms to be served by 10 years' incarceration).

CRISIS INTERVENTION. The development of approaches for defusing hostile dispute situations encountered in client supervision by applying techniques for restoring order and resolving conflicts. DEFENDANT. A person against whom an action is brought in a criminal case by the government (Federal, state or local) for an alleged criminal violation.

DETERRENCE. Punishment aimed at preventing future criminal behavior, both specifically (e.g., the person imprisoned), and generally (e.g., the population aware of the consequences).

DIVERSION. An administrative procedure which permits selected offenders to bypass formal adversary proceedings by participating in a treatment-oriented program, thus avoiding a formal conviction.

FELONY. A crime that generally is more serious in nature than a misdemeanor and has a harsher sentence.

FINE. A sum of money adjudged payable by the defendant to a public treasury, as a form of punishment for the commission of a crime.

FURLOUGH. A program that permits an inmate to be conditionally released to the community for a finite period prior to sentence completion.

GROUP COUNSELING. An experience-based model of counseling that relies upon group processes for a framework of problem-solving and human learning.

HALFWAY HOUSE. A place of residence for formerly institutionalized offenders that is designed to facilitate their readjustment to private life.

INCAPACITATION. Incarceration for purposes of physically restraining offenders and preventing further criminal behavior.

INMATE. A person confined in a penal institution.

INTERMEDIATE PUNISHMENT. A punishment option that is considered on a continuum to fall between probation and a sentence of incarceration.

JUDICIAL REPRIEVE. An early English practice that permitted a delay or suspension of punishment by the court when considered appropriate.

JURISDICTION. The legal authority of a court to hear and decide a case.

MISDEMEANOR. An offense that is less serious than a felony and generally is punishable by a fine or by imprisonment of less than one year in jail.

NARCOTICS ANONYMOUS. A program for recovery from addiction to drugs and problems related to addiction, usually involving steps or stages of behavioral change.

NOLLE PROSEQUI (or NOL. PROS.). A decision by a prosecutor not to prosecute or proceed with an alleged criminal case.

NOLO CONTENDERE. The Latin term meaning "no contest," which is an infrequent plea that normally has the immediate consequence of a guilty plea, but may benefit the defendant in subsequent civil actions or lessen the social stigma associated with confessed guilt. By pleading *nolo contendere* the defendant admits the facts of the case to be true, but nothing further.

PAROLE. The conditional release to the community of a prisoner prior to completion of the original sentence by a parole board.

PAROLE BOARD. An official body which determines whether inmates will be released from incarceration to the community prior to completion of criminal sentences.

PLEA BARGAINING. An agreement entered into by a prosecutor and a defendant whereby concessions are generally made, e.g., reduced charges or sentences, in return for a guilty plea.

PRESENTENCE INVESTIGATION. An investigation by a probation officer that serves as a basis for a formal report given to the court to assist in sentencing.

PRE-TRIAL RELEASE. A process that permits a defendant to be released to the community prior to trial, and sometimes in lieu of trial.

PRIOR RECORD. The criminal history of an individual frequently reviewed in presentence investigations and considered in the sentencing process.

PROBATION. A sentence given to a convicted offender which is to be served in the community without incarceration, under conditions of supervision by probation officers.

PROSECUTOR. An attorney representing the government with the responsibility of initiating and pursuing criminal proceedings against accused criminals.

PSYCHODRAMA. A counseling technique involving the reenactment of life situations which reveals personal difficulties through role portrayals, and leads to improved self-understanding and reorientation.

RATIONAL EMOTIVE PSYCHOTHERAPY. A therapy which assumes that many disturbing behaviors result from irrational thinking which can be converted to rational thinking through reorganizing perceptions and promoting logical self- verbalizations.

REALITY THERAPY. A modern counseling approach which assists individuals to accept reality and gain self-respect through greater involvement with others.

RECIDIVISM. A return to criminal behavior.

RECOGNIZANCE (RELEASE ON OWN RECOGNIZANCE). An obligation in a court of law to perform a specified duty, e.g., to appear in court, as a condition for release.

REFERRAL. A process used by probation and parole authorities in arranging appropriate treatment and assistance programs beyond their agencies for probation and parole clients.

REHABILITATION. An approach to punishment which attempts to change the offender's criminal behavior through appropriate treatment.

RESTITUTION. A sentencing alternative that requires an offender to compensate a victim or society for the damage incurred by the offender's crime.

RETRIBUTION. A philosophy that punishment should fit the crime, and that society is morally justified in exacting proportionate penalties for wrongdoing.

REVOCATION. An action taken by the court or the parole authority which removes a person from probation or parole, because of a violation of conditions of release.

RISK PREDICTION SCALE. A device used by probation or parole authorities to determine the appropriate level of client supervision.

SALIENT FACTOR SCORE. A measurement device that is part of a statistically-based instrument for predicting and recommending the length and severity of sentences.

SHOCK INCARCERATION (or BOOT CAMP). An intermediate sanction that typically includes a highly disciplined, military-type curriculum for youthful, nonviolent first-time offenders.

SHOCK PROBATION. A punishment technique that requires an offender to serve a short prison term prior to release on probation for purposes of encouraging future crime avoidance and behavior changes.

STARE DECISIS. A Latin term meaning "let the decision stand," which is used as a rule for applying precedents in legal reasoning.

SUSPENDED SENTENCE. A process whereby the court delays or stays the execution of a sentence and usually imposes conditions of probation.

TICKET-OF-LEAVE. An historic conditioned release of an offender that was granted for good behavior and revoked for misconduct.

TRANSACTIONAL ANALYSIS. A counseling theory aimed at improving interpersonal relationships by focusing on three primary ego states (parent, adult, child) which are used in analyzing human transactions and behaviors.

VICTIM IMPACT STATEMENT. A report typically used in presentence investigations which assesses the impact of a crime on the victim.

VOLUNTEER. A possible alternative resource for probation and parole systems which involves using non-paid staff to assist in performing various office responsibilities.

WORK RELEASE. A program that permits an inmate to be conditionally released to the community for a finite period prior to sentence completion for purposes of engaging in productive employment.

INDEX

EXERCISES

EXERCISE 1

Presentence Investigation (PSI) Report (Traditional)

Instructions: Prior to completion of this exercise, the student should review the discussion of presentence investigations and examples A, B and C. Having completed the review, the following hypothetical presentence report worksheet and final presentence report is to be read thoroughly by the student. The hypothetical reports are based on information that is typical of that required in many state probation settings. The reports are designed from the forms that were used in the U.S. Federal Probation System prior to the recent adoption of new sentencing guidelines. The proper completion of the reports is one of the major responsibilities of the probation officer (PO), and serves as an important factor in the final sentencing of the defendant. Now, using the information below (along with additional information), complete the blank PSI worksheet in its entirety. Following its completion (at the discretion of the course instructor), use this information as a basis for a final PSI report, similar to the one performed on John Doe (hypothetical defendant). Be sure to recommend a final sentence for the defendant. Clarity and conciseness are of tremendous significance, as these reports are generally reviewed by the Chief Probation Officer and the presiding judge. For the items of information not provided, use information about yourself or hypothetical information as required. Reasonable and creative thoughts are encouraged. Be sure to leave no item unanswered.

Hypothetical Facts: The defendant is charged with a violation of 21 USC 844(a) (Simple possession of marijuana -- 1st offense; maximum sentence: 1 year/$5,000 fine). The defendant was arrested on September 1, 19__ and released on a personal recognizance bond the following day. The defendant advises defense counsel, J. Lee Baity, to notify the Assistant U.S. Attorney, I. Gotchew, that a plea of guilty is desired.

Exercise 1 *(continued)*

PROB 1 (Rev. 11/78) UNITED STATES DISTRICT COURT Federal Probation System **WORKSHEET FOR PRESENTENCE REPORT** *(See Publication 105 for Instructions)*	DISTRICT	DOCKET NUMBER
	SENTENCING JUDGE	SENTENCING DATE

1. IDENTIFYING DATA

COURT NAME (Last, first, middle) AKA	DATE OF FIRST INTERVIEW
	REPORT DUE
TRUE NAME (Last, first, middle)	RECORDED BY

CURRENT ADDRESS (Directions, how long)	LEGAL ADDRESS (if different)	CONSENT FORMS SIGNED ☐ YES ☐ NO
		RACE
		CITIZENSHIP

PHONE NO.	AGE	BIRTHDATE	BIRTHPLACE	SEX	MARITAL STATUS
NO. OF DEPENDENTS	SOC. SEC. NO.		FBI NO.		OTHER IDENTIFYING NO.

2. OFFENSE

OFFENSE AND DATE OCCURRED	DATE, BY WHOM AND WHERE ARRESTED
PLEA OR VERDICT	CUSTODIAL STATUS
PENALTY	
ASST. U.S. ATTORNEY	DEFENSE COUNSEL (Name, address, & phone no.) ☐ APPOINTED ☐ RETAINED

3. DEFENDANT'S VERSION (Summary of offense and arrest by defendant/explanation and reasons for involvement)

4. OTHER DEFENDANT INFORMATION (Relative culpability of all the defendants)

Exercise 1 *(continued)*

5. PRIOR RECORD (List below all other arrests whether convicted or not including juvenile adjudication)						COUNSEL		
DATE	AGE	OFFENSE	REASON FOR INVOLVEMENT	COURT OF CONVICTION	DISPOSITION	YES	NO	WAIVED

6. ADDITIONAL DATA (Detainers or charges pending; previous probation/parole and institutional history, dates, report of adjustment, present release status)

6. PERSONAL AND FAMILY DATA (If essential, include home and neighborhood, religion, previous addresses, interests and use of leisure time)

Exercise 1 *(continued)*

6. PERSONAL AND FAMILY DATA (Cont.)

6. Cont. NAMES OF IMMEDIATE FAMILY (List spouse & children under Item 7. MARITAL)

NAME	RELATIONSHIP	AGE	PRESENT ADDRESS	OCCUPATIONAL	PRIOR RECORD YES	NO

7. MARITAL (Present and previous marriages, including cohabitation)

NAME OF SPOUSE	AGE	PLACE AND DATE OF MARRIAGE	No. of Children	Outcome of Marriage

NAMES OF CHILDREN (Including those from previous marriages)	AGE	ADDRESS, SCHOOL, CUSTODY, SUPPORT

ATTITUDE OF SPOUSE AND CHILDREN TOWARD DEFENDANT AND HOME ATMOSPHERE

Exercise 1 *(continued)*

8. EDUCATION				
HIGHEST GRADE COMPLETED	AGE LEFT SCHOOL	REASON FOR LEAVING		
OTHER TRAINING RECEIVED (Business or trade)				
NAME OF SCHOOL (List schools attended; start with last school)		LOCATION	ATTENDED FROM/TO	DEGREE RECEIVED
SUMMARY OF SCHOOL DATA (Test Results, Academic Rating, Class Standing, Behavior)				

9. EMPLOYMENT (Cover last ten years including reasons for periods of unemployment or disability)		
DATES	NAME AND ADDRESS OF EMPLOYER	NATURE OF WORK, WEEKLY WAGE, REASON FOR LEAVING
STARTED		
ENDED		
STARTED		
ENDED		
STARTED		
ENDED		
STARTED		
ENDED		
STARTED		
ENDED		
STARTED		
ENDED		
STARTED		
ENDED		
OCCUPATIONAL SKILLS, INTERESTS, AND AMBITIONS		

Exercise 1 *(continued)*

10. HEALTH
PHYSICAL DESCRIPTION (Height, weight, scars, illnesses being treated; health problems, and all past and present treatment and medication)
DRUG ABUSE, ALCOHOL, NARCOTICS (Age use began, frequency/cost, type of drug, past and present treatment)
MENTAL AND EMOTIONAL (Self evaluation, personality traits, disorders, treatment)

11. MILITARY SERVICE				
SERVICE NUMBER	BRANCH OF SERVICE	DATE OF ENTRY	DATE DISCHARGED	TYPE OF DISCHARGE
HIGHEST RANK HELD	RANK AT SEPARATION	DECORATIONS AND AWARDS		VA CLAIM NUMBER
SUMMARY OF MILITARY DATA				

Exercise 1 *(continued)*

12. FINANCIAL CONDITION

LIST FINANCIAL ASSETS (Real estate, insurance, real and personal property, stocks, bonds, checking and saving accounts, income from pensions and compensation, rentals, and family income, net worth, ability to pay fine or restitution)	LIST FINANCIAL LIABILITIES (INCLUDING BALANCE DUE AND MONTHLY PAYMENTS FOR home mortgage, rent, utilities, medical, personal property, home repairs, charge accounts, loans, taxes, fines, restitution, pending civil suits)

13. EVALUATION (the probation officer's professional assessment of the defendant)

14. SENTENCING DATA (Use appropriate forms and charts)

15. ALTERNATIVE PLANS (Provide a statement of realistic sentencing alternatives available to the court and treatment plan)

EXERCISE 2

Sentencing Recommendations (Traditional)

Instructions: As demonstrated in the first exercise, the sentencing recommendation is one of the most important, yet difficult, responsibilities of the PO. In making his recommendation, each element of information gathered on the defendant must be checked for accuracy and then carefully weighed by the assigned officer. Depending upon the PO's overall evaluation of all the pertinent data, a final sentencing recommendation is made. It is this decision-making process which tests the true abilities and professionalism of the officer. Most studies have shown that the judge places great emphasis and reliance on the recommended sentence (following the advice of the PO in approximately 90 percent of the cases). Understanding the importance of this assignment, the following three hypothetical cases are provided which contain limited, yet important, information to be considered by the PO. The student should review each case carefully and then complete the recommended sentence with reasoning to support the recommendation in each case. At the discretion of the course instructor, students with conflicting recommendations should be prepared to argue in support of their recommendations. In defending their decisions, the students may find a review of the primary justifications and rationales for punishment in general to be helpful.

Exercise 2 *(continued)*

JOHN QUE CASE

OFFENSE: Theft of U.S. Treasury Check (18 USC 1708)

PENALTY: Fine of not more than $2,000, or imprisonment for not
more than five years, or both.

PLEA/JURY: Mr. Que plead guilty to the offense.

DETAILS OF   He stole a check for $300.00 and cashed the check at a
OFFENSE: local liquor store. He claims that he stole the check
to support his heroin habit.

PRIOR RECORD:

Charges	Disposition
Larceny under $100.00	6 months probation
Robbery - Holdup	Dismissed
Receiving Stolen Property	Nolle Prossed

MARITAL   Wife and three daughters reside with Mr. Que in a two
HISTORY: -bedroom apartment.

EDUCATION: Dropped out of the eleventh grade.

EMPLOYMENT: Mr. Que has been unemployed for one year. His last job
was that of a house painter.

MILITARY   Mr. Que served in Vietnam in a Special Forces Army
RECORD: Unit. He received the Purple Heart medal -- special
commendation for being wounded.

FINANCIAL   He owns a sports car and has two hundred dollars in
CONDITION: his bank account.

MR. QUE'S   He showed no remorse for taking part in the crime.
ATTITUDE

Your sentence recommendation: _____
_____
_____
_____

Why did you recommend this sentence?_____
_____
_____

Exercise 2 *(continued)*

SUSIE SMART CASE

OFFENSE: Unlawful Distribution of a Controlled Substance (21 USC 841 (a)

PENALTY: Up to 5 years imprisonment and/or a fine of up to $250,000

DETAILS OF OFFENSE: Sold two phenmentrazine (prescribed) tablets to an undercover detective for $20.00. She claims she sold the tablets to earn money for her graduate studies at Big Town University.

PLEA/JURY: Ms. Smart plead guilty to the offense.

PRIOR RECORD:

Charges	Disposition
Unlawful Distribution of A Controlled Substance (21 USC 841(a))	No papered (Nol. Pros.)

MARITAL HISTORY: Ms. Smart has been married three times. She said she divorced each husband because they would not allow her to complete a master's degree in English.

EDUCATION: Ms. Smart was a Phi Beta Kappa graduate. She is now working on a master's degree in English.

EMPLOYMENT: She has been employed part-time as an exotic dance at the Shakespeare Bar.

RELIGION: She is a member of the First Communal Church. She stated that this is the only church that encourages dancing.

FINANCIAL CONDITION: She earns $500.00 per week, but spends much of her income on literature books.

MS. SMART'S ATTITUDE: She has been writing poems of depression since her arrest. She is remorseful for her crime.

Your sentence recommendation: _____

_____

_____

_____

Why did you recommend this sentence?_____

_____

_____

Exercise 2 *(continued)*

DAVE SMITH CASE

OFFENSE: Simple Assault

PENALTY: Not more than one year or a fine of not more than $500.00, or both.

DETAILS OF   He attacked an IRS agent who tried to close down his
OFFENSE: shop. Mr. Smith owes the IRS $5,000 in back taxes. He claims the tax laws are unfair.

PLEA/   Mr. Smith denied guilt. He was found guilty of the
JURY: offense by a federal judge.

PRIOR   Charges   Disposition
RECORD: Disorderly Conduct   Fined $100.00

MARITAL   He has a wife and no children.
HISTORY:

EDUCATION: He attended two years of college. He dropped out of college to open a health food shop.

EMPLOYMENT: Mr. Smith has owned a health food store for five years. His store has now been closed by the IRS. He is currently receiving unemployment checks.

MILITARY   He has never served in a military unit.
RECORD:

FINANCIAL   He owes $20,000.00 on his house and has no savings.
CONDITION:

MR. SMITH'S   Mr. Smith has a very hostile attitude toward the Federal
ATTITUDE: government. He shows no remorse for his assault on the IRS agent. The agent received no serious injury as a result of the fight.

Your sentence recommendation: _____

_____

_____

_____

Why did you recommend this sentence?_____

_____

_____

EXERCISE 3

Conditions of Probation

Instructions: As demonstrated and discussed throughout this text, probation is an important and frequent alternative to incarceration. By all indications, probation will continue to serve as an important sentencing alternative in the future. Exercise 2 provided some examples of criminal behavior for which probation might be considered. Was probation recommended in any of the hypotheticals? If so, refer back to the example for purposes of completing this exercise. If not, select the example in which probation would appear most appropriate if mandated. The student should note that the Conditions of Probation Form contains numerous standard conditions applicable to all probationers. An additional section is provided for special conditions which the Court may use in "tailoring" the conditions of probation to the special needs/problems of the defendant. An example of such a special condition might be a provision mandating participation in a drug abuse program. After carefully considering the limited information provided on a hypothetical defendant (and assuming additional facts as necessary), complete special conditions. Be prepared to explain the reasoning behind each condition and the time limitations (if any) for each.

Exercise 3 *(continued)*

PROB 7
(3/73)

Conditions of Probation

UNITED STATES DISTRICT COURT
FOR THE

_____

To _____   Docket No.

Address _____

    In accordance with authority conferred by the United States Probation Law, you have been placed on probation this date,   , for a period of   by the Hon.   United States District Judge, sitting in and for this District Court at

CONDITIONS OF PROBATION

It is the order of the Court that you shall comply with the following conditions of probation:

    (1) You shall refrain from violation of any law (federal, state, and local). You shall get in touch immediately with your probation officer if arrested or questioned by a law-enforcement officer.

    (2) You shall associate only with law-abiding persons and maintain reasonable hours.

    (3) You shall work regularly at a lawful occupation and support your legal dependents, if any, to the best of your ability. When out of work you shall notify your probation officer at once. You shall consult him prior to job changes.

    (4) You shall not leave the judicial district without permission of the probation officer.

    (5) You shall notify your probation officer immediately of any change in your place of residence.

    (6) You shall follow the probation officer's instructions.

    (7) You shall report to the probation officer as directed.

The special conditions ordered by the Court are as follows:

    I understand that the Court may change the conditions of probation, reduce or extend the period of probation, and at any time during the probation period or within the maximum probation period of 5 years permitted by law, may issue a warrant and revoke probation for a violation occurring during the probation period.

    I have read or had read to me the above conditions of probation. I fully understand them and I will abide by them.

(Signed) _____   _____
                          Probationer   Date

You will report as follows:

_____   _____
       U.S. Probation Officer   Date

EXERCISE 4

Determination of Supervision Level

Instructions: When a client is assigned to PO, a determination must be made concerning the appropriate level of supervision to be accorded the client. A review of supervisory responsibilities from Chapter 4 should remind the student of the importance and scope of this responsibility. One method of assessing the appropriate level of supervision involves the use of predictive instruments based upon proven indicators of probable performance. Many probation agencies have devised "risk prediction scales" (RPS) to determine whether low activity (minimal supervision requirements) or high activity (intense supervision requirements) levels are required. The following RPS 80 Form is one adopted by the U.S. Probation Office and will serve as a guide for this assignment. Review the factual information provided for a hypothetical defendant profiled in the previous exercises and determine the level at which he or she should be supervised. Be prepared to discuss whether this mechanism for determining supervision levels appears to be beneficial to the PO. Does it reduce the discretion of the PO to an acceptable level? Is it an accurate guide to future behavior patterns of the probationer?

Exercise 4 *(continued)*

PROB 40
(1. 81)

RISK PREDICTION SCALE (RPS 80)

NAME	PROBATION OFFICER	DATE

I. Automatic Assignment

> If "yes" is checked for both A and B, place in Low Activity Supervision.

A) Individual has completed high school education   YES ☐   NO ☐

B) Individual has history free of opiate usage   YES ☐   NO ☐

II. Risk Score Determination

> If not automatically assigned, use items C through G to determine risk score and supervision activity level.

C) Twenty-eight years or older at time of instant conviction . . . . (7) ____

D) Arrest-free period of five (5) or more consecutive years . . . . (4) ____

E) Few prior arrests (none, one, or two) . . . . (10) ____

F) History free of opiate usage . . . . (9) ____

G) At least four (4) months steady employment prior to arraignment for
present offense . . . . (3) ____

Scale for Potential Adjustment (For Presentence Purposes)

RISK		SUM OF POINTS (33) ____
(0 - 9)	Poor	
(10 - 19)	Good	
(20 - 33)	Excellent	

RISK SCORE RANGE   **SUPERVISION LEVEL**

Automatic Assignment
or   >————————————————————→   Low Activity ☐
20-33

0-19   >————————————————————→   High Activity ☐

EXERCISE 5

Monthly Supervision Report

Instructions: The responsibilities of the PO are continuous in nature, especially that of supervision. Most probation/parole authorities require frequent reports on the performance of the client. Generally, this information is gathered in the form of a monthly supervision report. This report serves to update the PO on the client's progress or any material changes in his or her status. This information may be of value to the judge in considering modifications to the client's sentence, as well as to the probation/parole authority in documenting the client's behavior. This information is also very important to the PO in counseling and advising the client during office visits. Of course, the failure of the client to provide accurate information for the reports may result in a revocation proceeding if the omissions are material and substantial. The PO generally reviews the report with the client to ensure that it is accurate and complete. This exercise will involve selecting a previous hypothetical client from the preceding exercises and the assignment of that role to a classmate. Next, interview the classmate who has assumed the client's identity. The client should feel free to supply additional hypothetical information as needed. On the basis of this interview, complete the monthly supervision report. Upon final completion, determine the impact of this information on the future supervision of the client. Is any special counseling mandated? If so, what type and for what purpose?

219

Exercise 5 (continued)

PROB 8
(3.88)

MONTHLY SUPERVISION REPORT

INSTRUCTIONS

Submit this report to the Probation Office as directed.

REPORT FOR MONTH OF

CHECK TYPE OF SUPERVISION

PROBATION	MANDATORY RELEASE
PAROLE	MILITARY PAROLE
SUPERVISED RELEASE	DEFERRED PROSECUTION

FULL NAME

REGISTER NUMBER (if any)   TELEPHONE NUMBER (if any)

ADDRESS   MAIL ADDRESS

Zip Code   Zip Code

DID YOU MOVE DURING THE MONTH?   IF YOU HAVE MOVED, EXPLAIN WHY
☐ YES ☐ NO

NAME AND ADDRESS OF YOUR EMPLOYER (or school)   IF EMPLOYED, WHAT IS YOUR JOB?

HAVE YOU CHANGED JOBS DURING THE MONTH?   WHAT WAS THE TOTAL AMOUNT YOU EARNED FROM EMPLOYMENT DURING THE MONTH BEFORE DEDUCTIONS?   HOW MANY DAYS DID YOU WORK (or attend school) DURING THE MONTH?
☐ YES ☐ NO

IF YOU ARE NOT WORKING, OR HAVE CHANGED JOBS, EXPLAIN WHY

DID YOU RECEIVE ANY MONEY OTHER THAN FROM EMPLOYMENT, SUCH AS LOANS, RELIEF BENEFITS, ETC?   IF SO, GIVE AMOUNTS AND FROM WHOM RECEIVED
☐ YES ☐ NO

DO YOU HAVE ANY DEBTS WHICH ARE PAST DUE?   IF SO, GIVE AMOUNTS AND TO WHOM OWED
☐ YES ☐ NO

WERE YOU ARRESTED DURING THE MONTH?   IF SO, GIVE DATE OF ARREST   PLACE OF ARREST
☐ YES ☐ NO

WITH WHAT OFFENSE WERE YOU CHARGED? (explain)   DISPOSITION MADE (fine, jail, dismissed, etc.)

REMARKS, INCLUDING EXPLANATION OF ARRESTS, IF ANY (use reverse side for additional space)

SIGN HERE ▷ _____   DATE ▷ _____

DO NOT WRITE BELOW THIS LINE

ADVISER'S COMMENTS:

I have seen the above named personally
_____ times during the month.   _____
                    SIGNATURE OF ADVISER   DATE

PROBATION OFFICER'S COMMENTS: RETURN THIS REPORT TO:

_____   _____
SIGNATURE OF PROBATION OFFICER   DATE

EXERCISE 6

Sentencing Guidelines Application

The following exercise is to be used as an aid in learning how to apply sentencing guidelines. The exercise is not complex and the reader should read it carefully. The exercise will be useful as a learning tool if the reader applies the guidelines to the facts. Using the sentencing table, the reader can then ascertain the appropriate sentence (in months) an offender may receive. (Use Example F, Sentencing Guidelines Table on p. 191.)

Exercise 6 (*continued*)

Offense: <u>Fraudulently Acquiring or Improperly Using a United States Passport</u>

   Base Offense Level: 6

<u>Statutory Provisions</u>: 18 USC 1543, 1544.

<u>Application Notes</u>:

   In the case of a defendant who is an unlawful alien and has been deported (voluntarily or involuntarily) on one or more occasions prior to the instant offense, the Commission recommends an upward departure of 2 levels.

<u>Conviction</u>: Count 1:   Fraudulently Acquiring or Improperly Using a United States Passport (18 USC Secs. 1543, 1544)

   Penalty: A fine of not more than $250,000 or imprisonment for not more than 5 years, or both.

   The defendant was charged in a one-count indictment with fraudulently acquiring or improperly using a United States passport. Official documents reflect that on July 20, 19__, the defendant arrived at Dulles International Airport from Bogota, Colombia, and presented a U.S. passport in the name of Enrik Lorenza. A computer readout subsequently revealed that the defendant had previously obtained the passport using false and altered documentation and that a warrant had been issued for his arrest. The subject was identified as being an illegal alien who had been previously deported.

Using the Sentencing Guidelines Table:

Calculate the adjusted offense level for the defendant:

_____

With a Category V criminal history, calculate the sentence to be imposed:

_____

Exercise 6 *(continued)*

<u>Offense:</u>   <u>Laundering of Monetary Instruments</u>

(a)   Base Offense Level:

    (1)   23, if convicted under 18 USC Sections 1956(a)(1)(A) or (a)(2)(A):

    (2)   20, otherwise.

(b)   Specific Offense Characteristics

    (1)   If the defendant knew that the funds were the proceeds of an unlawful activity involving the manufacture, importation, or distribution of narcotics or other controlled substances, increase by 3 levels.

    (2)   If the value of the funds exceeded $100,000, increase the offense level as follows:

	Value	Increase in Level
(A)	$100,000 or less	no increase
(B)	$100,001 - $200,000	add 1
(C)	$200,001 - $350,000	add 2
(D)	$350,001 - $600,000	add 3
(E)	$600,001 - $1,000,000	add 4
(F)	$1,000,001 - $2,000,000	add 5
(G)	$2,000,001 - $3,500,000	add 6
(H)	$3,500,001 - $6,000,000	add 7
(I)	$6,000,001 - $10,000,000	add 8
(J)	$10,000,001 - $20,000,000	add 9
(K)	$20,000,001 - $35,000,000	add 10
(L)	$35,000,001 - $60,000,000	add 11
(M)	$60,000,001 - $100,000,000	add 12
(N)	more than $100,000,000	add 13

Conviction: Count 2:   Laundering of Monetary Instruments (18 USC Sec. 1005)

          Penalty: A fine of not more than $250,000 or imprisonment for not more than 5 years, or both.

Exercise 6 (*continued*)

The defendant was charged in a two-count indictment with the laundering of monetary instruments. The subject subsequently pled guilty to Count Two of the 2-count indictment.

In reference to Count Two of the 2-count indictment, on October 15, 19__, the defendant, while president of the First National Bank of Miami, accepted $1,000,000 from Leon Willis, a widely known drug dealer. Official documents reflect that these monies were subsequently laundered through a Swiss bank account and the defendant was paid $100,000 by Willis for his assistance in the instant offense.

Using the Sentencing Guidelines Table:

Calculate the adjusted offense level for the defendant:

With a Category II criminal history, calculate the sentence to be imposed: